Circular Migration between Europe and its Neighbourhood: Choice or Necessity?

Circular Migration between Europe and its Neighbourhood

Choice or Necessity?

Anna Triandafyllidou

UNIVERSITY PRESS

Great Clarendon Street, Oxford, OX2 6DP,
United Kingdom

Oxford University Press is a department of the University of Oxford.
It furthers the University's objective of excellence in research, scholarship,
and education by publishing worldwide. Oxford is a registered trade mark of
Oxford University Press in the UK and in certain other countries

© Oxford University Press 2013

The moral rights of the author have been asserted

First Edition published in 2013

Impression: 1

All rights reserved. No part of this publication may be reproduced, stored in
a retrieval system, or transmitted, in any form or by any means, without the
prior permission in writing of Oxford University Press, or as expressly permitted
by law, by licence or under terms agreed with the appropriate reprographics
rights organization. Enquiries concerning reproduction outside the scope of the
above should be sent to the Rights Department, Oxford University Press, at the
address above

You must not circulate this work in any other form
and you must impose this same condition on any acquirer

British Library Cataloguing in Publication Data

Data available

ISBN 978-0-19-967451-0

Printed and bound by CPI Group (UK) Ltd, Croydon, CR0 4YY

For my brother Alexandros

Preface

I first came across the notion of circular migration when reading a European Commission Communication on Mobility Partnerships and Circular Migration in 2007. I then discovered that there was a wealth of policy documents and literature that discussed circular migration and saw in it an opportunity for effectively regulating temporary and more medium term migration, combating irregular movements and flexibly responding to the needs of the European Union countries' labour markets. Although the idea of regulated circularity seemed to me quite unfeasible (as also discussed in this book) I thought that this was an idea worth studying more in depth as earlier studies indicated that circularity had existed in formal and informal ways for many decades between some countries. In addition I realized that there was little agreement as to what circular migration involved—who qualified as a circular migrant, or who was a long-term migrant that simply spent longer periods of vacation at the country of origin or again who was simply a temporary/seasonal but not circular migrant.

It was in 2009 that I had the opportunity to work more in depth and at a comparative level on circular migration: I applied for the METOIKOS research project (http://metoikos.eui.eu) which was selected after a competitive call. METOIKOS was co-funded by the European Integration Fund for Third Country Nationals under the Community Actions budget line. Indeed, this book would not have come to fruition if it was not for the METOIKOS project that gave several of the authors the opportunity to conduct extended fieldwork in both the countries of origin and those of destination and find out more about who are the circular migrants, how do they circulate and why, how do they feel about it, and what are the views of the local and national policymakers and civil society actors involved also in the largely uncharted territory of circular migration.

While the METOIKOS project concentrated more on issues of migrant integration (at the country of destination) and reintegration (at the country of origin) and at developing recommendations for policymakers on how to best regulate and manage circular migration, this book goes a step further: it brings in a larger theoretical framework as to how circular migration relates

Preface

to the current system of production and the wider priorities of EU migration policies.

I would like to thank here the contributors to this volume for their patience and perseverance during the fieldwork, the analysis, the writing and rewriting of the various chapters; Vicky Valanos for carefully copy-editing this manuscript; and, most importantly, the circular migrants interviewed who allowed us to glimpse into their lives. This book is dedicated to my brother, Alexandros, who circulates in Europe (not for work but for family reasons) and who has been a lighthouse for me since we were children and still today.

Florence,
25 September 2012

Table of Contents

List of Figures and Tables   x
Notes on Contributors   xii

1. Circular Migration: Introductory Remarks   1
   Anna Triandafyllidou

2. The Drive for Securitized Temporariness   22
   Jean-Pierre Cassarino

3. Flexible Circularities: Integration, Return, and Socio-Economic Instability within Albanian Migration to Italy   42
   Nicola Mai and Cristiana Paladini

4. Albanian Circular Migration in Greece: Beyond the State?   68
   Thanos Maroukis and Eda Gemi

5. Circular Economic Migration between Italy and Morocco   90
   Camilla Devitt

6. Circularity in a Restrictive Framework: Mobility between Morocco and Spain   114
   Carmen González Enríquez

7. Circular Migration between Hungary and Ukraine: Historical Legacies, the Economic Crisis, and the Multidirectionality of 'Circular' Migration   141
   Ayşe Çağlar

8. Circular Migration Patterns between Ukraine and Poland   166
   Krystyna Iglicka and Katarzyna Gmaj

9. A Transnational Double Presence: Circular Migration between Ukraine and Italy   187
   Francesca Alice Vianello

10. Circular Migration at the Periphery of Europe: Choice, Opportunity, or Necessity?   212
    Anna Triandafyllidou

Index   237

List of Figures and Tables

Figures

3.1	Map of Italy	43
3.2	Map of Albania	44
4.1	Albania and its neighbours: main migration routes	69
5.1	Map of Moroccan regions	92
5.2	Distribution of Moroccans resident in Italy based on regions of residency	93
5.3	Regional distribution of self-employed Moroccans in Italy	94
6.1	Moroccan immigrants in Spain	119
6.2	Seasonal work permits in Huelva for foreign workers	127
6.3	Who takes care of the children?	134
6.4	Plans for the investment of savings: absolute numbers	135
6.5	Evaluation of the programme	135
9.1	Map of Ukraine, highlighting the regions of L'viv (Львівська область) and Ivano-Frankivsk (Івано-Франківська область) where in-depth interviews were conducted	189
9.2	Map of Italy, highlighting the region of Veneto where in-depth interviews were conducted	190

Tables

2.1	List of mobility partnerships	32
4.1	Stay permits for seasonal and temporary employment	70
4.2	Typology of circular migration between Greece and Albania	73
Annex 4.1	Socio-demographic characteristics of the sample	87
Annex 4.2	Sector and type of occupation	88
Annex 4.3	Interviews with key informants in Greece and Albania	88
5.1	Typology of Moroccan economic circular migrants circulating between Morocco-Italy with main residence in Italy	98
5.2	Typology of Moroccan economic circular migrants circulating between Morocco and Italy with main residence in Morocco	99

List of Figures and Tables

Annex 5.1	List of interviews with policymakers, stakeholders, key informants, and researchers	113
6.1	Temporary work and residence permits assigned to the agricultural sector of Huelva, by countries of origin	126
7.1	Number of foreigners holding a permanent residence permit	157
7.2	Number of foreigners holding a short-term residence permit	157
7.3	Number of applicants for permanent residence card	157
7.4	Third-country national family member of EEA citizen	157
7.5	Third-country national family member of Hungarian citizen	157
7.6	Cumulative number of applications for residence under Act ll of 2007	157
8.1	Types of Ukrainian economic circular migrants circulating between Ukraine and Poland	174
9.1	Socio-demographic characteristics of the migrant women interviewed I	188
9.2	Socio-demographic characteristics of the migrant women interviewed II	188
9.3	Interviews with key informants	190
9.4	Ukrainian citizens with a permit of stay by purpose of presence, and sex as of 1 January 2009—male and female: absolute numbers	198
9.5	Ukrainian citizens who entered in 2008 and were legally resident as of 1 January 2009, by sex and marital status: absolute numbers and percentages	199
9.6	Ukrainian citizens entered in 2008 and legally present as of 1 January 2009, by sex and age group: absolute numbers and percentages	199
9.7	Types of Ukrainian migration	201

Notes on Contributors

Ayşe Çağlar was Research Group Leader holding a Minerva Fellowship at the Max Planck Institute for the Study of Religious and Ethnic Diversity. In February 2011, she obtained a Chair at the University of Vienna. Previously she was University Professor at the Central European University, Budapest since 2003. She obtained a PhD in Anthropology from McGill University, Montreal, Canada in 1995 and completed her Habilitation in Anthropology and Sociology at the Free University Berlin in 2004. Her recent books include *Encountering States in Transnational Migration* (forthcoming), *Locating Migration: Rescaling Cities and Migrants* (edited with Nina Glick Schiller, 2010).

Jean-Pierre Cassarino is a political scientist who has been working on labour migration issues, particularly as applied to the Euro-Mediterranean area, for more than twelve years. He is currently part-time professor at the Robert Schuman Centre for Advanced Studies (RSCAS) where he has been directing the Return Migration and Development Platform (RDP). Jean-Pierre Cassarino is also associated with the Border Crossing Observatory at Monash University (Melbourne, Australia) and with the Migration Industry and Markets for Managing Migration research programme hosted at the Danish Institute for International Studies (Copenhagen, Denmark). He is also a research associate at the Institut de Recherche sur le Maghreb Contemporain (IRMC, Tunisia). He has published extensively on how policy transfers are administered through processes of bilateral and multilateral consultations mobilizing countries of destination, of transit and of origin.

Camilla Devitt gained her doctorate in political and social sciences at the European University Institute in 2010. Her research interests encompass labour migration, immigration policies in Western Europe and North African political economy. Recent publications include 'Varieties of Capitalism, Variation in Labour Migration' (*Journal of Ethnic and Migration Studies,* 37(4), 2010) and 'The migrant worker factor in labour market policy reform' (*European Journal of Industrial Relations*, 16(3), 2010).

Eda Gemi is a research assistant at the ELIAMEP (Hellenic Foundation for European and Foreign Policy) and PhD candidate at the University of Athens, Institute for Migration and Diaspora Studies (EMMEDIA). She was a research assistant at the European University Institute, Robert Schuman Centre for Advanced Studies, in Florence, Italy, in 2010–12. Her main area of research is migration studies, with a particular focus on social integration, political participation, circular migration and gender.

Notes on Contributors

Katarzyna Gmaj holds a PhD in sociology (Warsaw University). Currently she works as a lecturer at Lazarski University, Warsaw. Since 2001 she has been collaborating with various NGOs, including the Institute of Public Affairs and the Centre for International Relations, as a researcher. Her main interests include migration, ethnic, and national minorities. She has also worked on research projects within the sixth and seventh framework programmes of the European Commission, namely MIGSYS, CLANDESTINO and EMILIE, and has published numerous academic and policy papers on migration.

Carmen González Enríquez is Full Professor at the Universidad Nacional de Educacion a Distancia (UNED), Department of Political Science. She is also Senior Analyst on Immigration at the Spanish thinktank Real Instituto Elcano. She has directed various research projects on migration such as 'Immigrants and trade unions', 'Immigration and political parties system', 'Preventing ethnic conflict in immigrants`neighbourhoods', 'Immigration in Spain-Morocco relationship', and has taken part in several European research projects on immigration dealing with the trafficking of human beings, irregular migration, civic participation of immigrants, and circular migration.

Krystyna Iglicka is Rector and Professor at Lazarski University, Warsaw, and a Polish government expert on migration policy. She obtained a PhD in Economics from the Warsaw School of Economics (1993) and her Habilitation with a degree in Economics at Warsaw University (2003). She has taught at various Polish universities and also at University College London (UK), University of Glasgow (UK), and University of Birmingham (UK). She has served as a consultant and expert to various international organizations such as the European Commission, International Organization for Migration, OECD and Polish government agencies. Since 2002, she has combined her academic work with the work at various Polish thinktanks, such as the Institute of Public Affairs and the Centre for International Relations. Her pubished works include ten academic books, nearly forty research papers/articles in academic journals published mainly in the USA, UK, and Poland and numerous policy oriented expertise, reports, and analysis.

Nicola Mai is Reader in Migration Studies at ISET, the Institute for the Study of European Transformations of the London Metropolitan University. He has researched several aspects of the Albanian post-communist transformation, with a particular focus on the role played by Italian media in the eliciting of migration and in stigmatizing Albanian migrants in Italy. His current research focuses specifically on the global sex industry as a space within which migrants (and non-migrants) both challenge and reproduce established intersections between social mobility, gender, and sexuality.

Thanos Maroukis is Marie Curie Research Fellow at the University of Bath, UK, working on migration and temporary agency work in the EU. He holds an MS degree from the University of Bristol, and a PhD from Panteion University in Athens. He worked as a researcher at the Hellenic Foundation for European and Foreign Policy (ELIAMEP) in 2007–12 and as a research assistant at the EUI in the METOIKOS project in 2010–11. His principal areas of research are migration studies and the sociology of work, with a special focus on undocumented migration, circular migration, labour issues, and

Notes on Contributors

migrant smuggling. He has authored several articles in scientific journals, book chapters and newspaper articles. His books include *Migrant Smuggling: Irregular Migration from Asia and Africa to Europe* (2012, co-authored with A. Triandafyllidou), *Migration in 21st century Greece* (2010, co-edited with A. Triandafyllidou, in Greek), *Economic Migration in Greece: Labour Market and Social Inclusion* (2009, in Greek).

Cristiana Paladini completed her doctorate in communication and intercultural studies in 2007 at the Lumsa University of Rome, where now she is a contract professor. She has been researching various aspects of migration and social studies such as the role of civil society in the inclusion of migrants in urban territories, and the rule of media in constructing stereotypes. From 2010 she has lived in Albania where she collaborates with several NGOs and international organizations as a field researcher on migration studies and as an expert on social context analysis. Her research is mainly focused on migration patterns, returning migrants, and the impact of migration on countries of origin.

Anna Triandafyllidou is Professor at the Global Governance Programme of the Robert Schuman Centre for Advanced Studies where she directs the Research Strand on <http://globalgovernanceprogramme.eui.eu/researchpublications/strands/cultural-pluralism/>. She was Senior Research Fellow at the Hellenic Foundation for European and Foreign Policy (ELIAMEP) in Athens from 2004 to 2012, where she headed a strong migration research team. She has been teaching as Visiting Professor at the College of Europe in Bruges since 2002. Her main areas of research and teaching are migration, nationalism, and European integration, media and discourse studies. Her recent books include: *Muslims in 21st Century Europe* (2010), *Irregular Migration in Europe: Myths and Realities* (2010), *European Multiculturalism(s)* (with T. Modood and N. Meer, 2011), *Migrant Smuggling. Irregular Migration from Africa and Asia to Europe* (with T. Maroukis, 2012), *The Greek Crisis and Modernity in Europe* (with R. Gropas and H. Kouki, 2013), *Irregular Migrant Domestic Workers in Europe: Who Cares?* (2013), *What is Europe?* (with R. Gropas, 2013).

Francesca Alice Vianello holds a PhD in Sociology. She is post-doctoral fellow at the Department of Philosophy, Sociology, Pedagogy, and Applied Psychology (FISPPA) of the University of Padua. Her main areas of research and teaching are migration, gender and labour. She is responsible for the research project 'Translocational positionality and multi-layered citizenship in Europe: everyday life strategies of migrant families across borders' (2011–13). She collaborates with the Daphne III Project 'Speak Out! Empowering Migrant, Refugee and Ethnic Minority Women against Gender Violence in Europe' and with the Research Project of Relevant National Interest 'Conditions for recognition. Gender, Migrations, Social Spaces'. She is member of the 'Interdepartmental Centre of research: Studies on gender policies' (CIRSPG). She has published the monograph *Migrando sole. Legami transnazionali tra Ucraina e Italia* [Migrating alone. Transnational ties between Ukraine and Italy] (2009) and articles and chapters in edited volumes.

1

Circular Migration: Introductory Remarks

Anna Triandafyllidou

1.1 Introduction

The term circular migration has become a buzzword among European and international policy and academic circles since 2007 when the European Commission issued the Communication 'Mobility Partnerships and Circular Migration', which highlighted the advantages and challenges of this type of migration and put forward specific policy ideas on how to implement it. Many national and European Union (EU) policymakers have heralded the idea of 'circular' migration with great enthusiasm as the solution to many of 'our' migration 'problems'. This EU policy would supposedly address both labour market shortages—by quickly providing a flexible labour force on demand—and migrant integration challenges concurrently (circular migrants are not there to stay and hence will create very limited, if any, integration challenges). Nonetheless, four years later, circular migration schemes such as those envisaged in the EU Communication have been hard to get off the ground, not least because of the acute global financial crisis that started in 2008 and is still ongoing. An additional problem is perhaps that EU policymakers were too ambitious from the start and also that they misunderstood the real needs and aims of migrants themselves (see Triandafyllidou 2009).

Despite this recent interest in circular migration by policymakers, and to a certain extent by scholars too, little is known about the realities of circular migration on the ground in Europe or between European and neighbouring countries. This book aims to contribute towards filling this gap by specifically concentrating on circular migration between EU member states and the region surrounding the EU. Chapter 2 examines circular migration vis-à-vis the larger institutional and policy framework that guides EU policies on circular and temporary migration by analysing critically the political agenda and 'vision' of migration that is behind these schemes. The remaining chapters concentrate on real cases of circularity between EU member states and countries outside the EU. In particular, we have conducted in-depth case studies of seven pairs of countries. Five of these pairs involve neighbouring countries: Greece and Albania, Italy and Albania; Spain and Morocco; Hungary and Ukraine, and Poland and Ukraine. In the other two pairs (Italy–Morocco, and Italy–Ukraine) the two countries involved are not neighbours. However in all seven sets of cases, the countries involved have experienced different forms of temporary, seasonal, circular or indeed more long-term migration. By studying the different forms of circular migration that develop within each pair of countries, we seek to better understand the employment prospects and realities of circular migrants, their motivations, the problems that they face as well as the factors that influence circular migration. A major focus of this book is on how legal status and overall migrant integration policies impact on the development of different forms of circular migration.

We thus eventually propose a full fledged typology of circular migration and assess the factors that create/promote circularity vs. those that prevent it from developing. We assess the importance of the migrant's agency, of the policy framework and we highlight how migrants and their families seize specific windows of opportunity offered to them or indeed create the opportunities and 'right' conditions themselves.

While in the introductory chapter of the book we start with a discussion of the scholarly literature on circular migration and propose a working definition and a tentative typology of circular movements, the concluding chapter completes the circle and provides for a critical assessment of the assumptions made by policymakers and scholars as to what circular migration is, how it develops, and who benefits from it. Our analysis is placed within the wider framework of contemporary transformations of migratory movements as a result of regional integration (within the EU and also between the EU and its neighbourhood), migratory restrictions (which actually prevent rather than encourage spontaneous circularity) and segmented labour markets (where migrants are employed in the secondary labour market).

Six out of the seven case studies presented in this volume are based on empirical research conducted within the METOIKOS research project, a comparative project funded by the European Integration Fund for Third Country Nationals for the period 2009–11 (http://metoikos.eui.eu).[1] In the sections that follow, we offer a critical review of the relevant scholarly literature, and also outline and criticize the policy approach adopted on matters of circular migration by the European Commission. We then propose a working definition of circular migration and a set of dimensions that in our view organize circular migration. The chapter concludes with the presentation of the book contents.

1.2 Circular migration: a buzzword or a new concept and policy framework

The realities of circular migration on the ground have been researched only sporadically since the late 1990s in the Mediterranean and Central and Eastern Europe (Peraldi 2001, 2002; Iglicka 2000, 2001). What research was done mainly highlighted the new patterns of mobility emerging in the European continent after the implosion of the communist regimes in Central and Eastern Europe. More recently, attention has been paid to circular movements of citizens from associated countries to the EU—for instance Polish migrants going to Italy, Germany or Greece in the late 1990s and early 2000s (see Triandafyllidou 2006; Duvell 2006) and to migration between the two coasts of the Mediterranean (Fargues 2008; Cassarino 2008; CARIM Proceedings 2008). Migrants' 'circulation' between their country of origin and their destination country has been taken into account in some preliminary studies on the impact of the global financial and economic crisis on immigration to Europe (Papademetriou et al. 2009).

Vertovec (2007: 2–3, and 5) notes that while scholars have been interested for more than twenty years in migrant transnationalism (Glick Schiller et al. 1992; Portes et al. 1999; Vertovec 2004) and in temporary, cyclical, circular or seasonal migration (see for instance Massey 1987; Massey and Espinosa 1997; Duany 2002; Constant and Zimmerman 2004; Ruhs 2005), policymakers have come to realize the recent fact that migrant transnationalism is intertwined with forms of circular and temporary mobility.

Policymakers have seen in circular mobility the answer to migration and development dilemmas for developing countries. Indeed circular migration has mainly been defined as a new mode of migration management that can provide triple-win solutions—for countries of origin, for countries of destination and for migrants themselves and their families—to the challenges that international migration brings with it. As Venturini (2008) rightly points out, circular migration belongs to the flexibility paradigm which prevails in the European post-Fordist economies during the last few decades. Circular migration fits with the new idea that positions may be temporary both on the high and the lower end of the labour market and that there is a need to respond to the demand and supply sides of labour markets and labour forces in an increasingly globalised world. It should however be also noted that circularity as a migratory phenomenon has existed for a long time between certain countries, in the post Second World War period, and was curtailed with the restrictive immigration policies of the late 1970s which indirectly 'obliged' migrants to stay in the destination country (Venturini 2008; Plewa 2010).

Ideally, circular mobility can or should promote brain circulation instead of brain drain. At the same time, circular and temporary forms of migration are seen to respond better to the swings of markets and the shifting needs of employers as well as to the desires and plans of migrants who are not aiming at settling down in the destination country. Last but not least, circular migration schemes appear to pose a very limited integration burden on destination countries while maximizing transnational transfers (not only in individual/family remittances but also in terms of wider efforts by diaspora groups and hometown associations to promote the development of their regions and countries of origin).

A brief survey of policy and scholarly documents that use the term circular migration (Martin 2003; GCIM 2005; Ruhs 2005; Sandu 2005; Dayton-Johnson et al. 2007; Vertovec 2007) shows that the term remains largely undefined and synonymous to temporary and seasonal migration. The term is sometimes used as an umbrella term for all forms of mobility that involve the repeated crossing of borders (back and forth) are not aimed at long term migrant settlement, and generate some degree of economic and social transnationalism in the form of participation in transnational migration networks that actually facilitate circular migration (moving and returning).

Indeed, in most of these documents, transnationalism is seen as closely intertwined with circular mobility, most importantly with return, not only with leaving the country of origin (Sandu 2005; Vertovec 2007). While the terms circular and temporary are often used (see for instance GCIM 2005; Dayton-Johnson et al. 2007) in a slash fashion 'temporary/circular' without distinguishing whether these are simply two words for describing the same phenomenon, or whether they refer to different social and economic realities.

Vertovec (2007) and related European Commission documents (EC 2005a and EC 2005b) note that circular mobility involves not only temporary stays and returns but also the repeated movement of the same person across borders. Indeed, the European Commission indirectly defines circular migration when it proposes what circular migration policies should promote:

> Policies to maximise the developmental impact of temporary migration ... should focus on encouraging circular migration, by giving a priority for further temporary employment to workers who have already worked under such schemes and have returned at the end of their contract, and also by offering appropriate rewards to participating migrants. (EC 2005a: 7)

The views expressed here emphasize that the same person will move repeatedly and also that circular migration policies should reward those who comply with the conditions of circular mobility.

In their overview of circular mobility and proposals for related policy developments, Dayton-Johnson et al. (2007) implicitly note another feature of circular migration: the fact that circular migrants move back and forth within the same year, over a period of several years in succession and may also change sector of employment. Thus, these authors indirectly point out that circular migration involves short-term or medium-term movement, flexibility in the type of work and type of permit that the migrant has, and facilitation of re-entry. Similarly to the European Commission documents (2005a and 2005b), the study by Dayton-Johnson et al. (2007) sees circular migration as a form of organized mobility scheme rather than as a set of unregulated 'spontaneous' movements initiated by migrants themselves. Vertovec (2007) by contrast, notes that early research on circular migration (referred to by a range of terms such as temporary, repeat, rotating, multiple, cyclical, or shuttle migration modes) concentrated on 'unregulated' rather than formal regulated systems of migration.

The view of circular migration as a regulated system is also adopted by the International Organisation for Migration (IOM) (2005) which, in its 'World Migration 2005' report, implicitly defines circular migration as regular, repeat temporary labour migration which should involve the government's offering to the circular migrant the option of returning to the same job in the future.

It is only in Newland et al. (2008: 2) that we encounter a first attempt at providing a working definition of the term circular migration. Newland and her co-authors note that:

> [W]e have developed a more dynamic notion of circular migration as a continuing, long-term and fluid pattern of human mobility among countries that occupy what is now increasingly recognised as a single economic space.

Indeed, Newland, Agunias, and Terrazas (2008) are the first to recognize the importance of a pre-existing economic space, even if they do not clarify whether this common economic space is a prerequisite or a condition for circular mobility to start, or an outcome of circular mobility. At this point, we may consider the different patterns of circular migration outlined by Cassarino (2008), who identifies three types of circular migration. First, *hindered circular migration*: people who would have an interest to circulate are hindered by the existence of closed or rigidly controlled borders (closed borders may result from political tensions or military conflicts while highly controlled borders are usually related to restrictive migration policies). Secondly, e*mbedded circular migration*: people engage into circular migration patterns despite and because of a border since in reality they cohabit a territorial space and economic area that extends into two neighbouring countries. And thirdly, *regulated circular migration*: when people are selected at the country of origin and move within the framework of a bilateral (or multilateral) agreement.

A question that arises from this discussion concerns the distinction between circular and temporary migration since, as most authors note (Cassarino 2008; Newland et al. 2008), circular and temporary migration share a temporary nature. Newland et al. (2008: 2) argue that:

> Circular migration is distinct from temporary migration in that circular migration denotes a migrant's continuous engagement in both home and adopted countries; it usually involves both return and repetition.... Beyond economic considerations, people also circulate to pursue philanthropic activities, to be close to family, and to seek educational opportunities, among many other reasons. Positive outcomes are less likely to occur when migrants are compelled to return periodically to their home countries simply to avoid permanent settlement.

Indeed, in relation to this point and in seeking to distinguish between circular and temporary migration, Annelies Zoomers notes that 'circular migration means that migrants are free to come and go, whereas the others [temporary, cyclical or contract migration] are more or less forced and managed forms of temporary residence' (cited in Skeldon 2009: 3). Going a step further, Newland and her co-authors (Newland et al. 2008) characterize as 'de facto circular migration' the movement within larger areas with high levels of regional integration, such as the European Union, the Nordic countries, Australia and New Zealand; where borders have been defined as permeable to human mobility. Here they further distinguish between areas such as the European Union or the Nordic countries where borders are to a large extent abolished, and areas united by common trade agreements which trigger as a by product frameworks for labour circulation. Such labour circulation may concern specific groups for limited periods or a wider range of groups for both short and long periods.

The authors cited above (Newland et al. 2008 and Zoomers, cited in Skeldon 2009) agree with Vertovec (2007) that circular migration is largely about unregulated or rather less regulated, non-compulsory mobility, and it extends to the social and cultural sphere, beyond mere employment purposes and economic transfers. This definition of circular migration, however, runs counter to the definition provided by the European Commission in its own documents (2007).

In relation to the more or less regulated nature of circular migration, Cassarino (2008) emphasizes that circular migration (but then also temporary migration) is part of larger frameworks of cooperation and exchange, regardless of whether such frameworks are necessarily fully regulated or whether they have more to do with pre-existing economic and cultural ties between the countries involved.

Circular Migration

Skeldon (2009), on the other hand, emphasizes the bi-local character of circular migration. The circular migrant belongs to both countries those of origin/return, and of destination. However, he notes that such bi-locality cannot be maintained for very long, and actually that circular migration necessarily involves only one generation of migrants. The second generation will either settle in the destination country or stay in the country of origin.

1.3 The EU's attempt to regulate circular migration

In the light of the above, it is worth looking more closely at the European Union's attempt to promote a regulated form of circular migration in the context of what has been termed:[2] mobility partnerships between countries of origin (outside the EU) and countries of destination (within the EU). As stated in section 1.1, the European Commission's Communication on circular migration and mobility partnership had as its primary aim to foster legal migration opportunities for non-EU workers to find employment in the EU, mainly through schemes of circular and temporary migration and through the so-called mobility partnerships. The two aspects developed in the Communication are distinct even if interrelated as the Commission intends to develop new instruments for managing legal migration and combating irregular migration.

1.3.1 *Mobility partnerships and circular migration*

The general aim of the *mobility partnership* approach adopted by the EU is to establish cooperation on a 'balanced partnership with third countries adapted to specific EU member state labour market needs'. The first instrument proposed to give legal shape to these partnerships is the idea of developing 'mobility packages', that is, legal schemes that would frame legal migration, preferably of a circular or temporary character. The Communication specifies that such legal schemes will be complex as they will have to duly balance and regulate the components of these schemes that will belong to the remit of the EU and those that will be in the remit of the member states.

An important part of the Communication is dedicated to explaining how third countries will be motivated—or rather obliged—to implement these temporary mobility schemes. While third countries are named as 'partners' with the EU in the context of these schemes, they are certainly not on an equal footing. As the Communication specifically notes:

> Mobility partnerships...will be tailored to the specifics of each relevant third country, to the ambitions of the country concerned, and of the EU, and to the

level of commitments which the third country is ready to take on in terms of action against illegal migration and facilitating re-integration of returnees, including efforts to provide returnees with employment opportunities.

It is clear from the vocabulary used in the Communication that these partnerships are highly unequal. They reflect power relations where the EU sets the rules of the game and third countries have to abide by these rules. However, third country governments will only have a genuine interest in implementing these partnerships if they can influence, at least to a certain extent, their content and scope, in line with their own interests and needs. Too much weighing of EU interests in this respect is contradictory to the idea of forging a 'partnership' with neighbouring countries.

While the Communication clarifies that mobility partnerships will take different shapes and will depend on the specific situation, a long list of commitments expected from the third country concerned are listed in point B of the Communication (2007: 4). These commitments are all related to readmission of own nationals as well as third country nationals, efforts to improve border control and security of travel documents, to cooperate with the EU on border management issues, and to take up concrete measures for combating trafficking and human smuggling. A last commitment is also added that relates to the third country's obligation to promote 'productive employment and decent work' as a means, among others, to reduce incentives for irregular migration. Moreover, the above will have to be implemented in full respect of human rights. Reading this list, one wonders which third country in the Eastern and Southern European neighbourhood has the capacity to fulfil these commitments. In other words, these commitments are desirable but not realistic.

The unrealistic nature of the Communication's goals is one of the main flaws of the mobility partnership idea. If third country authorities and public administrations were so well organized and effective, they would have probably solved many of their political and economic problems, thus reducing the motivations for migration already at its source. Some countries of origin may lack the technical know-how or indeed the human and economic capital to invest in this cooperation with the EU, regardless of their political will to do so or not. In other words, the mobility partnership concept may be unrealistic as it asks too much from the EU's neighbouring countries.

Migrants leave their homelands not only because of severe economic hardship; they often leave because they see no future in their country for themselves or their children, or because they do not trust the state, and feel insecure and at the mercy of their very own government. It is thus logical that prospective emigrants will not consult their state authorities before leaving. To put it differently, third-country authorities are not the right or at least not the sole actors with whom to sign a mobility partnership agreement. Migrants are likely to mistrust their own governments, consider them as 'hurdles' to overcome, just like the restrictive immigration policies of the destination countries.

Mobility partnerships as proposed, although innovative as a policy idea, do not seem to act in the right direction. Instead of targeting the source of the problem, notably the lack of economic and political opportunities in the countries of origin and the lack of human and financial security, they target the symptoms of it. The inability of both source countries, outside the EU and destination countries in the EU, to manage their borders and prevent unauthorized entry and stay is especially notable. Mobility partnerships seem to put the carriage in front of the horse. They externalize the implementation of border management to third country governments instead of giving priority to EU policies for social and economic development in neighbouring regions, which will collaterally also reduce migration pressures towards the EU.

This brings us to the second part of the Communication that deals with the notion of circular migration. The Commission considers circular migration strictly within the framework of labour market supply and demand (supply by the non-EU countries, labour demand by the EU Member States) largely ignoring any possible problems involved in circular migration. It emphasizes that circular migration in the sense of repeated temporary migration for employment purposes is potentially beneficial both to the EU, because it can respond faster to labour market shortages in high skill sectors, and to countries of origin, as they can avoid brain drain effects. The Communication argues that the promotion of circular migration will have beneficial effects for the involved persons as they will be able to spend limited periods of time in the EU acquiring new skills, improving their training and professional experience, or indeed earning extra money.

The whole concept is based on the idea of a well regulated circular migration that is monitored both by the EU and the country of origin and involves strong incentives also for the individual migrant to comply with the idea of returning back to her/his country when her/his working/training time in the EU is up. These individual incentives are similar to the state incentives for participating in mobility partnerships: the individual who participates in circular migration and complies with the rules may benefit from facilitated and repeated entries in the future. In other words, people who have stayed in the EU and worked or trained there will find it easier to return to an EU country for purposes of employment or study, provided they have respected the conditions of circular migration. The notion of circular migration also foresees schemes promoting reintegration of third country nationals into their country of origin after a stay in the EU. While these are important measures foreseen in the Communication, it remains to be seen how 'real' these benefits of return will be for migrants, given that the idea of returning to the EU in the future will remain an abstract concept rather than a concrete option in the near future (as it is in seasonal migration in agriculture).

While the proposal for developing circular migration schemes targets the individual workers and responds to the rapidly changing conditions in EU labour markets, it remains to be seen how such a scheme could be effectively enforced. It is likely that medium or high skilled professionals will prefer to migrate to countries which allow them to make long-term plans if they wish to settle (US, Canada, Australia, etc.). Concerning skilled and semi-skilled professionals, the idea of circular migration is unlikely to help the EU compete in the global labour market for the best and brightest. The German experience with the IT experts' scheme is a good example of how such controlled mobility cannot work, especially for people who feel they have other migration options available. When Germany launched its IT expert invitation scheme, it stated clearly that the skilled workers would be allowed to stay and work in the country for five years, after which period they would be invited to leave. This rather unwelcoming attitude and the fact that many skilled professionals from Asia or Africa do not speak German (while they speak English) have rendered the scheme so unattractive that its 5,000 positions were not filled. Later Germany has had to modify the scheme and allow for third country nationals completing a degree in German universities to apply.

The close connection that the Commission Communication on Circular Migration and Mobility Partnerships seeks to create between legal and irregular migration is misconceived. It is unclear in what ways irregular and legal flows are inter-related. It may be reasonable to assume that when restrictive policies and highly bureaucratic procedures are in place, making legal migration impracticable (i.e., in several Southern European countries), migrant workers and their native employers will prefer irregular entry and work.

Hence, it is clearly necessary that EU member make sure that their legal entry channels are simple and fast, so that migrant workers can satisfy the demands of domestic labour markets in several sectors where shortages are identified. A step in this direction has been implemented since 2006 in Spain when a long list of jobs was exempted from a labour market test. This has simplified and shortened the procedure for inviting a migrant worker for employment in these sectors. Britain had in 1999 actually liberalized its economic immigration policies by allowing employers to issue themselves work permits, notifying only afterwards the appropriate department of the Home Office. Indeed, innovative policies and cutting down the red tape is crucial in promoting legal channels of migration. Actually, past experience probably suggests that while common standards and principles are possible at the EU level, policies and practices need to remain tailored at the national level as public administration structures and practices remain national too. What can be transferred in this respect is know-how, both technical and legal, and lessons learned from the success or failure of a given policy (taking of course due account of the national context in which it was implemented). One-size-fits-all labour migration schemes or categories are unlikely to be implemented any time soon and may be harmful rather than beneficial to individual member states or the EU as a whole.

Having said this, it is not yet clear how specific forms of legal temporary migration will on the whole discourage irregular movements. A mobility partnership and the opportunity for legal circular migration will affect differently migrants with various types of human, social and economic capital. People who have relatively high social and human capital are likely to be encouraged to wait for an opportunity to migrate legally, but the cost-benefit calculation for low skill migrants may not be altered much by these partnerships. People with low social and human capital may find that the mobility partnership regime in place is not giving them any chance to migrate legally and hence may continue to try the irregular migration route. If this turns out to be the case, one fears that the mobility partnerships will have largely missed their target.

Moreover, it remains unclear whether countries of origin or of transit are able to implement both policies at the same time: to institute and take advantage of mobility partnerships while also ensuring increased levels of enforcement and close cooperation with the EU in the area of migration control and border management. It is interesting to note that in the early 2000s Spain signed agreements of cooperation with important countries of origin in particular Colombia, Ecuador, and Poland (then still a candidate country for EU accession). Spain reserved its annual immigration quotas for citizens of these countries. Despite the fact that the two countries had no past historical or cultural ties, the scheme worked well with Poland for a few years, as Polish authorities had the administrative capacity to cooperate with their Spanish counterparts. By contrast, Colombia, which has strong historical and cultural links with Spain and shares a common language, was unable to implement the agreement due to red tape. This shows that we should not overestimate the source and transit countries' capacity to govern and shape their citizens' plans. Therefore, mobility partnerships need to include a strong element of administrative capacity building through concrete measures, which is not yet foreseen in the Communication.

1.3.2 *Towards a typology of circular migration*

After reviewing the European Commission's view of circular migration and outlining the links between circular migration and wider issues such as migration and development, brain drain or brain circulation, the link between irregular and legal economic migration, we would like now to turn to our own conceptual interest on further developing the concept of circularity. Newland and her co-authors (2008: 3) provide for a short typology of circular migration based on two dimensions: the seasonal (or not) character of movement, and the level of skills of the migrants involved. They thus distinguish between circularity that relates to repeated seasonal employment (in agriculture or tourism for instance). and circularity that is non-seasonal such as contract work for relatively short periods of time (e.g., one or two years) which does not start as a circular pattern but ends up in forming one because the interested migrant is not able to make a living upon return to her/his country of origin, and hence seeks again to participate in the short or medium term migration scheme to which he had taken part before, this becomes some sort of a circular mobility pattern.[3]

The authors also distinguish (Newland et al. 2008: 14–18) between low and semi-skilled circular migration such as seasonal agricultural, tourism, or non-seasonal construction and other semi-skilled work, and high skill circular mobility which concerns professionals, scientists, and entrepreneurs—the kind of people that destination countries seek to keep and that origin countries seek to attract for repatriation. Here circular mobility involves their periodic movement back and forth between the country of origin and one or more destination countries and the related economic, human and social capital transfers that these people can effect.

In this book we consider four dimensions that define circular migration:

- *Space*: The circular migration that is of concern in this project is international, as it involves the crossing of borders.
- *Time*: Circular migration involves stays of limited duration. Each stay may vary from several weeks, to several months to a few years. However, circular migration is not about movements that extend over several years or over a decade.
- *Repetition*: Circular migration is about repeated movements. For mobility to qualify as circular mobility the immigrant in question must have moved at least twice back and forth between country of origin and country of destination.
- *Scope*: Circular migration is not only about employment but it is mainly about economic activities: employment, trade, investment, or otherwise. While social and cultural aspects are involved in circular migration, economic motivations (economic survival, higher earnings, socio-economic mobility, better working conditions, etc.) qualify as circular migration. People who move back to their country of origin to visit relatives for an extended period (for instance two or three months per year are not circular migrants).

Thus circular migration is defined in this book as international, temporary, repeated migration for economic reasons. On the basis of this working definition, we can also further specify the four dimensions that organize circular migration. First is the legal or irregular nature of movement, and hence the regulated or unregulated character of the phenomenon. Here we can distinguish among circular mobility taking place under the framework of bilateral agreements between two countries; circular migrants who hold permits/identity documents that allow them (generally or under certain conditions) to engage into circular mobility between the country of origin and the country of destination; and circular migrants that cross borders illegally.

Second, as regards the level of skills and education of the people involved, we shall distinguish the circular migration movements of unskilled manual workers (e.g., men and women employed as farm workers, cleaners, or men employed as unskilled builders), or that of semi-skilled workers (people working in tourism, catering, construction or caring/cleaning jobs in specialized positions), from the circulation of highly skilled workers (entrepreneurs, scientists, managers).

Third, the time length of each stay and return introduces another dimension. Circular migration may take the form of repeated short stays taking place within less than a year; short stays of between six months and a year that follow an annual cycle; and long-term circular migration that involves stays of a couple of years in each country (origin and destination).[4]

In order to consider the length of each stay, one needs to also identify where the migrant (and her/his family) has their 'home', meaning which country they consider as their 'base'. While for policymakers circular migration is assumed to start from the home country and involve repeated stays at destination, qualitative studies on new European migrations (see also King 2001; Triandafyllidou 2006) suggest that circular migration may also involve people who are already settled in the destination country.

1.4 Factors that influence circular migration

Several factors have been identified in recent studies as conducive to the development of circular migration. Sandu (2005) and Vertovec (2007) note that there are certain demographic factors that characterize circular mobility. Notably, young people tend to engage more in circular mobility. Vertovec (2007: 5) notes that marriage decreases the likelihood of circular mobility but the arrival of children increases it again.

Sandu (2005) underscores the importance of the local hometown/village context in promoting circular mobility. He finds that large Romanian villages in more developed/less poor counties, with a higher percentage of youth population and where circular mobility has already taken place tend to further develop circular migration patterns. He also notes that when Romanian emigration first emerged in the early 1990s ethnic and religious ties with neighbouring countries and related support networks played a major role in the migrants' decision to migrate. As time passed, it was more the collective experience of a community (a village) towards migration and the related 'relational social capital' (Sandu 2005: 571) that people accumulated (through their individual, family and community transnational networks) that mattered much more than ethnic or religious ties. He also finds that human capital (in the form of skills and education) did not increase the likelihood of a person to engage in circular mobility. Rather human capital mattered once the movement and the stay abroad were repeated and prolonged, as it provided for better employment and socio-economic mobility opportunities (Sandu 2005: 571).

Interestingly, both Sandu (2005) and Vertovec (2007) note that the legal or irregular form of the border crossing and the overall movement seems to decrease in importance as experience in migration and in particular in circular mobility increases. Vertovec (2007) argues that the legality of the movement is of limited importance when other conditions tend to favour circular mobility (e.g., employment opportunities and previous experiences of moving, knowledge of how to find accommodation and a job). He argues that the more experienced a 'mover' is, the less s/he pays attention to the legal or irregular conditions of her/his movement. He also notes however that as human capital rises, concerns with being legal are also higher. In the case studies presented in this volume, we specifically analyse how factors such as the legal status of the migrant when circulating, her/his level of education and skills, her/his family situation and age, and her/his previous experience of migration impact on her/his propensity to circulate and the type of circularity that s/he engages in.

It is in the light of the above considerations about what circular migration means, how it is different from temporary or seasonal migration, whether it can better develop into spontaneous or regulated forms, and the review of some concrete examples related to circularity and its advantages and disadvantages, that this book approaches the topic.

1.5 Contents of the book

This book is organized into ten chapters. Chapter 2 places circular migration into its European institutional and policy context while chapters 3 to 9 concentrate on a pair of countries each: Chapter 3 on Albania and Italy;

Chapter 4 on Albania and Greece; Chapter 5 on Morocco and Italy; Chapter 6 on Morocco and Spain; Chapter 7 on Ukraine and Hungary; Chapter 8 on Ukraine and Poland; and Chapter 9 on Ukraine and Italy. In five out of the seven sets of cases studied the two countries involved are neighbours (with the exception of Italy–Morocco and Italy–Ukraine, which are further apart), and have experienced different forms of temporary, seasonal, circular or indeed more long-term migration. The three countries of origin, notably Albania, Ukraine and Morocco have been selected because of their relevance as source countries for economic immigrants, their geographical proximity with the destination countries and because of recent research suggesting that circular migration does take place in these countries, albeit assuming different forms in different labour market contexts and with regard to different types of migrants (low, semi- or high-skilled). Hence, the relevant integration and reintegration challenges and policies are also likely to differ (Triandafyllidou 2009b).

In each pair of countries we have conducted between ten and fifteen interviews with stakeholders, and between thirty and fifty interviews with circular migrants. These interviews took place in both countries of each pair with a view to including stakeholders (state officials, NGOs, trade unions, experts) from either country, and also with a view to capturing the viewpoint of migrants on both sides of the border, and hence at different 'moments' of their circular migration experience. Interviews at the country of origin were conducted in the mother tongue of the interviewees in most cases (i.e., Albanian in Albania, Arabic or French in Morocco, Ukrainian in Ukraine), while in some cases (Italian team research in Morocco) a local researcher facilitated the fieldwork, the contacts and sometimes acted as an interpreter at the interviews. Interviews at the country of destination were conducted mainly in the language of that country or in the language of the country of origin or indeed in a third language (e.g., French for Moroccans). In the case of Spain for instance, interviews with Moroccan women were conducted in Arabic by a Moroccan researcher.

The book concludes with a comparative chapter (Chapter 10) which brings together and compares the circular migration patterns and dynamics among the seven pairs of countries studied, discusses their similarities and differences, constructs a revised typology of circular migration, compares the factors and policies that affect circular migration patterns within each pair of countries. This chapter pays special attention to the role of the migrant's agency and the ways in which migrants not only react and seize the opportunities available to them but also create opportunities under the pressure of economic uncertainty.

1.5.1 *Chapter outline*

In Chapter 2, Jean-Pierre Cassarino discusses critically the wider policy and institutional set-up that frames circular migration and highlights the contradictions built into it. This chapter sets out to contextualize the introduction of EU-sponsored circular migration programmes. It explains that circular migration programmes do not only build upon past practices designed to regulate the movement of international migrants (e.g., with temporary labour migrant schemes); they also embed the adoption of temporary and circular migration programmes within new security-driven agendas. This unquestioned though questionable linkage between (circular) migration and security reflects the predominant schemes of understanding that today structure migration policy discourses and shape the management of international migration.

In Chapter 3 Nicola Mai and Cristiana Paladini look at flexible circularities between Italy and Albania. The chapter argues against the politicized celebration of the 'circularisation' of migration as a win-win situation for both countries of origin and destination. The findings of our study show that the majority of research participants were reluctantly and ambivalently oscillating between Albania and Italy. For most, circulating is a way to achieve the migratory flexibility they need to negotiate their livelihoods between societies and labour markets characterized by the different opportunities, predicaments and degrees of socio-economic and political instability. Most Albanian migrants do not choose to circulate, but accept to do so in order to secure the sustainability of projects of settlement abroad and/or return home which are still not completed or which became unsustainable in the context of the global financial crisis of the late 2000s. For younger people and women, particularly if they are studying, oscillating between Albania and Italy is both a way to reconcile the contradictory moral worlds brought together by their diasporic trajectories and a way to gain the socio-cultural capital to bypass widespread dynamics of corruption and preferential access to the labour market in Albania.

In Chapter 4 Thanos Maroukis and Eda Gemi look at the circularity patterns that develop between Albania and Greece. Albanians have been moving back and forth between Greece and their home country throughout the last two decades. Doing so, often, was part of different migration plans. Nowadays, after two decades of immigration experience and in the context of the economic crisis and the different crossroads that these two countries stand before the EU, the options of return and circular migration become all the more pertinent in the agenda of the Albanian migrant household. This chapter brings up the diversity of the circular patterns of mobility of the Albanian migrants, and discusses the scope of spontaneous versus state-managed forms of circularity with a view to understanding the prospects of this circularity for the parties involved (the migrant, the employer, the host country and the country of origin).

Camilla Devitt (in Chapter 5) provides an analysis of Moroccan circular economic migration between Italy and Morocco. Interestingly, the study shows that circularity does not necessarily start from the country of origin but may also be the conclusion of a migratory experience (i.e., after a long stay in Italy the migrant goes back to Morocco and then engages into circular migration to work for the summer season in Italy in street peddling), or just an intermediate step during the course of a longer stay at the destination country (e.g., the migrant has a long term stay permit in Italy but because of unstable employment or insufficient income engages into transport and trade activities with Morocco to sustain himself and his family). The significance of such movements in the overall context of Moroccan migration to Italy is evaluated and explained, with a particular focus on the role of various Italian and Moroccan policies in fostering or indeed impeding this kind of circular migration. In particular they look at the importance of residence security in Italy as a factor for fostering circularity as well as the need for economic reintegration policies in Morocco.

Chapter 6 (by Carmen González Enríquez) points to a totally different reality between Spain and Morocco. Indeed, although the two countries are neighbours and more than 760,000 Moroccans live in Spain, the strong limitations to circulation among them have reduced circular migration to seasonal agricultural work. The chapter describes the institutional framework which restricts circularity and explains it in the context of past experiences related with the arrival of big numbers of irregular Moroccan migrants and the fear of opening legal ways of entry which could become doors to new irregular staying. The main features of Moroccan migration to Spain are presented as social framework, underlying the striking absence of a qualified migration. Moroccan-Spanish experience on seasonal agricultural circularity is broadly evaluated as positive among stakeholders in both countries and it has constituted itself into a 'model' which European and international institutions try to diffuse in other countries. The chapter describes the origin, organization, and functioning of this managed circularity, the impact on the home country, and the challenges it faces.

In Chapter 7, Ayşe Çağlar discusses the complicated circularities that characterize the migratory movements between Hungary and Ukraine. The chapter points to this region's historical specificities and legacies and also to the role played by the Hungarian state politics and national ideology vis-à-vis Hungarian minorities abroad. It focuses on the impact of Hungary's EU membership and the economic crisis of 2008 on the volume, composition and the directionality of migration from Ukraine to Hungary. The findings of this case study open up questions about the temporal dimension and the directionality of flows which are substantial to the concept of circular migration. By drawing attention to the increasing multidirectional nature of the migrants' mobility from Ukraine to Hungary, this chapter raises critical questions about the concept of 'circular' migration.

Chapter 8 (by Krystyna Iglicka and Katarzyna Gmaj) points to short-term employment and circular migration as a survival strategy among Ukrainian women in Poland. These women follow established patterns elaborated by their networks instead of searching for longer stay possibilities. They are often not aware of other options or they are convinced that these options are beyond their scope. Periodic returns to Ukraine are necessary for legal reasons too; to renew their short term stay visas. However, engaging into circular migration allows Ukrainian women to reconcile their income from employment abroad with family roles such as looking after young children, elderly parents and husbands.

Chapter 9, by Francesca Alice Vianello, looks at circular migration between Ukraine and Italy. Here too circularity is predominantly a female domain, and actually concerns approximately 80 per cent of the 170,000 Ukrainians officially resident in Italy. The chapter casts light on the main factors hindering or facilitating circular migration between Ukraine and Italy such as the restrictive Italian immigration policies, the features of the Italian and Ukrainian labour market, and the migrants' family ties back home in Ukraine.

In the concluding chapter (Chapter 10), Anna Triandafyllidou develops a typology of circular migration patterns identified in the seven pairs of cases presented in Chapters 3 to 9. She discusses the similarities and differences within each set of countries, notably between Italy, Albania and Greece, between Morocco, Italy, and Spain; between Hungary, Poland, Italy, and Ukraine with a view to identifying their specificities but also their common elements. She argues that the role of policies is important in fostering circular migration, for instance: promoting secure long-term residence to settled immigrants who then engage in circular migration, or allowing for repeated temporary/circular migration. However, circularity is largely conditioned by human agency and should thus not be seen entirely within the policy and structure paradigm, but rather be analysed in relation to the role of human agency in international migration.

References

CARIM Proceedings (2008). *Circular Migration Meetings*, CARIM Proceedings 2008/01 [online report], http://www.carim.org (10 December 2009).

Cassarino, Jean Pierre (2004). 'Theorising Return Migration', *International Journal on Multicultural Societies*, 6(2), 253–79.

Cassarino, Jean Pierre (2008). 'Patterns of Circular Migration in the Euro-Mediterranean Area. Implications for Policy Making', *CARIM Analytic and Synthetic Notes, CARIM-AS 2008/29* [online], http://www.carim.org (accessed 9 January 2010).

Castles, Stephen (2006). 'Back to the Future? Can Europe Meet its Labour Needs through Temporary Migration?' *Oxford: International Migration Institute Working Paper no. 1.*

Constant, Amelie and Zimmerman, Klaus F. (2004). 'Circular Movements and Time Away from the Host Country', London: Centre for Economic Policy Research, Discussion Paper 4228.

Council of the European Union (2009). *The Stockholm Programme. An Open and Secure Europe Serving and Protecting the Citizens.* Document no. 17024/09, Brussels, 2 December 2009.

Cremona, Marise (2008). 'Circular Migration: A Legal Perspective', *CARIM Analytic and Synthetic Notes*, CARIM-AS 2008/30 [online], www.carim.org (accessed 11 June 2010).

Dayton-Johnson, J. et al. (2007). *Gaining from Migration: Towards a New Mobility System.* Paris: OECD.

Duany, Jorge (2002). 'Mobile livelihoods: The Sociocultural Practices of Circular Migrants between Puerto Rico and the United States', *International Migration Review*, 36(2), 355–88.

Duvell, Franck (2006). *Illegal Migration in Europe: Beyond Control.* Basingstoke: Palgrave Macmillan.

Erzan, Refik (2008). 'Circular Migration: Economic Aspects', *CARIM Analytic and Synthetic Notes*, CARIM-AS 2008/31 [online], www.carim.org (accessed: 8 June 2010).

European Commission (2005a). *Migration and Development: Some Concrete Orientations.* Brussels: Communication from the Commission to the Council, the European Parliament, the European Economic and Social Committee and the Committee of the Regions, COM (2005) 390 Final.

European Commission (2005b). *Policy Plan on Legal Migration.* Brussels: Communication from the Commission, COM (2005) 669 Final.

Fargues, Philippe (2008). 'Circular Migration. Is it Relevant for the South and East of the Mediterranean?' *CARIM Analytic and Synthetic Notes, CARIM-AS 2008/40* [online], www.carim.org (accessed: 5 January 2010).

Fargues, Philippe (2009). *Irregularity as Normality among Immigrants South and East of the Mediterranean*, CARIM 2009/02 [online background paper], www.carim.org (accessed: 3 December 2009).

GCIM, Global Commission on International Migration (2005). *Migration in an Interconnected World: New Directions for Action.* Geneva: Global Commission on International Migration.

Glick-Schiller, N. et al. (1992). 'Transnationalism: A New Analytic Framework for Understanding Migration', in N. Glick Schiller, L. Basch, and C. Szanton Blanc (eds), *Towards a Transnational Perspective on Migration.* New York: New York Academy of Sciences, 1–24.

Iglicka, Krystyna (2000). 'Mediterranean Migration of Poles in the 1990s: Patterns and Mechanisms', *Studi Emigrazione/Migration Studies*, xxxvii(139), 651–63.

Iglicka, Krystyna (2001). 'Shuttling from the Former Soviet Union to Poland: From "Primitive Mobility" to Migration', *Journal of Ethnic and Migration Studies*, 27(3), 505–18.
IOM (International Organization for Migration) (2005). *World Migration 2005: Costs and Benefits of International Migration*. Geneva: IOM.
Kosic, A. and Triandafyllidou, A. (2004). 'Albanian and Polish Migration to Italy: The Micro-Processes of Policy, Implementation and Immigrant Survival Strategies', *International Migration Review*, 38(4), 1413–46.
Lutz, Helma (2008). 'Gender in the Migratory Process', paper presented at the Conference on Theories of Migration and Social Change, St Ann's College, Oxford, 1–3 July 2008.
Martin, Philip L. (2003). *Managing Labour Migration: Temporary Worker Programs for the 21st Century*, Geneva: International Institute for Labour Studies, ILO.
Massey, Douglas (1987). 'Understanding Mexican Migration to the United States', *American Journal of Sociology*, 92(6), 1372–403.
Massey, Douglas and Espinosa, Kristin (1997). 'What's Driving Mexico-U.S. Migration? A Theoretical, Empirical and Policy Analysis', *American Journal of Sociology*, 102(4), 939–99.
Metz-Göcke, S., Morokvasic M., and Senganata A. M. (2008). *Migration and Mobility in an Enlarged Europe: A Gender Perspective*. Leverkusen-Opladen: Budrich.
Newland, K., Rannveig Agunias, D. and Terrazas, A. (2008). 'Learning by Doing: Experiences of Circular Migration', *Migration Policy Institute, Insight*, September 2008, [online] http://www.migrationpolicy.org/pubs/Insight-IGC-Sept08.pdf (accessed 13 September 2012).
Papademetriou, Demetrios and Terrazas, Aaron (2009). *Immigrants and the Current Economic Crisis: Research Evidence, Policy Challenges and Implications*. Washington, DC: Migration Policy Institutes.
Peraldi, Michel (2001). *Cabas et Containers*. Paris: Maisonneuve and Larose.
Peraldi, Michel (2002). *La fin des norias?* Paris: Maisonneuve and Larose.
Portes, A., Guarnizo L. E., and Landolt, P. (1999). 'The Study of Transnationalism: Pitfalls and Promises of an EmergentRresearch Field', *Ethnic and Racial Studies*, 22(2), 217–37.
Ruhs, Martin (2005). *The Potential of Temporary Migration Programmes in Future International Migration Policy*. Geneva: Global Commission on International Migration.
Sandu, Dumitru (2005). 'Emerging Transnational Migration from Romanian Villages', *Current Sociology*, 53(4), 555–82.
Skeldon, Ronald (2009). *Managing Migration for Development: Is Circular Migration the Answer?* Paper presented at the Swedish EU Presidency Meeting on Labour Migration and its Development Potential in the Age of Mobility, Malmoe, Sweden, 15–16 October.
Triandafyllidou, A. (2006). *Contemporary Polish Migration in Europe. Complex Patterns of Movement and Settlement*. Lewiston, NY: Edwin Mellen Press.
Triandafyllidou, A. (2009). 'Managing Migration in the EU: Mobility Partnership and the European Neighbourhood', ELIAMEP Thesis, 1/2009 [online policy paper] www.eliamep.gr/en/ (accessed: 24 July 2012).

Venturini, Alessandra (2008). 'Circular Migration as an Employment Strategy for Mediterranean Countries', *CARIM Analytic and Synthetic Notes*, CARIM-AS 2008/39 [online], www.carim.org (accessed:11 June 2010).

Vertovec, Steven (2004). 'Migrant Transnationalism and Modes of Transformation', *International Migration Review*, 38(3), 970–1001.

Vertovec, Steven (2007). 'Circular Migration. The Way Forward in Global Policy?', International Migration Institute, University of Oxford, Year 2007, Paper 4.

Notes

1. The Chapter on Italy and Ukraine is based on Francesca Vianello's PhD dissertation.
2. This section largely borrows from Triandafyllidou (2009).
3. Newland et al. (2008) use the example of Asian migration to the Gulf countries as typical of circular non-seasonal mobility. They also however outline related non-seasonal schemes adopted in the UK, Spain, New Zealand, and by the Philippines as a country of origin that seeks to be actively involved in the management of its emigrants.
4. Venturini (2008) argues that an extended definition of circular migration may also include return migration. In other words, it may include migrants who only went and returned once in a lifetime. Provided the return took place during their working age and not after they retired. However, for the purposes of this project we are concentrating on migrants who moved back and forth more than once.

2

The Drive for Securitized Temporariness

Jean-Pierre Cassarino

2.1 Introduction

Never before has the term 'circular migration' been used and mentioned by so many diverse actors ranging from scholars, thinktank experts, policymakers, migration stakeholders, and officials from the European Union (EU), the United Nations and the World Bank. Over the last seven years or so, a plethora of studies, reports, policy briefs, communications and recommendations have been produced to address the logic and relevance of circular migration. Clearly, in the West this plethoric production coincides with the renewed attention paid by European leaders to the regulated temporary stay of foreign workers. In 2005, the Global Commission on International Migration (GCIM) underlined 'the need to grasp the developmental opportunities that this important shift (i.e., circular migration) in migration patterns provides for countries of origin' (GCIM 2005: 31), even if, as noted by Stephen Castles, this positive assumption of circular migration remained undefined in the GCIM Report (Castles 2006: 12). The same year, the European Commission presented policy recommendations aimed at 'encouraging circular migration, by giving a priority for further temporary employment to workers who have already worked under such schemes and have returned at the end of their contract, and also offering appropriate rewards to participating migrants' (European Commission 2005: 7). Later, in May 2007, the European Commission defined circular migration 'as a form of migration that is managed in a way allowing some degree of legal mobility back and forth between two countries' (2007a: 8).

The objective of this chapter is not to review the literature on circular migration that has proliferated like a ripple effect over the last few years, nor is it aimed at explaining whether 'circular migration programmes' are a winner in the so-called management of international migration, serving the interests of countries of destination and of origin as well as those of migrants. Rather, this chapter sets out to contextualize the introduction of EU-sponsored circular migration programmes, while explaining that something anchored in the past may account for policymakers' current focus on temporary *and* circular migration. In other words, this chapter shows that circular migration programmes do not only build upon past practices designed to regulate the movement of international migrants (e.g., with temporary labour migrant schemes); they also react against such inherited practices in a subtle manner by linking the adoption of temporary and circular migration programmes with new security-driven safeguards. This unquestioned though questionable linkage is reflective of the consolidation of powerful drivers and predominant schemes of understanding that today structure migration talks and orient policy options as applied to the management of international migration.

2.2 The circularity issue

What circular migration precisely implies and how it differs from migration *tout court* is rather clear for migration scholars. It is, however, unclear how and what governmental and intergovernmental institutions intend to promote and implement when talking about circular migration.

People moving across borders may, through their mobility, be involved in a form of back and forth movement between their places of origin and of destination. Because of their repeated and fluid cross-border mobility, they are circular migrants. Migrants' countries of origin and destination may cooperate with a view to developing circular migration programmes. However, the premises of these bilateral schemes may turn out to be so constraining and restrictive in terms of participation that, in practice, the bilateral cooperation might promote the selective temporariness of labour mobility more than its fluid circulation.

Frank Bovenkerk (1974) defined circulation as 'the to and fro movement between two places, [this movement] includes more than one return [to the place of origin]'. Repeated movements are the ingredients leading to circulation. These may include stays in one or various countries abroad with repeated return movements back to the country of origin. Bovenkerk describes a pendulum-like movement between migrants' country of origin and one or various destination countries. This means that migrants may circulate abroad or reside in various destination countries before returning more than once to their home country. In other words, circular migration cannot be viewed in the limited sense of a binary movement between the country of origin and one country of destination. There are additional elements inherent in the dynamics of circular migration that need to be stressed.

First, circular migration does not involve legal migrants only. As emphasized by Amelie Constant and Klaus Zimmermann (2007), 'circular migration is even an issue for illegal migrants'. Their assumption implies that circular migration movements are not necessarily managed as a result of state policies.

Second, not all migrants are circular migrants. In other words, not all migrants (can easily) circulate between their origin countries and abroad. There are migrants who leave for abroad and stay abroad (i.e., they emigrate). There are migrants who leave for abroad once before returning for good and staying in their home countries (i.e., they return on a permanent basis). Conversely, there are migrants who leave for abroad before returning to their home countries on a temporary basis, and then decide to move again (i.e., they return on a temporary basis and circulate across borders).

Third, there exist various patterns of cross-border circularity which are shaped not only by the mobility strategy of migrants but also by state policies in the field of migration management and border controls. Against this background, the circular migration programmes, which have been extensively discussed by European policymakers and migration stakeholders, constitute just one pattern of circular mobility.

2.3 Patterns of circularity

Laying emphasis on the existence of various patterns of circular migration is key to understanding that the repeated cross-border movements of persons may be shaped and reshaped by changing circumstances and structural factors which sometimes foster and disrupt migrants' mobility. Patterns of circularity vary across time, space and as a result of migrants' agency. These preliminary remarks are important to further the reflection on circular migration between destination and origin countries while showing that patterns of circularity may be hindered, embedded and regulated.[1]

Firstly, circular migration may be hindered when major obstacles prevent people from circulating across the border. Obstacles are diverse. They may stem from severe political tensions and military disputes between two countries, making the crossing of their adjacent border barely impossible.[2] Obstacles may also result from restrictive immigration policies and strengthened border controls which prevent the repeated back and forth movements that inhere in circular migration; emigration (whether legal or unauthorized, whether temporary or permanent) is the only option.

Secondly, circular migration is embedded into the lived reality of a given territorial area when a form of symbiotic relationship exists between people and territories, when people cohabit with a border which (administratively but not physically) demarcates two territorial entities that are characterized by frequent exchanges of goods, contacts and interaction, and when frequent circular movements exist despite and because of the border. Circular migration may also be embedded in the consolidation of a regional trading bloc, because the fluid movement of people is viewed as being conducive to a reinforced integration process between the member states of a trading bloc and to an area of stability and enhanced economic exchanges. Circulation is fostered by the lowering of national barriers or by granting preferential free-entry visa regimes between member states. The European Union is probably the most emblematic example of this embedded circularity. Circularity exists because of the existence of a coherent and stable bloc of countries which mutually agree to lower their barriers. Vice versa, the bloc of countries exists because of the internal circularity which nurtures its cohesion and unity.

In different settings, circular migration may be viewed as being embedded because it is or has always been part of the reality of a geographical area covering various national territories. In this case, repeated cross-border movements of people precede and survive the formation of the nation-state. Whether states decide or not to foster, from a top-down perspective, the mobility of their citizens, circular migration remains part and parcel of grass-roots dynamics sustaining the mobility of people across borders.[3] The repeated back and forth mobility of people is emblematic of a self-sustaining cross-border circulation, which is viewed and perceived by some segments of the population as being a natural off-shoot of the historical regional context.

Crisis, in all its dimensions, is more often than not the key factor that turns the repeated to and fro movement of migrants into a visible, if not a problematic, phenomenon. What was viewed as being part of the lived reality of a cross-national context (i.e., embedded circular migration) may be viewed as being disruptive because of changed circumstances. As mentioned above, the embeddedness of some circular movements may be questioned by crisis elements at national and international levels. The state may respond by adopting restrictive provisions aimed at controlling and regulating the entry and residence of migrants while showing to its constituency that it has the capacity to do so. Similarly, the host society may respond with strong xenophobic perceptions and discriminatory attitudes *vis-à-vis* circular migrants with a view to (re)constructing boundaries of distinctiveness as a reaction to the perceptible porosity of the national border.

Thirdly, circular migration may be managed and regulated when institutional mechanisms are implemented to determine the number of admitted migrants (e.g., with entry quotas), to monitor their limited duration of stay abroad, and to select their profiles and skills. Regulated circular migration involves the prior selection of migrants in their country of origin.

It is important to stress that the above-mentioned three different patterns of circular migration are not mutually exclusive. Circular migration may be abruptly hindered (owing to tense diplomatic relations, restrictive immigration policies, closure of the border), and be gradually and potentially conducive to e*migration* or even to no mobility at all. Furthermore, the reference to the notion of embedded circular migration is important to show that grass-roots patterns of circular mobility may be self-sustaining and unmanaged, for they are part and parcel of the lived reality of an area spanning national territories. Finally, circular migration may be promoted and regulated at a top-down level when governmental institutions decide to organize the temporary recruitment of specific categories of migrants in response to labour needs in destination countries. The next section sets out to explain the rationale for regulated circular migration while laying emphasis on how past practices have impacted on the current configuration of circular migration programmes.

2.4 A historical perspective

Just like temporary migration programmes (e.g., Germany's *gastarbeiter* programme), circular migration programmes respond to the need for foreign manpower in destination countries' labour markets. Memoranda of understanding, exchanges of letters, and agreements may be concluded at a bilateral level to match labour needs in specific sectors of industry. Another characteristic shared by temporary migration programmes (TMPs) and circular migration programmes (CMPs) lies in the fact that they are part and parcel of broader patterns of bilateral cooperation.

Another common denominator between TMPs and CMPs is that both programmes often involve countries that are characterized by strong differentials in terms of living conditions, wages, economic development, education, the rule of law, and political governance, to mention just a few. The resilience of such differentials makes the temporariness of labour migration an extremely tricky issue, not only because migrants may be tempted to seek permanent settlement abroad, but also because migrants' countries of origin and destination may not share the same vision and interests in managing temporary migration.

Short-term employment is a declared objective shared by both TMPs and CMPs. In practice, however, the return and rotation of foreign workers, on which TMPs were premised, did not occur systematically. With reference to the German guest worker programmes, Philip Martin explains that such programmes lasted longer than expected because 'employers often encouraged migrants to stay longer, saving them the cost of recruiting and training a replacement' (Martin 2003: 10). At the same time, two additional effects contributed to the time extension of TMPs. In Martin's opinion, the first one relates to 'dependence', namely the fact that migrants and their families could come to depend on foreign jobs through family reunification. The second effect pertains to 'distortion', which, to rephrase Martin, refers to 'the fact that employers make investment decisions on the assumption that migrants will continue to be available' (Martin 2003: 1), leading to an adjustment of domestic labour markets to the presence of foreign workers. Both the dependence and distortion effects prevented the rotation of foreign labour and the expected return of foreign workers to their home countries. Other unintended consequences also included the capacity of foreign workers to organize themselves through trade unions and to voice their claims for equal treatment through strikes.

Martin's assumption is important to understand that a combination of economic and non-economic factors combined together, making the temporary stay of foreign workers *less* temporary, if not permanent. Of course, the oft-cited maxim that 'there is nothing more permanent than temporary foreign workers' is certainly convenient for some analysts and policymakers to rationalize the so-called 'failure of temporary migration programmes' and to subtly justify the introduction of additional legal and administrative restrictions designed to ensure the short-term admission of foreign labour. This maxim is also suitable to reify the managerial centrality of the state and of its law-enforcement agencies, with a view to showing to constituencies that 'past policy mistakes' (Ruhs 2005: 7)—if these were at all mistakes—will not occur any longer. At the same time, one is entitled to wonder whether it is reasonable to focus exclusively on the need to limit at all costs the duration of stay of foreign workers, when we learn from past experience that the root causes of their prolonged stay stem, among others, from a mix of economic performance and a complex socialization process, whereby migrant workers were encouraged by their employers to stay for longer.

To grasp such systemic causes, the most adequate maxim is certainly not the one mentioned above; rather, it is Max Frisch's 'we wanted a labour force, but human beings came' with their own qualities, skills, and aspirations for stability in their lives, advancement, and rights. This maxim reflects a truth that political and economic elites in many Western countries realized one century ago: the 'impossibility of separating the marketable resource (labour services) from the human beings who offered them' (Crouch 2008: 4–5). This specific context favoured the adoption of regulations aimed at protecting workers' labour rights and at reducing their life uncertainties (with reservation wages,[4] protective employment laws, social insurance arrangements, and welfare benefits).

Colin Crouch remarks that such labour security measures started to be under strong political pressure following the 1973 oil crisis, rising unemployment and inflation, leading to the gradual prioritization (and acceptance) of job flexibility over protection from uncertainty. This gradual shift in priority could be summarized by saying that 'if earlier labour law was concerned with human rights, today's law is concerned with human resources' (Crouch 2008: 7). Manifestly, this shift did not occur overnight. To date, it has contributed to making the current emphasis placed by economic and political elites on workers' employability more acceptable and thinkable. The recurrent reference to employability in public discourse reflects the 'adjustment of labour supply to the requirements of the market, deregulation and rising labour market flexibility' (Burroni and Keune 2011: 76). The next section sets out to analyse how this neo-liberal shift in labour market policies has impacted on the ways in which circular migration programmes have been thought and configured, particularly regarding migrants' 'employability' and their labour rights.

2.5 Old and new priorities

The abovementioned shift that occurred as a result of the 1973 oil crisis had a decisive impact on the gradual commodification of labour, while exposing it at the same time to market competitiveness and uncertainty. For migrant workers in European destination countries, this shift also entailed a process of market deregulation which, quite paradoxically, went hand in hand with the reinforced regulation of migration by the state administration. The international agenda for the management of migration, which was introduced in Bern in 2001, is most emblematic of the reinforced regulatory function of public administration. I will get back to its implications for the way in which circular migration programmes have been configured at a later stage.

As of the mid-1970s, restrictive immigration laws were adopted not only to channel given human resources to given sectors of industry, but also to turn migrant workers into a vulnerable commodity, subject to 'market forces' and political discretion. For example, in France the right to stay became subordinated to migrant workers having a job contract. Moreover, family reunification was made more difficult following the introduction of restrictive criteria. Later on, these restrictions were accompanied by the implementation of state-led 'return' programmes aimed at inducing migrants to leave French territory. Such programmes were initially questioned and subsequently suspended. Then, during the late 1980s, they were reintroduced by the French government. This was not just a response to the resilient economic downturn in France and to the growing politicization of such domestic concerns as the 'integration of immigrants', citizenship and identity, as well as the separation between religion and the state (France's *laïcité*). These programmes also constituted and still constitute the most explicit form of state interventionism designed to make constituencies (more) aware of the presence of the sovereign, above all in a context marked by growing globalization, including economic deregulation, industrial delocalization and calls for state divestiture. These coercive practices soon became suitable for policymakers to express the resilience of state authority and sanction, when needed, and to classify aliens and citizens alike (Engbersen 2009).

As early as the 1990s, particularly following the 1993 entry into force of the Treaty on European Union (TEU), the EU intended to play a major role by turning migration into an issue of 'common interest' and by obliging member states to better cooperate on (and harmonize their national) migration policies.

In January 1994, the European Commission (EC) set out to propose three main areas of action, including the creation of new rights for legally resident immigrants, reinforced integration policies, and tougher measures against unauthorized migration. The EU's call for policy harmonization reflected the initial desire to adopt supranational common standards on legal immigration in order to 'enhance the social integration of legally resident immigrants through equal opportunities in employment, education, housing, social policy and health care'.[5] The attempt of the EC to spread its influence into areas viewed as being under the sovereign preserve of the member states was met with strong reluctance, if not stark criticisms on the part of the Council. In July 1998, a strategy paper on immigration and asylum policy, submitted by the then Austrian Presidency, emblematically reflected such criticisms towards the full harmonization of migration laws in Europe. While recognizing 'a thoroughly respectable achievement and an essential step towards approximation of the law in Europe', the Council added:

> The European Union has not really managed to influence sustainably the reality of immigration in a manner that can be ascertained empirically. Neither the potential will to emigrate nor actual emigration from the main regions of origin has decreased in the past five years (rather the opposite) [...] The incessant influx of illegal migrants and the effects of migration crises on demographic policy have been major contributing factors to the absence of any prospect, even now, of uniform EU-wide rights of legal immigrants. (European Council 1998: § 5)

> The initiatives taken in the Union to harmonise the available data on migratory movements and to improve the quality of data were only partly successful. (European Council 1998: § 10)

> Effective measures to combat illegal employment have still not been taken [by the Union]. However, to reduce the pull factors of illegal migration and to promote social stabilisation of the host societies, this aspect is extremely important, and increasingly so in view of unemployment trends. If the Union now devotes itself

to fighting unemployment as a priority objective, considerable importance will also have to be attached in this context to a strategy to counter illegal immigration. (European Council 1998: § 18)

It has to be stressed that member states have expressed their concern in numerous ways regarding the capacity of the EU institutions to deal 'effectively' with unauthorized migration, including the thorny issue of readmission. In 2003, the G5 (today's G6) was founded, bringing together the interior ministers of France, Spain, the United Kingdom, Italy, Germany, and Poland (since 2006). On 27 May 2005, the Prüm Treaty was signed.[6] This treaty is aimed at stepping up cross-border police cooperation and exchanges between member states' law enforcement agencies to combat organized crime, terrorism, and unauthorized migration. In September 2006, an open letter was addressed to the then Finnish Presidency of the Council of the European Union, calling for reinforced common concrete actions to 'counter mass arrivals' in Southern Europe. The open letter came from the heads of state of Cyprus, France, Greece, Italy, Malta, Portugal, Slovenia, and Spain. On 13 January 2009, a document was delivered to the then Czech Presidency of the Council of the European Union, pressing for the conclusion and effective implementation of Community readmission agreements.[7] Cyprus, Greece, Italy and Malta decided to coalesce in order to form the Quadro Group during the French EU Presidency (July–December 2008) with a view to keeping unauthorized migration on the EU agenda in the offing of the entry into force of the Treaty of Lisbon (Cassarino 2011).

These developments clearly show that the existence of an exclusive Community competence on immigration has been an issue of contention between the EU on the one hand and its member states on the other. The 2009 entry into force of the Treaty of Lisbon clarified, to some extent, the scope of Community competence by stating that the Union shall develop a common immigration policy without affecting 'the right of member states to determine volumes of admission of third-country nationals coming from third countries to their territory in order to seek work, whether employed or self-employed' (Art. 79, § 5 TFEU); and without harmonizing the laws and regulations of the member states regarding the integration of third-country nationals residing legally in their territories (Art. 79, § 4 TFEU).

Such limits clearly illustrate the difficult path towards the creation of a fully fledged EU immigration policy based on harmonized standards, as well as the resilience of bilateralism (Cassarino 2011). Attempts to harmonize migration policies have been confronted with the resilient sovereign right of each EU member state to require third-country nationals to comply with national integration laws (as stated in the 2003 Family Reunion Directive), or to determine the volume and skills of qualified foreign nationals admitted, on a temporary basis, in their territories (as foreseen in the 2009 Blue Card Directive).[8]

Such developments have also had serious implications for the way in which the EU has responded to the need for migration management, whether legal or unauthorized. Against this backdrop, it is no accident that the EU initiatives have been, as it were, regimented by the security-oriented concerns and recurrent criticisms of the EU member states (particularly but not exclusively France, Germany, Greece, the United Kingdom, Italy, and Spain). It could even be argued that a form of policy convergence as applied to migration issues has taken place between the EU and its member states, through recurrent dialogues and meetings, leading to a form of alignment prioritizing security concerns (Cassarino 2010).

This gradual alignment found its full expression in the adoption in December 2005 of the Global Approach to Migration (GAM)—an approach which had already been put forward by the Council in its July 1998 Strategy paper (see above). The GAM was described as 'a comprehensive approach [combining] measures aimed at facilitating legal migration opportunities with those reducing illegal migration' (European Council 2007: 3). There is no question that this dual combination has had a certain bearing on how circular migration programmes were designed and implemented through the introduction of mobility partnerships.

2.6 Mobility partnerships and circular migration programmes

Mobility partnerships form an integral part of the GAM (European Commission 2007a: 4). They encompass a broad range of issues ranging from development aid to temporary entry visa facilitation, circular migration programmes,[9] and the fight against unauthorized migration, including cooperation on readmission. They are selective in that they are addressed to those third countries once certain conditions are met, such as cooperation on unauthorized migration and the existence of 'effective mechanisms for readmission' (European Commission 2007a: 19). The EU's attempt to link mobility partnerships with cooperation on readmission reflects how this issue has become a central component of its immigration policy. This conditional link is also stressed in the European Pact on Immigration and Asylum, which was sponsored by France and endorsed by the twenty-seven EU member states in October 2008.

Additional factors explain this security-driven conditionality. First, readmission is all the more central for the EU and its member states as the control of the European external borders and border restrictions affect the fluid and repeated back and forth movements inherent in the cross-border movement

Table 2.1 List of mobility partnerships

Third country	Mandate	Date of signature
Armenia	May 2009	27 October 2011
Cape Verde	December 2007	5 June 2008
Georgia	June 2008	30 November 2009
Moldova	December 2007	5 June 2008
Senegal	June 2008	suspended

of people. The EU and its member states are aware that, because of border restrictions and the difficult access to labour markets in destination countries, migrants might be tempted to extend their stay abroad or to overstay and become irregular.[10] Second, the resilient differentials in standards of living, economic development, working conditions, welfare, and political governance between origin and destination countries cannot be overlooked. Third, countries of origin might be tempted not to respect their commitment, above all when it comes to dealing with the readmission and redocumentation of their nationals. This explains why mobility partnerships are assessed on a regular basis by the parties involved (European Commission 2007b: 4).

Since late 2007, the Commission has been invited by the Council to launch pilot mobility partnerships with a few countries. In June 2008, Cape Verde[11] and Moldova[12] signed partnerships with the EU, Georgia[13] in November 2009 and Armenia[14] in October 2011, whereas the accord with Senegal stalled. It is interesting to note that negotiations on mobility partnerships have been successful so far, with third countries having, as it were, a weak leverage on European affairs.

Clearly, it is still too early to assess the extent to which such pilot mobility partnerships will sustain the concrete implementation of circular migration programmes. For now, they show that the European Commission is intent on adaptively revamping its cooperative framework on readmission in an *ad hoc* and more flexible manner while 'taking into account the current state of the EU's relations with the third country concerned as well as the general approach towards it in EU external relations' (European Commission 2007b: 3). Importantly, member states are free to take part in mobility partnerships if they consider that the partnership adds value to their current bilateral relations with a given partner country or not. Moreover, implementation remains the exclusive bilateral prerogative of the member states.

Mobility partnerships are not only designed to foster cooperation on various migration-related areas, while proposing incentives in terms of legal circular migration and visa facilitation to cooperative third countries. When viewed as a platform for dialogue and consultations, such partnerships are also deemed to consolidate, through repeated exchanges among officials, a dominant scheme of understanding, if not a system shaped by beliefs, values, and priorities that continue to impact on the ways in which the EU's circular migration programmes have been configured.

In previous works (Cassarino 2010; 2011), I analysed the existence of dominant schemes of understanding as applied to migration management, laying emphasis on the need to consider the existence of a causal link between beliefs and (perceived) interests, subjectivities, and priorities, as well as between dominant values and policy agendas. I took the international agenda for the management of migration as the most emblematic expression of a belief system whereby common orientations and understandings as to how the movement of all persons should be organized and influenced gradually consolidated in migration talks. Repeated consultations and policy meetings gathering officials from countries of destination, of origin, and of transit have to date played a key role in instilling guiding principles, which in turn have been erected as normative values that shape how international migration should best be administered, regulated, and understood.

In addition to their recurrence, I also stressed that such consultations have gradually introduced a new lexicon including such words and notions as *predictability, sustainability, orderliness, interoperability, circularity, flexibility, comprehensiveness, illegal migration, prevention, shared responsibility, joint ownership, balanced approach,* and *temporariness*. There is no question that this lexicon, endorsed and used by governmental and intergovernmental agencies, among others, has achieved a terminological hegemony in today's official discourses and rhetoric as applied to international migration. It has also been critical in manufacturing a top-down security paradigm while reinforcing, at the same time, the managerial centrality of the state and of its law-enforcement bureaucracy.

One major implication of this pervasive lexicon lies in having homogenized our perceptions and viewpoints as applied to migration issues. To rephrase Pierre Bourdieu (1982), the production and reproduction of the above-mentioned lexicon have contributed to creating a predominant 'linguistic market', codifying human as well as state-to-state interactions. Not only has this hegemonic lexicon been conducive to consensus formation, it has also contributed to dispossessing those who received (and assimilated) the above-mentioned predominant lexicon from their own realities and contingencies. I am particularly, though not exclusively, referring to officials from countries of origin who hail the 'effectiveness' of their EU-sponsored circular migration programmes while minimizing, if not disregarding, their effects on (low-cost) migrant workers' working conditions and restricted labour rights.[15]

2.7 The drive for securitized temporariness

Beyond the 'joint-ownership' rhetoric, circular migration programmes result from an (EU) receiving-country bias that would never have made sense without the production and reproduction of the above-mentioned lexicon. The latter was of course a precondition to turn circular migration programmes (and their conditionalities) into a credible triple-win solution, by serving the interests of countries of destination, of origin, and of migrants themselves.

As mentioned in the introduction of this chapter, my point is not to argue against or in favour of the triple-win solution, on which circular migration programmes have been premised. Rather, it aims to show that the circular migration programmes put forward by the EU have not been immune to the predominant schemes of understanding described above. This has had serious implications for the respect of migrant workers' rights and aspirations.

Regardless of their skill level, it is a well-known fact that time impacts on migrant workers' experience of migration, in its broadest sense. Particularly, time impacts on the ability to benefit from economic and social rights, and to be protected from vulnerability. In his comprehensive study on circular migration, Pyasiri Wickramasekara demonstrates that the more temporary the employment of migrant workers, the more difficult the realization of their human and labour rights in destination countries.

Two conventions of the International Labour Organisation (ILO) deal explicitly with migrant workers' fundamental rights. The ILO Convention no. 97 dated 1949 and the ILO Convention no. 143 dated 1975 respectively deal with recruitment procedures and conditions of labour, and with equal treatment and opportunities between migrant workers and native workers. There is no distinction between permanent and temporary migrant workers in either ILO Convention. Nonetheless, faced with the growing interest in temporary and circular migration, the ILO made it clear in 2006 that 'all international labour standards apply to migrant workers', whether temporary or not (Wickramasekara 2011: 65). This clarification was an explicit call on destination countries to reaffirm their formal commitment to abide by their obligations under Conventions 97 and 143. Among others, and irrespective of the duration of stay abroad, such obligations include the respect for migrant workers' freedom of association, their participation in trade unions, the right for equal treatment in terms of salary, family allowances, working conditions and hours of work, training and apprenticeship, employment tax, accommodation, and social protection (Wickramasekara 2011: 73).

One is entitled to wonder how the drive for temporariness and job flexibility—the two pillars of circular migration programmes—facilitates the effective observance of such internationally recognized standards. It is precisely the drive for temporariness, not the repeated to and fro movements of migrants, that has configured the rationale for circular migration programmes. If it were the opposite, the issues of return and reintegration would have been dealt with more substantially by policymakers in countries of destination and of origin. Admittedly, return has often been cited as a key component of circular migration programmes. However, return is not viewed as a stage in the migration cycle; rather as the end of the temporary stay of migrants. Unsurprisingly, given the receiving-country bias mentioned above, reintegration—i.e., the process through which migrants take part in the social economic, cultural, and political life of their countries of origin—is glaringly overlooked. Moreover, since the early 2000s, the 'return' policies of the EU and its member states have been predominantly, if not exclusively, viewed as instruments aimed at fighting against unauthorized migration. This shortsighted approach has been detrimental to the exploration of the link between return, reintegration, and development;[16] just as it may explain the resilient reluctance of many countries of origin to adopt and implement mechanisms aimed at sustaining the temporary or permanent reintegration of their nationals.

For having focused exclusively on the security aspects of return, the EU and its member states find themselves with inadequate instruments aimed at supporting genuine circular migration programmes. Neither their national 'return' policies, as they stand now, nor the November 2002 Return Action Programme, nor the 'EU directive on common standards and procedures for returning illegally staying third-country nationals' provide compatible instruments for the promotion of genuine circular migration programmes. There is no question that giving circular migrants a concrete opportunity to go back and forth between their countries of destination and origin will depend on the extent to which these countries will be able to adopt adequate legal and institutional mechanisms aimed at supporting the (temporary and permanent) social and professional reintegration of circular migrants back home.

Among others, this situation stems from that the fact that circular migration programmes have been introduced by the EU as a means to further other security ends, i.e. enhanced bilateral cooperation on readmission and the fight against unauthorized migration, with a view to ensuring the temporariness of migrant workers' stay. This drive for securitized temporariness characterizes the rationale for circular migration programmes.

Moreover, had circular migration programmes been viewed as an end in themselves, not only would the EU member states have adopted legal provisions that specifically deal with circular migration, but non-EU countries would also have been more sensitive to the need for effective reintegration mechanisms addressed to their own nationals. To date, none of the above exists.

The drive for securitized temporariness has also a certain bearing on employers' low propensity to invest in the training of temporary workers.

A recent study conducted by the European Migration Network (EMN) has shown that skills acquisition, integration in the company, and employer-employee relationships are intensely shaped by the temporary duration of the job contract. The EMN study concluded that if the period of employment of migrant workers is too short, that is two years, there might be little gain for employers (EMN 2011: 61) to invest in the training of migrant workers. Admittedly, this assumption also holds true for temporary migration programmes in general. However, when temporariness turns out to be securitized, as explained above, it generates a form of containment with a double-edged effect. On the one hand, employers know that policy discretion, based on short-term security-oriented concerns, might abruptly jeopardize their ability to economically invest in migrant workers' training. On the other hand, migrant workers' aspirations for integration and level of socialization in the host country are subtly restrained, just as their rights for family reunification and professional advancement are limited.[17]

Likewise, temporariness may also shape the professional behaviours of migrant workers. The advocates of the New Economics of Labour Migration (NELM) argue that migrants' 'calculated strategy' has a stronger impact on their professional behaviours than temporariness *per se*. In other words, it is because of their ability to plan and to maximize their temporary stay abroad that migrants have the capacity to 'exert a higher level of work effort [in receiving countries] than that exerted by native-born workers' (Stark 1991: 392), and to save more money than native-born workers (Stark and Galor 1990). The planning of the migration project may have a bearing on the professional performance of migrant workers in host countries. However, this 'strategy' cannot be isolated from other consequences linked with the overriding influence of temporariness on migrant workers' professional behaviours and living conditions. Heinz Werner aptly remarks that temporary migrant workers 'try to earn as much money as possible and at the same time cut costs [...] working overtime, accepting more difficult working conditions, living in cramped cheap accommodation etc. The consequences can be health risks and social segregation and isolation' (Heinz 1996: 10). Whereas temporariness generates such consequences while exposing migrant workers to vulnerability, the drive for securitized temporariness, on which circular migration programmes are premised, makes such consequences more inevitable, if not acceptable.[18]

2.8 Conclusion

Has the possibility of questioning the drive for securitized temporariness become hopeless if it is true that we are confronted with predominant schemes of understanding where security concerns continue to shape policy options as applied to circular migration?

To reply to this uncomfortable question, we need to realize that circular migration programmes (CMPs) stem from the Global Approach to Migration (GAM), which was introduced in late 2005 with a view to 'brokering a new deal' with non-EU countries and to making the latter more cooperative on security concerns (i.e., enhanced cooperation on readmission, reinforced border controls, and the fight against unauthorized migration). As explained, the GAM was also a response to growing criticisms from some EU member states regarding the capacity of the European Union to tackle unauthorized migration effectively. CMPs have been, from the outset, shaped by non-economic concerns, namely security and the search for enhanced credibility on the part of EU institutions. As of the mid-1990s, this situation culminated with the perceptible, though gradual, alignment of the European Commission with member states' security concerns, together with the resilient controversy on Community competence, as explained above. This alignment took place through recurrent consultative processes and migration talks, at bilateral, regional, and international levels. They allowed an international agenda for migration management to be consolidated, and dominant schemes of understanding to be unquestioned.

Perhaps the most important implication of these developments lies in having built a hierarchy of priorities aimed at best achieving the objectives set out in the migration management agenda. The lexicon mentioned above was of course a prerequisite to giving sense to this hierarchy of priorities, which in turn has gradually been conducive to a process of consensus formation.[19] The drive for securitized temporariness, on which EU-sponsored circular migration programmes are premised, clearly results from this hierarchy of priorities. The latter has contributed to containing migrant workers' aspirations for stability in their lives, while exposing them to uncertainty and policy discretion.

Today, there is growing awareness of the need 'to go beyond the concept of managed circular migration which is hardly likely to lead to the promised win-win scenarios' (Wickramasekara 2011: 90). There are growing calls on decision-makers to further interact with trade unions and employers' organizations by involving them in the design of mobility partnerships and circular migration programmes.[20] Their participation would arguably enhance the responsiveness of such programmes to labour shortages as well as their adequacy to international labour standards.

However, questioning the drive for securitized temporariness will require more than that. In a context marked by predominant subjectivities, apodictic statements, and stereotypes, the production of critical knowledge constitutes the most daunting endeavour to debunk long-established official truths as applied to the management of international migration in general and to the acceptance of migrant workers in particular. Critical knowledge, that is the capacity to inform and act beyond or against predominant schemes of understanding, has become strategic, if not crucial, in political terms to unveil the neo-liberal drive for temporariness and its consequences on the destiny of migrant workers and workers in general.

References

Bourdieu, Pierre (1982). *Ce que parler veut dire. L'économie des échanges linguistiques*. Paris: Fayard.
Bovenkerk, Frank (1974). *The Sociology of Return Migration: A Bibliographic Essay*. The Hague: Martinus Nijhoff.
Burroni, Luigi and Keune, Maarten (2011). 'Flexicurity: A Conceptual Critique', *European Journal of Industrial Relations*, 17(1): 75–91.
Cassarino, Jean-Pierre (2008). 'Patterns of Circular Migration in the Euro-Mediterranean Area: Implications for Policy-Making'. Analytic and Synthetic Notes, 2008/29. Florence: RSCAS/EUI.
Cassarino, Jean-Pierre (2010). *Readmission Policy in the European Union, Directorate General for Internal Policies*, Policy Department C: Citizens' Rights and Constitutional Affairs, Civil Liberties, Justice and Home Affairs. Brussels: European Parliament. http://www.europarl.europa.eu/committees/en/studiesdownload.html?language-Document=EN&file=35488 (accessed 24 July 2012).
Cassarino, Jean-Pierre (2011). 'Resilient Bilateralism in the Cooperation on Readmission', in Marise Cremona, Jörg Monar and Sara Poli (eds), *The External Dimension of the European Union's Area of Freedom, Security and Justice*.Brussels: Peter Lang, 191–208.
Castles, Stephen (2006). 'Back to the Future? Can Europe Meet its Labour Needs Through Temporary Migration?', *IMI Working Paper*, International Migration Institute, University of Oxford. http://www.imi.ox.ac.uk/pdfs/imi-working-papers/wp1-backtothefuture.pdf (accessed 24 July 2012).
Constant, A. and Zimmermann, Klaus F. (2007). 'Circular Migration: Counts and Exits and Years Away from the Host Country', *Discussion Paper Series IZA DP* (2999). Bonn: Institute for the Study of Labour. http://ftp.iza.org/dp2999.pdf (accessed 24 July 2012).
Crouch, Colin (2008). 'The Governance of Labour Market Uncertainty: Towards a New Research Agenda', *Discussion Paper* 2008–08, Amsterdam: Hugo Sinzheimer Institute. http://sociologyofeurope.unifi.it/upload/sub/documenti/colin_crouch_%20the%20governance%20of%20labour%20market%20uncertainty.pdf (accessed 24 July 2012).
De Haas Hein (2007). 'Morocco's Migration Experience: A Transitional Perspective', *International Migration*, 45 (4): 39–70.
EMN (2011). *Temporary and Circular Migration: Empirical Evidence, Current Policy Practice and Future Options in EU Member States*. Luxembourg: Publications Office of the

European Union. http://www.emn.ie/files/p_201111110314492011_EMN_Synthesis_Report_Temporary_Circular_Migration_FINAL.pdf (accessed 24 July 2012).

Engbersen, Godfried (2009). 'Irregular Migration, Criminality and the State', in Willem Schinkel (ed.), *Globalization and the State: Sociological Perspectives on the State of the State*. Basingstoke: Palgrave Macmillan, 144–72.

European Commission (2002). *Green Paper on a Community Return Policy on Illegal Residents*, Brussels, COM (2002) 175 final.

European Commission (2005). *Migration and Development: Some Concrete orientations*, Brussels, COM (2005) 390 final.

European Commission (2006). *The Global Approach to Migration One Year On: Towards a Comprehensive European Migration Policy*, Brussels, COM (2006) 735 final.

European Commission (2007a). *On Circular Migration and Mobility Partnerships between the European Union and Third Countries*, Brussels, COM (2007) 248 final.

European Commission (2007b). *Applying the Global Approach to Migration to the Eastern and South-Eastern Regions Neighbouring the European Union*, Brussels, COM (2007) 247 final.

European Council (1998). *Strategy Paper on Immigration and Asylum Policy*, 9809/98, 1 July 1998, Brussels.

European Council (2009). *2927th Council Meeting Justice and Home Affairs*. Brussels, 26 and 27 February 2009.

GCIM (Global Commission on International Migration) (2005). *Migration in an Interconnected World: New Directions for Action*. Geneva: GCIM.

Hailbronner, Kay (2010). '*Implications of the EU Lisbon Treaty on EU Immigration Law*'. Presentation at the Transatlantic Exchange for Academics in Migration Studies, San Diego, 29–30 March 2010. http://eucenter.berkeley.edu/files/Hailbronner.pdf (accessed 24 July 2012).

House of Commons (2004). *Migration and Development: How to Make Migration Work for Poverty Reduction*, International Development Committee, Sixth report of Session 2003–4, vol. 1, 8 July 2004. http://www.publications.parliament.uk/pa/cm200304/cmselect/cmintdev/79/79.pdf (accessed 24 July 2012).

Martin Philip (2003). *Managing Labor Migration: Temporary Worker Programs for the 21st Century*. Geneva: International Institute for Labour Studies. http://www.ilo.org/public/english/bureau/inst/download/migration3.pdf (accessed 24 July 2012).

Ruhs, Martin (2005). *The Potential of Temporary Migration Programmes in Future International Migration Policy*. Geneva: Global Commission on International Migration. http://economics.ouls.ox.ac.uk/12666/1/TP3.pdf (accessed: 24 July 2012).

Stark, Oded (1991). *The Migration of Labor*. Cambridge: Basil Blackwell.

Stark, Oded and Galor, Oded (1990). 'Migrants' Savings, the Probability of Return Migration and Migrants' Performance', *International Economic Review*, 31 (2): 463–67.

Werner, Heinz (1996). '*Temporary Migration of Foreign Workers*' [online manuscript], http://doku.iab.de/topics/1996/topics18.pdf (accessed 24 July 2012).

Wickramasekara, Piyasiri (2011). *Circular Migration: A Triple Win or a Dead End?* Geneva: International Labour Organization. http://www.gurn.info/en/discussion-papers/no15-mar11-circular-migration-a-triple-win-or-a-dead-end (accessed 24 July 2012).

Notes

1. This section focuses on patterns of circular migration and draws on a previous working paper (Cassarino 2008).
2. As shown by Hein de Haas, 'after Morocco became independent from France in 1956, political and military tensions between Morocco and Algeria increased, leading to the closure of the Moroccan-Algerian border in 1962. This meant that circular migration to Algeria came to a definitive halt' (De Haas 2007: 45).
3. This embedded dimension of circular migration is described in Francesca Alice Vianello's chapter.
4. A reservation wage is the minimum wage a worker will accept for a given job.
5. Excerpt from the speech by Mr Pádraig Flynn—Joint Meeting of the European Parliament, Committee on Civil Liberties and the Migrants' Forum—15 December 1993—Strasbourg. http://europa.eu/rapid/pressReleasesAction.do?reference= SPEECH/93/151&format=HTML&aged=1&language=EN&guiLanguage=en.
6. The Prüm Treaty or Convention was initially signed by seven EU member states: Austria, Belgium, France, Germany, Luxembourg, the Netherlands, and Spain. The Convention aims at stepping up cross-border police cooperation and exchanges between members' law enforcement agencies with a view to combating organized crime, terrorism and illegal migration more effectively. Provisions of the Prüm Treaty dealing with police co-operation and information exchange on DNA-profiles and fingerprints were transposed in the legal framework of the European Union following a Council Decision dated 23 June 2008 (Council Decision 2008/606/JHA).
7. 'Cyprus, Greece, Italy and Malta Paper', Ministers of the Interior and (for Malta) Minister of Justice and Internal Affairs, 13 January 2009. Available at: http://www.cittadinitalia.it/mininterno/export/sites/default/it/assets/files/16/0970_Final_paper_Versione_firmata.pdf. This document was mentioned in European Council (2009), 2927th Council meeting Justice and Home Affairs Brussels, 26 and 27 February 2009: 9.
8. For a more technical and legal analysis, see Hailbronner, Kay (2010).
9. The communication of the European Commission entitled *Migration and Development: Some Concrete Orientations* (COM(2005) 390), dated September 2005, is probably one of the first EC documents which set out to present some policy recommendations regarding the promotion of circular migration (see its annex 5). Later, as a follow-up to the Hampton Court informal meeting of the Heads of State and Government (held in October 2005), the November 2005 Brussels Council of the EU invited the EC to further develop the idea of 'temporary and circular migration'. Further details were included in the November 2006 EC communication on *The Global Approach to Migration One Year On: Towards a Comprehensive European Migration Policy*, European Commission (2006) 735 final.
10. This point draws on Heaven Crawley's statement reported in the House of Commons (2004). 'When people come to a country [...] through a managed migration programme often they have had quite a difficult time getting onto that programme in the first place, and when they get to the [destination country] their

first thought is not to think about how to return, because they found it difficult trying to get here in the first place, it is more about how to stay' (see § 71, 40–1).
11. European Council (2008), Joint Declaration on a Mobility Partnership between the European Union and Cape Verde, 9460/08 Add 2, Brussels, 21 May 2008.
12. European Council (2008), Joint Declaration on a Mobility Partnership between the European Union and Moldova, 9460/08, Brussels, 21 May 2008.
13. European Council (2009), Joint Declaration on a Mobility Partnership between the European Union and Georgia, 16396/09, Brussels, November 2009.
14. European Council (2011), Joint Declaration on a Mobility Partnership between the European Union and Armenia, 3121st JHA Meeting, Luxembourg, 27–8 October 2011.
15. See Carmen González Enríquez' chapter, particularly the part on the Moroccan-Spanish agreement aimed at recruiting Moroccan female seasonal workers in the Spanish city of Cartaya known for its strawberry production.
16. It could even be argued that the April 2002 Green Paper on a Community Return Policy on Illegal Residents, presented by the Commission (European Commission 2002, 175 final), epitomizes this security-oriented vision of 'return'. The Green Paper acknowledged the existence of various categories of returnees, making a clear-cut distinction between those who decide autonomously to go back to their country of origin and those who are forced to. The focus was, however, on the latter, i.e. on the forced and assisted return of persons residing irregularly in the European Union. Admittedly, the Commission recognized that the return of persons who decide autonomously to go back to their countries of origin should deserve further attention, owing to its potential impact on return migrants' countries of origin, and that it should be 'subject to further reflection on the part of the Commission, at a later stage' (7). Today, this reflection is still missing in migration talks in general and in the EU's Global Approach to Migration particularly.
17. This is what Krystyna Iglicka and Katarzyna Gmaj (Chapter 8) remarked in this volume with reference to Ukrainian migrants in Poland.
18. For example, by assuming that 'migrant workers may sometimes be willing to trade economic gains for restrictions in personal rights to an extent that is likely to be considered unacceptable in most liberal democracies' (Ruhs 2005: 14). Willingness would make sense if migrant workers had the concrete opportunity to choose.
19. A hierarchy of priorities could be defined as a set of policy priorities whose main function is to delineate the contours of the issues that should be tackled first and foremost, while hiding or dismissing others.
20. Their involvement in migration talks and inter-governmental consultations on circular migration took place only when CMPs and their security-driven conditionalities were already established from the top and branded as a 'potential' triple-win solution.

3

Flexible Circularities: Integration, Return, and Socio-Economic Instability within Albanian Migration to Italy

Nicola Mai and Cristiana Paladini

3.1 Introduction

Albanian migration to Italy is a particularly strategic context for the study of circular migration for several interrelated reasons. Italy played an important historical role in the development of the Albanian national identity and in the emergence of a transnational imaginary that encompassed its post-communist migration experience. It was the second most important foreign destination (after Greece) for Albanian migrants and a very relevant geopolitical actor in the development of the Albanian migration and development agendas after 1991. Albanians in Italy were both intensely stigmatized and particularly integrated within Italian society. Our research findings do not support a politicized appreciation of circular migration as a win-win situation for all actors involved. They show that circular migration works only for the minority of Albanian migrants who were able to achieve permanent or long-term legal status and who are socio-economically integrated in both Albania and Italy. The majority of Albanian migrants are reluctantly and ambivalently oscillating between Albania and Italy. Most decided to circulate and/or to return to sustain migratory projects that are still not completed, or which became unsustainable in the context of the global financial crisis of the late 2000s.

3.2 A short history of Albanian migration to Italy

Because of their geographical proximity and their geopolitically and economically mutually strategic positions, the territories currently falling under the

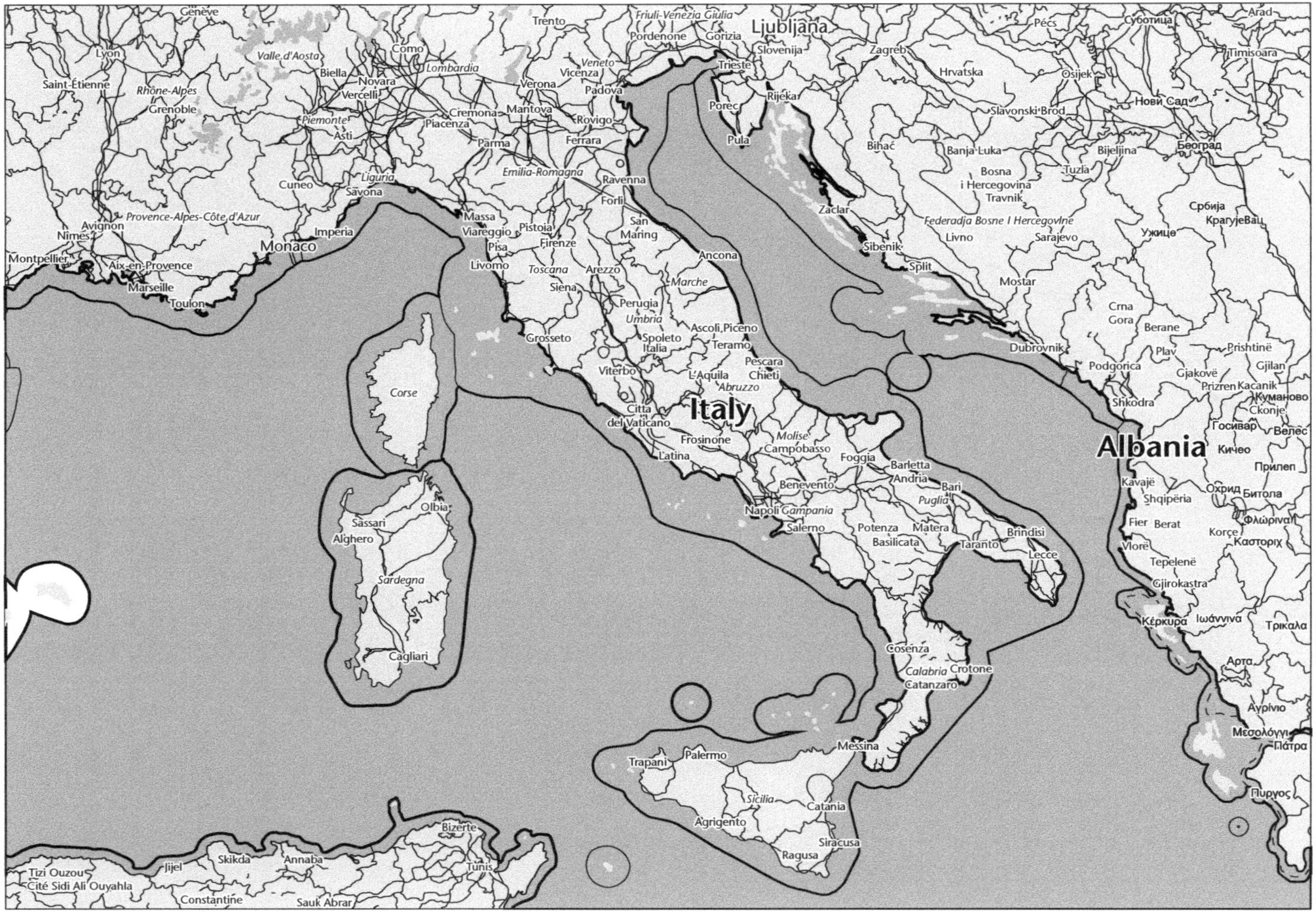

Figure 3.1 Map of Italy

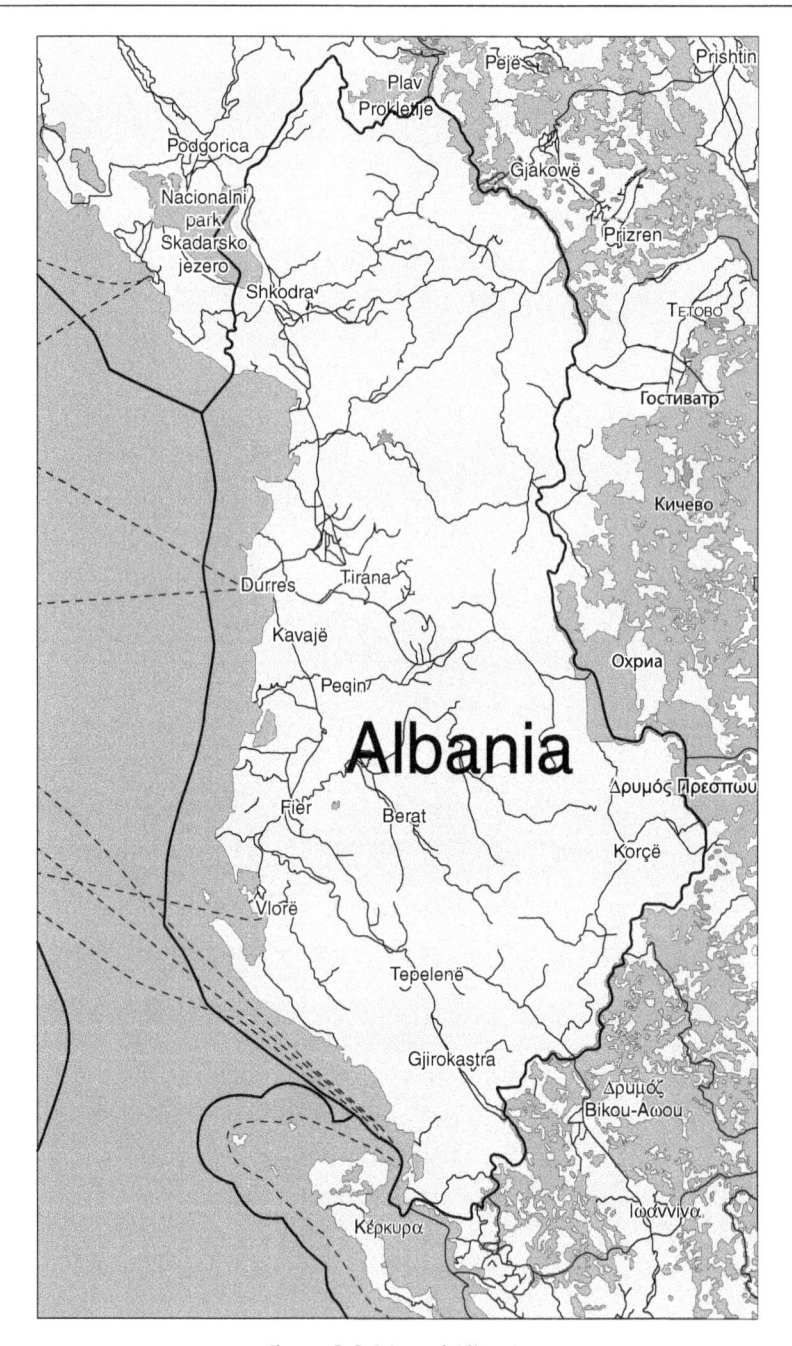

Figure 3.2 Map of Albania

jurisdiction of Italy and Albania have been historically part of a shared socio-cultural and economic space. The geopolitical, socio-economic and cultural relevance of this (unequally) shared space were discontinuous across different historical phases. The post-communist Albanian migratory crises of the 1990s inaugurated a new phase in the history of relations between Italy and Albania, which both built upon and transformed their imaginary, socio-economic, and geopolitical liaisons. Between 7 and 10 March 1991, as the Albanian communist state collapsed and the country was precipitated into a situation of violent political confrontation and extreme economic deprivation, some 25,700 Albanians crossed the Otranto Channel between Albania and Italy in boats and rafts of every type. A new crisis arose in August 1991 with the arrival of another 20,000 Albanian refugees on several overloaded ships. Whereas most of the Albanians who arrived in March 1991 were considered refugees and given legal immigration status, most of those who followed in August 2001 were repatriated as 'irregular migrants'. The two migratory waves of 1991 were just the beginning of a dramatic and controversial migratory flow, which has its roots in the prolonged economic and political instability of Albania throughout the 1990s. After March 1997, as Albania was on the verge of civil war as a consequence of the collapse of 'pyramid selling' schemes, there was another mass migratory crisis. Although there have been no further mass emigration episodes from Albania since 1997, because of the restrictive visa policies implemented by the Italian state in 1991, many Albanians resorted to illegal entry into the country, mostly through dangerous rides on speedboats across the Adriatic Sea to the Apulian shores, from Vlorë to Otranto. Throughout the 1990s, Italy promoted a number of migration amnesties, through which many irregular migrants were able to obtain legal status. By 2010, Albanians constituted the second largest community in Italy (466,684) after Romanians (887,763), and ahead of Moroccans (431,592) (ISTAT 2010). According to recent research Albanians are the most significant group of migrants in Italy, in relation to the overall size of the population of the sending country; 14 per cent of Albanians live in Italy (ISMU 2011).

3.3 Reasons to migrate

The main explanations for the extent to which Albanians migrated in the last two decades are rooted in the role of poverty, demographic factors, and political instability. Until recently, Albania has been characterized by the most widespread poverty of any country in Europe, the least diversified and most backward economic base, the enduring and pervasive threat of disappearing financial and human capital, inadequate fiscal resources, and the reluctance of foreigners to invest in the country (De Soto et al. 2002: 1).

Internal as well as international migration became a fundamental livelihood strategy for many households all around the country, and remittances determined the economic viability of many Albanian families (King and Mai 2008). A crucial demographic dimension of the Albanian migration phenomenon is its youthfulness. In 1998, 42 per cent of the total population was under nineteen years of age, and the average age was about twenty-four years (UNICEF 1998: 14–15). Both in 1990 and in 2000, nearly one third of the population was under fifteen, which means that there is still an abundance of potential young emigrants for the next ten to twenty years. Albanians between the ages of fifteen and forty-five have been, and continue to be, involved in migration; these age groups accounted for 94.6 per cent of the total number of migrants until the early 2000s (Gjonça 2002: 31). Migration accounted for the overall improvement of the living conditions of most Albanian households. Since 2005, the population in absolute poverty in Albania declined from 25 per cent in 2002 to 12.4 per cent, and in 2008, there was a marked decline in unemployment. However, these positive dynamics coincided with a heightened economic polarization among the population and refer to the central, more urbanized and prosperous area of the country (UN 2010). The growing inequalities and the relative poverty of Albanian society are likely to continue to fuel young people's need and desire to migrate. According to a survey carried out in 2007 (EFT), migration will continue to play a role in Albania in the short term, with 44.2 per cent of eighteen to forty year olds interviewed saying that they were thinking of migrating, and 17.8 per cent actually being able to do so because of their access to necessary social and economic capital.

3.4 Albanians in Italy: the paradox of differential integration

In Italy, a recent country of immigration, there is as yet no overarching model of immigrant incorporation. Policy measures have been ad hoc and frequently contradictory. There seems to be an acceptance of the economic rationale of harnessing migrant labour and of the inevitability of immigration in a scenario of enhanced global mobility; and yet the trend in legislation—from the Legge Martelli (1990) through the Turco-Napolitano (1998) to the Bossi-Fini laws (2002)—has been to pay lip-service to integration. This legal trend keeps immigrants as a marginalized, temporarily resident fraction of Italian society (Zincone 2006). Italian press and other media have reinforced this stance by continuously representing immigrants as outsiders and a threat to the nation. Throughout the 1990s and since, Albanians have been the main target of this negative discursive framing of immigration. Until 2008, more than any other group in recent years, Albanians were subject to a brutal campaign of stigmatization and criminalization by the Italian media (Mai 2002). As in Greece (cf. Lazaridis 1996), 'albanophobia', an all-encompassing and irrational fear of all things Albanian, became entrenched within the perceptions of the Italian population as a whole. This stigmatization clashed dramatically with Albanian migrants' expectations.

In Albania, by illegally watching Italian television in communist times, many young people internalized lifestyle models that were very different from those assigned to them by communism. In this way the idea of migrating abroad (above all to Italy) could be seen as the logical outcome of a wider process of the disembedding of Albanian young people's identities from the homogenous, moralized, collectivist-nationalist landscape that prevailed before 1991 (Mai 2001). Albanians, especially teenagers and young adults, had already undergone a process of anticipatory assimilation to Italy and its way of life even before their 'migratory projects' became realizable. The paradoxical coexistence (King and Mai 2009) between aspirational integration into and selective exclusion from Italian society underpinned Albanian migrants' partially successful assimilation into Italian society. Their fast progress along the assimilation-integration trajectory has been achieved in a short space of time compared with longer-established immigrants in Italy. Quantitative data on Albanians in Italy reinforce the impression that Albanians are becoming increasingly integrated within the host society. In fact, they are the most 'dispersed' of all immigrant nationalities in Italy (Bonifazi 2007). The evolving demographic structure of Albanians in Italy is another indicator of rapid stabilization and integration. By 2001, 40 per cent of Albanian migrants were women, a gender trend showing dynamic change towards demographic 'normalization' (Bonifazi and Sabatino 2003: 970). Data on pupil enrolments in the Italian school system also confirm these 'normalizing' trends, as Albanians are now the largest foreign-origin group in Italian schools, accounting for 17.7 per cent of all foreign pupils, well above their share of the overall immigrant population (11.3 per cent). During the academic year 2004–5 there were 9,522 Albanian students studying at Italian universities, comprising a quarter of all foreign students. At university level most students are not second-generation young people living with their immigrant parents, but 'primary' migrants. Nonetheless, the existence of so many third-level students is another facet of Albanians' close relationship to Italy across different age and social strata (Caritas/Migrantes 2006: 181).

These positive quantitative indicators of the outcome of migrant integration strategies need to be measured against the qualitative experience of the process of integration by migrants themselves. In this respect, the relentless stereotyping of Albanians as criminals and more generally as rough, uncivilized people has two main (and important) ramifications. The first is the behaviour of Italians towards Albanians in various spheres of life, such as employment and housing. Although Albanians have little difficulty obtaining low-status jobs in Italy, many instances of discrimination in the workplace were recorded, including the receipt of lower wages than Italians who were doing the same work. This becomes less common as time passes and Albanians get legalized and progress to more stable jobs, as is the case for all immigrants who start as undocumented workers in the informal labour market. More specifically, anti-Albanian discrimination arises when Albanians try to access qualified jobs: there appears to be a glass ceiling. The second ramification involves Albanians' internalization of the stigmatising discourse, so that it affects their own self-presentation and their behaviour towards both Italians and other Albanians. Sometimes parents want to ensure that their children are not identified as Albanian and picked on as a result, so they encourage them to speak Italian all the time at school and in public spaces (see also Zinn 2005).

Albanian associations that exist in Italy were not established in the early years of arrival, in order to reinforce Albanians' ethnic identity and help each other settle down. Rather, they were formed in the late 1990s in order to respond to negative media images by recovering positive elements of identification. This delayed ethnic mobilization is described in American sociological literature as 'reactive ethnicity', and arises out of the 'confrontation with concerted attitudes of prejudice on the part of the surrounding population' (Portes and Rumbaut 1996: 133; 222). The fact that Albanians' projective identification with Italians was not reciprocated and was met with stigmatization led some Albanians to adopt another, more extreme, assimilation strategy: mimesis (Romania 2004). This may be accompanied by an acceptance and internalization of the rationales for stigmatization. Others, instead, may be led to a reappraisal of their Albanian heritage, either through an embryonic and delayed growth of ethnic associations, and/or a return gaze to the homeland. But this is a confused gaze, for the homeland itself is full of contradictions—between its rejected communist past and an uncertain neoliberal future. The latter is characterized by a stark socio-economic polarization and by new rearticulations of long-standing tensions between the rural and urban dimensions and the traditional and modern aspects of Albanian society (Fuga 2000). These observations are very relevant for the scope of this research, as the idea of return, which often translates into circularity, was often embedded within people's desire not to be singled out or stigmatised as 'Albanians'.

3.5 Methodology

The research for this chapter was undertaken by two teams of local researchers in both Albania and Italy. We gathered eighty interviews with circular migrants and twenty interviews with key informants in the two countries.

In both Albania and Italy we cooperated with the Italian NGO IPSIA, which has offices in both Shkoder and Tirana, and was undertaking a parallel study on the dynamics of the return of Albanian migrants from Italy. Cristiana Paladini, the co-author of this article, a sociologist working for ACLI-IPSIA between Albania and Italy, conducted forty-five interviews.[1]

The composition and expertise available among the researchers involved allowed us to address diverse experiences of circularity, as well as different socio-economic and geographical areas in both Albania and Italy. In Albania, the research focused on the coastal area, the one more structurally and historically involved in migration to Italy, and covered the cities and areas of Shkoder, Tirana, Durres, Fier, and Vlore. In Italy, the majority of interviews were gathered in Rome, with some undertaken in Milan and in Calabria.

3.6 Institutional and legal constraints facilitating and hindering circular migration

Although facilitating circular migration remains a stated objective of both the Italian and of the Albanian government, at the moment there are no specific initiatives or legislation to support it. The only exceptions are the seasonal agricultural schemes foreseen by current immigration legislation, allocating a quota of approximately 4,500 seasonal permits to Albanian workers. For everybody else, circularity develops in the socio-economic and legal interstices produced by interrupted integration and settlement trajectories in both Albania and Italy. In most cases, as we will explain more fully below, circularity is resorted to as a fall-back strategy when people's projects to settle and 'make papers' in Albania or in Italy do not work out.

In Italy, very few migrants resorted to the services of Albanian associations and authorities as sources of information, support, or solidarity. Most relied on family and friends' networks, which guided them through very complex and often discouraging bureaucratic procedures. The amnesties that took place in the 1990s were the main sources of regularization for Albanian migrants, many of which opposed the restrictions posed by the 2001 Bossi-Fini revision of the 1998 Turco-Napolitano law. Seasonal migrants, who were the only interviewees whose circularity was supported by a specific legislative framework, often complained about the high costs involved in obtaining seasonal working permits. The impossibility to convert a seasonal permit into a yearly one and then upgrade gradually towards an indefinite leave to remain and citizenship, a restriction introduced by the Bossi-Fini law, is mentioned by many migrants, and by seasonal migrants in particular, as a key obstacle to their integration in Italy and to their return to Albania. Two migrants from Albania recounted their experiences:

> This year I decided not to go any more to Italy, as they only offered me short contracts and short permits to stay. It's not worth it in terms of money, the rules have changed now and it's not like before. They said you could convert the seasonal visa into a longer one, but this is not possible any more. Now, I have a job here, but... I am changeable, like the weather at the moment... I don't know if I am going to stay here as I am not used to work without rules and contracts. And the pay is low. Then the way of working is different. (circular migrant, Albanian male, 34, Albania)

> The main problem I had was documents; that's why I won't work as seasonal any more. They give you short term documents as a seasonal worker, for six to nine months only... and they cost more than documents for five to ten years!!! If I had a five years long permit it would be ideal, it would be cheaper, I could come here for a couple of months, then go home whenever I finished and then come back again. (circular migrant, Albanian male, 52, Albania)

The impediments introduced by the Bossi-Fini law to the process of regularization forced many Albanian migrants to stay in Italy even in times of crisis, or to circulate irregularly, in order to keep documented, because their mobility was *de facto* criminalized. On a positive note, the granting to migrants (particularly students) of the right to use the receipt of the permit to stay rather than the permit itself (which was often not ready until it was expired) when returning home on holiday, allowed many to circulate between Albania and Italy while they were documented and to remain in touch with their families and friends on both shores.

Because of the enduring economic and political instability in Albania, obtaining and keeping legal status in Italy (and abroad in general) is still an absolute priority for individuals and their families. 'Making papers' abroad has always been considered as a safety valve by most Albanian individuals and households, and was one of the main motives for migrating. Most interviewees waited to achieve legal status before considering returning to or investing in any economic activity in Albania. For many, circularity is the only way to remain legal by renewing their seasonal or two-year work permit until they can obtain more durable forms of documentation. An Albanian migrant explains the importance of maintaining legality:

> There are many who keep a relation with Italy in order to remain documented, long after they stopped working in Italy and returned to Albania. Here they don't spend much money, they try and get the odd job, many in construction... And they hope for the Italian economy to pick up again, because life there is less stressful, even if you work more, you feel safer in terms of work and everything else. (circular migrant, Albanian male, 55, Albania)

Continuing economic and political instability in Albania is one of the main reasons why assisted repatriation, which implies renouncing the residence permit, is the only option for people who would otherwise face forced deportation and expulsion.

In Albania, the government does not have any policies in place to assist repatriated migrants in establishing a business or in obtaining information about migration. Only one interviewee availed herself of a recruitment programme promoted by the government through the IOM (International Organisation for Migration). The networks associated with the Catholic Church offered significant opportunities for many migrants in Shkoder, a city where the Catholic Church has historically been more established. Providing assistance and support to returning migrants is seen as a priority for future governmental interventions, as most interviewees feel that such initiatives could attract resources and knowledge that would benefit the socio-economic development of Albania.

People dealing with import-export activities felt that the taxation regime was too high for them to break even, particularly in times of crises. All migrants thought that the lack of an efficient road network, and of regular electricity and water supply, was preventing Albania from developing an economy based on production, rather than on construction and import-export services fuelled by remittances. Some migrants appreciated the relatively low level of taxation for firms in Albania, whose potential for the setting up of new enterprises was seen as being undermined by a parasitical and inefficient bureaucracy, and by the widespread practices of favouritism and corruption. Continuing political instability and the lack of a culture of democratic governance were also blamed for the unavailability of foreign companies to invest their capital and knowledge in Albania. Most returnees complained about the endurance of a culture of nepotism and corruption, which was blamed for the unequal redistribution of already limited work opportunities.

The forthcoming liberalization of the EU Schengen tourist visa by 2012 was seen very favourably by all interviewees. Many felt that the associated advantages of the possibility for migrants in Italy to keep in touch with their families, and also for potential migrants in Albania to explore employment possibilities available in Italy, without having to commit to the social and cultural capital needed to obtain a work permit, were enormous. Most migrants felt that the liberalization of EU visas would not have coincided with an outflow of people, because they thought that Albanian people were more aware of the actual opportunities available in Italy, and also of the unfeasibility of working and living in Italy undocumented. At the same time, many migrants were also disappointed, but not surprised, with the rejection of Albania's application to be a candidate member of the EU. They saw Albania's candidacy to EU membership as a first step towards a higher degree of prosperity as well as recognition of their cultural and historical heritage, a higher level of employment possibilities, and a potential stabilization and democratization of their polity.

3.7 Types of circularity

The institutional and legal constraints and the socio-economic, geopolitical and cultural context presented above engendered different and interlinked circular forms of migration, corresponding to five circular migrant typologies:

1. *Seasonal workers* (agriculture, tourism, herding), both of a legal and technical type, the latter associated with residence and work permits that do not correspond to the seasonal character of the work undertaken.
2. *Students* returning to Albania in order to work in universities, in public administration, the third sector, and, less so in the private sector. This category includes students who study and live in Italy and who visit Albania regularly.
3. *Migrant entrepreneurs* residing in Italy and setting up a parallel firm in Albania, in order to start building a future between Italy and Albania and to employ their relatives, notably in the construction industry. This category includes returned or successful entrepreneurs whose base is in Albania and who need to be in Italy very often as part of their work (import-export, for example).
4. *Documented returnees*, meaning migrants with Italian citizenship or a permanent/long-term (five plus years) permit to stay, who returned to Albania as they felt their migratory experience was completed, but still retain structural links with Italy.
5. *Economic returnees* are migrants who, having returned to Albania as a consequence of the economic crisis in Italy, and because of the temporary and informal nature of their employment in Italy, are planning to return to Italy in order to keep documented and/or obtain Italian citizenship. This category includes migrants who were deported and/or decided to go back to Italy repeatedly and irregularly to earn a living for themselves and their families.

These forms of circular mobility are specific in terms of the duration and frequency of migratory periods and of the skills of migrants. However, they were all influenced and encompassed by these shared dynamics and factors, to which we now turn.

3.7.1 *The impact of the economic crisis*

According to a recent UN report (UN Albania 2010), the Albanian economy was not as adversely affected by the 2008–9 global financial crisis as were other economies in South East Europe. However, there was an important indirect impact of the crisis on neighbouring countries, which had a negative influence on 'remittances, commodities, the export-sensitive footwear and apparel industry, and migration' (UN Albania 2010: iii). As far as migration is more directly concerned, the same research underlines that the deepening of the crisis and planned austerity measures in Greece could translate to the return of low-skilled migrants working in construction and agriculture (UN Albania 2010: 4). While this might be true for Greece, we identified a different trend regarding the return of Albanian migrants from Italy.

The looming of the economic recession in both Italy and Albania encouraged people to stay put, rather than to engage in circularity. In Albania, key economic sectors such as the construction industry ground to a halt, particularly in the Tirana-Durres conurbation. Returning migrants mentioned that in Italy it became increasingly difficult to find, or even retain, a job, particularly without legal migration status. As a consequence, staying put in Italy and in Albania is still a reality when people have a job to hold on to. Those migrants who have a job abroad might have to be circular in order to maintain their families in Albania and Italy, as this interviewee working for an Albanian diaspora newspaper in Rome explains:

> People who did not make it come back...or people who lost the permit to stay. From what I have seen, people who are documented tend to stay here [Italy] because even if the crisis is bad here, and I have seen it impact on my work, there are still many more prospects in Italy than in Albania, it is a more secure and safe environment anyway. Those who are returning now it's because they are documented, maybe they open a small business, while they are unemployed here. Then there are those who became citizens, who go back home as Italians abroad. (Key informant, Rome)

The impact of the economic downturn that followed the global financial crisis of 2008 was often mentioned by migrants as one of the main reasons for their decision to return. However, as the previous quote shows, the crisis impacted differently on different groups of migrants, with the legal status being the second (after employment opportunities) most important variable in people's decision to stay put, migrate, return, and circulate. Migrants who had still not obtained the level of documentation they aspired to tended to either stay put in Italy or to 'go circular', in order not to lose the rights they had accumulated in relation to their legal status. Documented migrants with Italian citizenship or a *carta di soggiorno* (a five year valid permit to stay) tended to either stay put in Italy or in Albania, depending on their economic and family circumstances. However, since the last few months of 2011, because of the enduring economic and political crises in Italy, the number of returnees seems to have increased considerably. Even if we are not in possession of reliable quantitative data about this phenomenon, according to international observers and key informants in Albania, many families decided to return from Italy.

This trend, at the moment, seems to lead more to return patterns than to circularization ones.

3.7.2 Escaping Albanophobia and 'being over the migration experience'

Albanians are no longer the main scapegoat for long-standing problems within Italian society, which they were until recently. Nowadays, while new moral panics are erected regarding the presence of (Roma) Romanian migrants (Mai 2010), Albanians are increasingly and equally arbitrarily defined as a virtuous example of integration. While this has always been true, it has only been publicly recognized very recently, with the vast majority of Albanians being regularly resident in Italy. The dynamics of othering and marginalization are key in (particularly older) interviewees' decision to return to Albania and are often summarized (and glossed over) in terms of 'the migration experience being over'. Escaping stigmatization is one of the main reasons behind the decision to return, and can obfuscate, together with nostalgia, the limited opportunities offered by the Albanian socio-economic context. This nostalgic obfuscation and superficial knowledge of the actual opportunities available in Albania are major factors explaining the unfeasibility and failure of many of the return projects of migrant individuals and families. A migrant explains:

> I don't think I will go back and live in Italy for good. I thought about returning to Albania for a long time because it really gets at you all of this 'Albanese' talking. Even when they do not actually say it, you feel that they think it, that you are constantly prejudiced against and that gets difficult to bear in the long term. (circular migrant, Albanian female, 23, Albanian)

The existence of a more conservative mentality in Albania regarding established gender and family roles was mentioned by most migrants as an important factor in their decisions to migrate and to return. People above forty, particularly men, were ambivalent about the predicaments and opportunities posed by these values. Some felt that the 'openness' of Italian society was a threat to the gender and family roles they associated with being Albanian. Younger people and women, particularly if they are students, tended to be critical of Albanian gender and family values. Youth and females see gender as producing a lack of entitlement to individual self-expression in the name of sacrifice for the family, which translates into a neglect of professionalism for them. Younger interviewees were the most critical about the conservatism of Albanian culture, and the most sceptical about the possibility of any improvement in the socio-economic and cultural climate of Albania. Most of them wished to build a future bridging Italy and Albania in order to reconcile their contradictory expectations, values, and commitments, as two young migrants state:

> I really don't like one thing about Albanian culture, taboos. Like, 'don't talk to that one, don't say this, don't do that'. And what I hate most is people talking, talking, talking! I mind your business, you mind my business, together we mind everyone else's, sadly that seems to be the motto over here. (circular migrant, Albanian male, 28, Albania)

> I came back because we returned as a family, but as soon as I can I will return to Milan, I am used to that mentality, here it is completely different. I like this country but, to give you an example, I am friendly with everybody and they misunderstand it. I was with a guy for three months last summer and I could not show to be happy, he told me I had to show a sad face otherwise people would talk behind his back and look down on him for being with me! I mean, help! (circular migrant, Albanian woman, 27, Albania)

Young people's enduring oscillation between Albania and Italy not only reflects the problems they meet in finding work in both countries, but it also corresponds to their ambivalence towards the patriarchal and conservative values of Albanian culture, and their dissatisfaction with the lifestyles and opportunities they can enjoy at home. By occupying the socio-economic and cultural space emerging in between Albania and Italy, they fill 'a void inside', which is created by the gap existing between their aspirations for a more individualized and fulfilling lifestyle, and their marginalization in Italy. As a result, they 'can not find themselves' (settle down) culturally or economically neither in Italy, where they are marginalized, nor in Albania, where they feel culturally estranged (Mai 2002). Two examples of this dilemma are recounted here:

> I left when I was sixteen with the speed boat, I just wanted to leave, to go somewhere. I lived in many places in Italy and worked very hard... I got papers as a minor and worked all the time ever since. I mean, I work from 2am until 7pm... And sometimes I dream of escaping home. But when I come home I like it... but I could not live here any more. I don't know what I want to do, I have a void inside, I just go on and on. I know I could live back at the village, with nothing, doing little, but here in Italy we are more forward and even if I work too much... it's better. I think what I would like is to have an Italian lifestyle and Albanian rhythms... but that does not exist, does it? (circular migrant, Albanian male, 24, Italy)

> At the moment I feel in between the earth and the sky, suspended. I am twenty-seven and I don't know where to build a life for me, where to get married and set up a family. Here not for sure, but not even in Albania! Here in Italy it is not possible, because I am Albanian. I don't want to frame it in terms of racism but I went through quite a few episodes, even here at the university... And then there is the economic issue, it is difficult for Italians to find a job, can you imagine for an Albanian, and a woman on top of all, because there is a lot of machismo in Italian society... In Albania I can't find myself any more... I feel foreign now and

'Italianised!' I can't stand the prejudices people have against women, the mentality here... So I guess at the moment I feel like... mobile... in between Albania and Italy, but a bit confused. (circular migrant, Albanian female, 27, Italy)

Forms of circular migration can be the expression of an ambivalent passage to a more syncretic, that is a less oscillating and contradictory, assimilation of Albanian and Italian values, practices and opportunities, in the context of enduring economic instability and socio-cultural ambivalence and stagnation, both in Albania and in Italy. Many migrants, particularly students, highlighted their multiple belonging not only to both Albania and Italy but to an in-between *Italese* (a neologism formed out of *Italiano*—Italian and *Albanese*—Albanian, in Italian) diasporic space, subsuming the two national cultures, as well as more localised (i.e., regional, urban, etc.) identities within both Albania and Italy. However, the possibility of taking advantage of this multi-layered diasporic belonging is dependent on migrants' lived experiences of social inclusion and participation in Italy. Those who were most marginalized often experience the in-between space they were excluded from as a double loss of identity and belonging (Sayad 2002), from both Albanian and Italian societies.

A particularly recurrent criticism, and a parallel appreciation of the experience of emigration to Italy, highlighted the perceived 'lack of work culture' within Albanian society. Many migrants, in particular seasonal workers (documented) and migrant entrepreneurs, saw manual labour as undesirable for the fear of being stigmatized socially. More specifically, many 'returned' interviewees felt that the shame associated with 'humble' professions, such as cleaning or taking care of the elderly, in Albania was undermining the dynamism they felt the country needed to lift itself out of poverty and instability. A migrant entrepreneur now living in Italy explained her plight with workers in Albania:

> When we first opened the bar and the cinema once back here... it was very difficult. I should have been a tough boss from the very start, people wanted to get paid to sit down and knit. While I was doing everything, I cleaned, I managed... People had no respect for work, they were stealing money from the cash, they felt ashamed to be seen cleaning the floor by other people... And they were very poor too!!! I mean, I regret having invested all of that money in that experience, we should have bought a home instead... I mean, there is no respect for work in many people, there is no understanding of working, producing, which is why I am not thinking of going back there. (circular migrant, Albanian woman, 35, Italy)

At the same time, many 'returned' interviewees thought that the translation of the Italian 'culture of work' into Albanian society potentially brought about by returning migrants was a very important contribution to the improvement of the socio-economic situation at home, as a returned migrant recounts:

I only know people who came back because they had to... But I think people returning will determine a change is society, because they will have experienced the mentality and culture of work that is active in Italy and they will have brought it with them. They will reproduce it there and in the process produce something for themselves and others... Because in Albania... capitalism was misunderstood, it was translated in the worst possible form, as making money at all cost and in any possible way, without any plan or morals, and that has damaged society and the economy a lot.

Almost all migrants admired Italy's 'work culture', which they understood in terms of the valorization of the experience and value of professionalism and work *per se*. However, the possibility of capitalising on the work ethos of the country of destination is defined by the actual experiences of work encountered by migrants, some of which were marked by extreme marginalization and precarization. Undocumented economic returnees who are deported to Albania, or those returning because they lost their jobs in Italy, or those resettling in rural areas because they cannot afford to re-settle in urban areas, often worked in Italy in places where a positive work ethos and labour rights were not upheld. These underprivileged migrants tend to establish circular forms of migration between Albania and Italy as a way to sustain themselves and their families in a context of extreme socio-economic frailty and employment precariousness.

3.7.3 The unsustainability of return in times of socio-economic and political instability

As we highlighted above, there is a direct connection between legal status, social capital, and the possibility to resort to different forms of settlement and circularization. Migrants who have remained longer in Italy have greater chances of becoming regular and to build the socio-economic capital and skills. They also have the greatest nostalgia for the homeland, which underpins any project of return. In many cases, this involves opening, or the intention of opening, an economic activity as a way to:

1) maintain professional fulfillment, the working conditions and income level they could enjoy in Italy;
2) provide themselves and their relatives at home with employment opportunities, and;
3) reconcile their family responsibilities and attachments with their professional achievements and individual ambitions.

In general, migrants who are now in Albania try to reproduce the economic activities they were involved in while in Italy. They also tend to remain in touch and cooperate with their employers in Italy, through the exchange of equipment, technology, products, and know-how. The individual (or nuclear family) scale of investments combined with the fact that most migrants tended to work for small and medium enterprises while in Italy means that most 'diasporic' enterprises remain rather limited in scale and fragile in terms of financial sustainability and knowledge transfer. However, we encountered some more structured and larger-scale forms of cooperation, such as call centres and transportation firms, which are usually established in cooperation with Italian investors. Several migrants who established business tell about their experiences:

> I mean, it's a dream for each Albanian to bring the work experience they had in Italy back here, because they are proud of it! Like my idea, after having worked in the best bars, restaurants and clubs in Florence, after having worked as a DJ in Italy, I decided to open a lounge bar here. I mean, it will be a rustic lounge bar, because this is not Tirana, but it is important to try and bring back something, to change things. Here in Albania, lots of people complain about the lack of many things and then say it's not important. But it is very important! Everything is important, if you do something, you have to do it well, even the little leaf of basil is important. This is why I am trying to open a quality venue here, because we need to start from somewhere, for things to change. (circular migrant, Albanian male, 32)

> I have papers in Italy because I first went there as a minor. I learnt a lot there, by working in vineyards, wine bars, nice 'alternative' restaurants...That is where I got the idea of opening an agricultural tourism place, but I don't want to live there for the moment. I want to go there to keep updated, I would like to promote the slow-food concept in Albania, but I don't feel ready yet. This place is more ready that what it seems, it is less of a cultural desert than what it seems. I think there are possibilities here, but it is difficult to have changes fast because the place was devastated by a very violent consumerist and capitalist development. When communism went, everything went with it, values, morals... It's a bit like water, they say water is life, but when the dam breaks down it's another matter altogether. (circular migrant, Albanian male, 24)

Often, analysis of the feasibility of return is based on personal priorities rather than on actual evaluation of the economic and social context one returns to. For instance, most returning migrants want to set out as self-employed in order to avoid the poor working conditions and the authoritarian relations which often characterize employed work in Albania. In the absence of specific skills, or of the economic and social capital to invest in the sector they worked in while in Italy, many migrants have opened bars and restaurants, whose proliferation is currently not sustainable in Albania. A migrant who opened a restaurant in Albania explains the problems he faces:

> I live in Albania, but I go and come back from Italy every two months as I have people offering me work there as a painter, decorator, etc. Here in Albania, in Durres, we opened a restaurant, which is working mainly in the summer.

> We thought we had enough money when we returned, but then we had to get some credit and the restaurant alone is not enough to pay it back. (circular migrant, Albanian male, 45)

In some cases, returning migrants invested a considerable amount of hard-earned savings into the establishment of recreational venues which were out of sync with the conservative mentality and the socio-economic context they returned to in Albania. Again, the desire to reconcile 'being home' with the possibility of enjoying and offering more hedonistic lifestyles and diverse forms of consumption can fuel a potentially unfeasible project of return. Such a story is recounted by a migrant who returned to Italy:

> I mean I tried to invest in Albania, and so did my brother. They opened restaurants, but they will never get the license and...I invested in transport, with minibuses, fast delivery services. I was the first person to open a go-cart place here in Albania. But it never worked. The issue of the police, of corruption, documents... is very important. In the last two to three years I think Albania has been alienating all Albanians. Like me and my brothers we invested all our money and even went into debt, but then the first person who goes to the police can destroy you...Or like when you want to buy a house...I wanted to buy a flat in Tirana but in the end you will never be sure it is yours with the laws and the corruption we have...I'd rather buy it here in Milan, rent it out and live with the money, or not? (circular migrant, Albanian male, 37, Italy)

The lack of infrastructure and of credit opportunities, pervasive gender inequality and discrimination, unemployment, deskilling, corruption, and the impossibility of obtaining self-fulfilment through work are the most frequently mentioned problems encountered by migrant entrepreneurs. They also account for the main reasons for their return to Italy, which often translates into reluctant forms of circularity.

The rural-urban divide influences the development of specific forms of resettlement upon return. People from and returning to villages tend to be reabsorbed within family structures and to have looser contacts with Italy, mainly in the form of staying periodically in touch telephonically with their former employers and friends in order to keep the door open in case of future necessity, and also out of affection and respect. However, most returnees move from rural to peri-urban new settlements outside the city centres in Albania. The process of urbanization and of international migration are parallel strategies adopted by families and their individual members, and need to be analysed as parallel aspects of contemporary social transformations in Albania. In northern Albania, only people who were deported, or became undocumented, or faced emergencies returned to these rural or mountainous areas. Such migrants found that in these cases the family network protects 'failed' migrants from the economic consequences of their return, while the social and psychological impact of a failed migration project can be very hard. In the south of Albania, the relationship between the success of the migratory project and the return to a rural environment is more complex. Some 'successful returnees' managed to build a house in the city for their families, and chose to live in, or to commute from, the village of origin in order to run their business in agriculture and to enjoy a higher quality of life, which they associate with living in the countryside.

Students occupy the other extreme of the socio-economic spectrum encompassing return. They enter Italy documented; they avoid, to a certain degree, stigmatization and marginalization; and they gain skills and qualifications, enabling them to have better chances to find a good job back in Albania. However, their experiences of return are often marked by the frustration of their desire to find a job according to their qualifications. They are also more likely to feel very disconnected with the conservative mentality and the family-centred values of their country of origin. As a consequence, many try to maintain contact with Italy, aim to go back to Italy to work regularly, and aim to attain skills and specialization that will enable them to meet their professional ambitions back home. By obtaining more cultural capital abroad, Albanian students attempt to overtake the impediments to social mobility that they meet at home. Impediments can be a limited job market, in which the allocation of work opportunities according to personal liaisons and not merit (which they describe in terms of 'corruption') rule. At the same time, they negotiate an in-between socio-economic and cultural space, enabling them to enjoy selective aspects of the homes between which they circulate.

3.7.4 *Family and circular migration*

In the Albanian case, family dynamics cannot be meaningfully separated from the labour-economic dimension when trying to understand the main forces behind the migration/circularization nexus. Family networks are the main support and solidarity structure through which the Albanian migration phenomenon unfolded in Italy and in the rest of its diasporic ramifications. At a deeper level, and besides the logistical implications of people's reliance on family networks, most migrants referred to themselves as part of their extended or future families. The case of a young migrant is illustrated here:

> I left with my family when I was seven. It was a family reunification visa, seventeen years ago... My father found a job as a caretaker in a building in Milan. My mother was working as an assistant to elderly people, in a home; she even got a diploma to do that. Then, a few years ago, because of the crisis, my father lost his job and my mum started having back problems, so we all came back. It was a real shame for me because I had almost got all the criteria to ask for citizenship, I have now lost them. They are lucky as they have long-term permits, which they keep

updated by going to Italy often. But I will go back at the first opportunity because I can't get used to the mentality here, it is too different from how I was brought up in Italy. (circular migrant, Albanian female, 24, Albania)

This last excerpt show that it is not only the individual migrant experience, but the system of family affiliations and livelihoods that is vital to understanding the nexus between circularity, legal documentation, and socio-economic sustainability. For instance, one spouse of the same family unit, usually the husband, can work in Italy, while the other, usually the wife, takes care of children/the elderly in Albania. At the same time, one spouse, or partner in the case of younger unmarried couples, can work in Albania, while the other completes his/her studies in Italy, in hope of obtaining a better career, which will benefit the family in the longer term. Being close to an ageing parent, to a partner, a spouse, and/or children are often the main motivations stimulating people to return and/or engage upon circularity, and sometimes override economic and migration legal status considerations.

3.8 Striving for migrant flexibility in uncertain times: is circularity good, and for whom?

The two main dimensions underpinning Albanian migration to Italy are the enduring socio-economic disparity between the two countries and the difficult socio-economic and political situation Albania still finds itself in. As a result, emigration to Italy, rather then return to Albania, remains the prevailing trend. The World Bank estimated the number of migrants returning to Albania in 2005 at around 83,000 (2008). IOM (2007) research highlights several points:

1) the majority of returning migrants are from Greece;
2) there is a positive attitude in Albania towards return within families with a history of migration, and;
3) return is conditional to the availability of secure employment.

However, the same research shows that 60 per cent of respondents felt that reintegration upon their return was difficult, and only 8 per cent reported receiving any assistance (IOM 2007). Although the idea and the intention to return is still mentioned by at least half of Albanian migrants, and there is some return to Albania 'after all' (Labrianidis and Hatziprokopiou 2005), other existing studies (Barjaba 2000; King and Mai 2008) confirm a weak propensity for Albanian migrants in Italy and elsewhere to return. Above all, this is because the current state of the Albanian economy offers little encouragement to do so.

King and Vullnetari (2003) highlight how Albanian migration can be seen as constantly evolving, and therefore how return migration can be seen as interlinked with the emergence of circular patterns. Existing research has highlighted that the length of stay abroad reduces the propensity to return, as mentioned earlier in the chapter (Markova and Black 2005; Bonifazi et al. 2006). Albanian migrants in Italy, as well as being from relatively less underprivileged backgrounds than those in Greece, also earn and remit more, but are less likely to be able to reintegrate when they return to Albania (Labrianidis and Lyberaki 2004; Labrianidis and Hatziprokopiou 2005; see also de Zwager et al. 2005). This confirms the contrast between the back-and-forth nature of much Albanian migration to Greece (see Maroukis and Gemi in this volume) and its more permanent character in Italy. The different resources and patterns available to Albanians migrating to Greece and Italy are implicitly confirmed by Vadean and Piracha's analysis (2009) of the specific determinants of return and circular migration in Albania. Vadean and Piracha highlight the relationship between lack of education, seasonal work, and circularity, as 'being a male, having a lower education level, originating from a rural area and having a positive temporary migration experience in the past are factors affecting circular migration'. The amount of time spent abroad, legal residence, and accompanying family are positively related to permanent migration; while age, secondary education, failed migration, or fulfilment of a savings target determine permanent return after the first trip. Finally, a survey undertaken in 2007 on 'The Contribution of Human Resources Development to Migration Policy in Albania' (ETF 2007) highlights three main aspects characterizing the relation between return and circular migration: the higher rate of success of educated returnees, the relevance of socio-economic and cultural factors other than employment in the decision to re-emigrate, and according to Kilic et al. (2009) the possibility that many returning migrants had not yet attained an appropriate target level of savings and skills to successfully reintegrate in Albania to engage in self-employment activities upon their return.

The findings of this study confirm these broad trends and analyses, and offer more nuances regarding the intricate relationship between return, socio-economic integration (whether at home or abroad), and the circularisation of migration. The majority of migrants interviewed in this research were reluctantly and ambivalently oscillating between Albania and Italy. For most, circulating is a way to achieve the migratory flexibility they need to negotiate their livelihoods between societies and labour markets. Both societies and markets are characterized by different opportunities, predicaments, and degrees of socio-economic and political instability. In other words, for most interviewees circularity is a necessity, rather than a choice. While some interviewees, usually students (and particularly women), underlined the positive aspects associated with living in between the Albanian and Italian socio-cultural settings, most people involved in circular patterns emphasize the toll that going back and forward takes on their lives in economic and emotional terms.

Many interviewees first decided to return and live in Albania, and then felt that they had to keep working/studying in Italy as a way to support their return in the short to medium term, since the economic and professional opportunities in Albania could not meet all of their needs and aspirations, as explained by two migrants:

> For a few years we had two activities, one in Italy and one in Albania and we kept going back and forward all the time... It was good in a way as we could keep both of our social lives here and there, but then it started also being stressful, living in two places means double worry and double work. Then with my child I could not move as freely because of school and everything else, so we decided to return. (circular migrant, Albanian female 27, Albania)

> It is a difficult question, whether I am thinking of returning or not. In a moment like this, in which Italy is not doing very well and I am having problem with my papers, I am considering returning to Albania. But then as soon as I fix the papers I will give myself some more time here. I am at the third year of my doctorate. I don't know what to say as I want to try both here and there. I mean I want to follow a double track and get the best option available between the two countries. (circular migrant, Albanian female, 30, Italy)

In many cases, interviewees were in the process of negotiating a return home or settlement abroad through circularity, rather than aiming at building a circular future for themselves. Only a minority of interviewees decided to build a professional and emotional life stretching across Albania and Italy. This minority tended to be skilled, documented, and integrated in either one or both countries, and is the only group for whom circularity can be seen as 'being good'. The majority that have oscillated between Albania and Italy returned or are considering return for an inextricable mix of reasons, including: wanting to escape stigmatization or even 'being abroad', nostalgia of homeland, being closer to the family at home or abroad, building one's family at home or abroad, having access to key health services in Italy, keeping legally resident in Italy, maintaining one's family at home or abroad, exploring new situations and social settings, and studying in order to improve one's employability in Albania and/or Italy. The combination of these factors sometimes obliterates an objective evaluation of the sustainability of the project of return, which then makes circularity necessary to sustain life at home and/or abroad.

3.9 Conclusion

The specificity of the diasporic experience and of the socio-economic and cultural capital accumulated by Albanian migrants in Italy offers an ideal background for the study of circularity, especially in a comparative perspective to the experience of Albanians in Greece. As in the cases of the Morocco-Italy and Albania-Greece migrations discussed in this book (see Devitt; Maroukis and Gemi), within the Albanian migration to Italy the interplay between migration, integration, return, and circularity unfolds notwithstanding the lack of supporting policies and targeted initiatives at a governmental level. The absence of an overarching model of immigrant incorporation in Italy and of policies supporting returning migrants in Albania has meant that networks of family members and friends have been the most important source of information, support, and solidarity for Albanian migrants, both at home and abroad. The paradoxical coexistence between aspirational integration into and selective Albanophobic exclusion from Italian society underpinned Albanian migrants' partially successful integration into Italian society. The majority of Albanians were able to extricate themselves from poverty and marginalization. However, their experiences of emigration and return have been marked by extreme forms of stigmatization, and by the absence of support for their integration in Italy or their reintegration in Albania. In the process, many Albanian migrants continue to be ambivalently integrated, documented and marginalised within and between Albania and Italy. As a result, they resort to circulating between the two countries while waiting for sustainable opportunities of more permanent integration in Italy and/or reintegration in Albania.

The findings of this study do not corroborate politicized celebrations of the circularization of migration as a win-win situation for both countries of origin and destination, as the policies of the European Commission state (for a discussion of EC policies see the chapters by Devitt and Cassarino in this volume). For most, circulating is a way to achieve the migratory flexibility they need to negotiate their livelihoods between societies and labour markets characterized by different opportunities, predicaments, and degrees of socio-economic and political instability. Most Albanian migrants do not choose to circulate, but accept to do so in order to secure the sustainability of projects of settlement abroad and/or return home, which are still not completed or which became unsustainable in the context of the global financial crisis of the late 2000s. For younger people and women, particularly if they are studying, oscillating between Albania and Italy is both a way to reconcile the contradictory moral worlds brought together by their diasporic trajectories and a way to gain the socio-cultural capital to bypass widespread dynamics of corruption and preferential access to the labour market in Albania.

In the last ten years, returning to Albania has become a priority for many older and younger migrants who want to capitalize at home on the knowledge and experiences they gained in Italy, while being in the company of their family and friends, and living in a context in which they are not made to feel like undesirable foreigners. However, these ambitions are at odds with the enduring political instability and economic underdevelopment in Albania. This instability makes obtaining and keeping legal documentation in Italy a priority for the socio-economic survival of families and individuals. In the present context, therefore, those who are fully documented tend to either stay put in Italy or return to Albania. Those who are not, have to circulate in order to meet the legal, social, and economic requirements of sustainable integration in Italy and/or return to Albania.

References

Barjaba, K. (2000). *Ondate senza Ritorno*. Rome: International Organization for Migration.

Bonifazi, C., Conti, C. and Mamolo, M. (2006). *Balkan International Migration in the 1990s*, Demobalk Working Paper 8.

Bonifazi, C. and Sabatino, D. (2003). 'Albanian Migration to Italy: What Official Data and Survey Results can Reveal', *Journal of Ethnic and Migration Studies,* 29(6): 967–95.

De Soto, H., Gordon, P., Gedeshi, I. and Sinoimeri, Z. (2002). *Poverty in Albania: A Qualitative Assessment*, Washington, DC: World Bank Technical Paper 520.

De Zwager, N., Gedeshi, I., Germenji, E. and Nikas, C. (2005). *Competing for Remittances*, Tirana: International Organization for Migration.

ETF (2007). *The Contribution of Human Resources Development to Migration Policy in Albania*. Tirana: European Training Foundation.

Fuga, A. (2000). *Identités Périphériques en Albanie*. Paris: L'Harmattan.

Gionça, A. (2002). 'Albanische Emigration in den Neunziger Jahren—eine neue ära in der demographischen Entwicklung' in Kaser, K., Pichler, R., and Schwandner-Sievers, S. (eds) *Die Weite Welt und das Dorf. Albanische Emigration am Ende des 20. Jahrhunderts*. Vienna, Cologne, and Weimar: Böhlau Verlag, 15–38.

IOM (2007). *Enhancing the Impact of Migrant Remittances in Albania*. IOM/ILO Working Paper: Geneva.

ISMU (Fondazione Iniziative e Studi sulla Multietnicitá) (2011) ISMU Newsletter 16 March 2011 [online]. http://www.ismu.org/ISMUnews-notizia.php?id_notizia=220 (accessed 24 July 2012).

ISTAT (2010). *La Popolazione Straniera Residente in Italia*, Rome: ISTAT.

Kilic, T., Carletto, G., Davis, B. and Zezza, A., (2009). 'Investing Back Home: Return Migration and Business Ownership in Albania', *Economics of Transitions* 17(3): 597–623).

King, R. and Mai, N. (2008). *Out of Albania*, Oxford: Bergharn.

King, R. and Mai, N. (2009). 'Italophilia Meets Albanophobia: Paradoxes of Asymmetric Assimilation and Identity Processes Among Albanian Immigrants in Italy', in *Ethnic and Racial Studies*, 32(1), 117f–138.

King, R. and Vullnetari, J. (2003). *Migration and development in Albania*, Working Paper C5, Development Research Centre on Migration, Globalisation and Poverty. Sussex University, Brighton UK.

Labrianidis, L. and Hatziprokopiou, P. (2005). 'The Albanian Migration Cycle: Migrants Tend to Return to Their Country of Origin After All', in R. King, N. Mai, and S. Schwander-Sievers (eds), *The New Albanian Migration*. Brighton: Sussex Academic Press, 93–117.

Labrianidis, L. and Lyberaki, A. (2004). 'Back and Forth and In-Between: Albanian Return-Migrants from Greece and Italy', *Journal of International Migration and Integration*, 5(1): 77–106.

Lazaridis, G. (1996). 'Immigration to Greece: A Critical Evaluation of Greek Policy', *New Community*, 22(2): 335–48.

Mai, N. (2001). 'Italy is Beautiful': The Role of Italian Television in the Albanian Migratory Flow to Italy', in R. King and N. Wood (eds), *Media and Migration: Constructions of Mobility and Difference*, London: Routledge, 95–109.

Mai, N. (2002). 'Myths and Moral Panics: Italian Identity and the Media Representation of Albanian Immigration', in R.D. Grillo and J. Pratt (eds.) *The Politics of Recognising Difference: Multiculturalism Italian Style*. Aldershot: Ashgate, 77–95.

Mai, N. (2010). 'The Politicisation of Migrant Minors: Italo-Romanian Geopolitics and EU Integration', AREA 42(2): 182–9.

Markova, E. and Black, R. (2005). *New European Immigration and Social Cohesion in Britain*. Final report prepared for the Joseph Rowntree Foundation [online report]. http://www.jrf.org.uk/publications/east-european-immigration-and-community-cohesion (accessed 24 July 2012).

Portes, A. and Rumbaut, R. (1996). *Immigrant America: A Portrait*. Berkeley: University of California Press.

Sayad, A. (1999). *La double absence. Des illusions de l'émigré aux souffrances de l'immigré*. Paris: Seuil.

UN Albania (2010). Albanian National Report on Progress towards achieving the Millennium Development Goals, Tirana: UN [online]. http://intra.undp.org.al/ext/elib/download/?id=1058&name=Albania%20National%20MDG%20Report%20%2D%20July%202010%2Epdf (accessed 24 July 2012).

UNICEF (1998). *Situation Analysis 1998: Children's and Women's Rights in Albania*, Tirana: UNICEF.

Vadean, F. and Piracha, M. (2009). Circular Migration or Permanent Return: What Determines Different Forms of Migration? Bonn: IZA Discussion Paper No. 4287 [online]. http://ftp.iza.org/dp4287.pdf%20(accessed 24%20July%202012).

World Bank (2008). *Migration Remittances Factbook* [online]. www.worldbank.org/prospects/migrationandremittances (accessed 24 July 2012).

Zincone, G. (2006). 'The Making of Policies: Immigration and Immigrants to Italy', *Journal of Ethnic and Migration Studies*, 32(3): 347–75.

Zinn, D. L. (2005). 'The Second Generation of Albanians in Matera: The Italian Experience and Prospects for Future Ties to the Homeland', *Journal of Southern Europe and the Balkans*, 7(2): 259–77.

Note

1. IPSIA (Istituto Pace Sviluppo Innovazione—Institute Peace Development Innovation ACLI) is the Italian development NGO we cooperated with in Albania in the context of the research project whose findings inform this chapter. It is part of the ACLI (Associazioni Cristiane Lavoratori Italiani—Christian Associations Italian Workers) network of associations supporting Italian and migrant workers in Italy. For more information, see: http://www.ipsia-acli.it/ipsia/

4
Albanian Circular Migration in Greece: Beyond the State?

Thanos Maroukis and Eda Gemi

4.1 Introduction: a brief history of Albanian migration to Greece

The explosive mass emigration flows of Albanians in the beginning of the 1990s were considered to be both a unique case and an 'exceptional' type of international migration (Barjaba and King 2005, King and Vullnetari 2009). Between 1991 and 1992, an estimated 300,000 Albanians left the country, of whom 150,000 crossed the border to Greece (Carletto et al. 2006). Irrespective of the stabilization that seemed to take place between 1993 and 1996, Albanians continued to emigrate on a large-scale, particularly to Greece. In 1995 alone, 295,000 Albanian migrants arrived in Greece, while in 1996 the number of migrants reached 428,000. Following the collapse of pyramid schemes in early 1996, about 70,000 Albanians left the country. As in the past, a larger though unquantifiable number of Albanians crossed the Greek borders (Vullnetari 2007). In the first decade of the twenty-first century Albanian migration has continued, albeit at a lower scale, thus marking the end of highly intense mass emigrations from the previous decade (Migrant Remittances 2010: 7).

In total, over a million Albanians—almost 30 per cent of the population or 35 per cent of its active population (IOM 2008)—have emigrated abroad. According to the OECD database on immigrants and repatriates, almost 64.4 per cent of Albanian migrants abroad live in Greece, which corresponds to approximately 577,500 people in total (Eurostat 2009).[1] On the other side of the border, the Greek Labour Force Survey (Triandafyllidou and Maroufof 2011) estimated their number to be about 501,000, which amounts to around 60 per cent of the total immigrant population (out of 839,000) living in

Albanian Circular Migration in Greece: Beyond the State?

Greece, as well as 5 per cent of the total native Greek population. It should be noted that among these legally residing Albanians there are 197,000 who hold special permits as Albanian citizens of ethnic Greek descent.

The back-and-forth movements of Albanians to Greece throughout the 1990s were temporary, predominantly irregular, and involved semi-skilled, low-skilled, or unskilled migrants. These migration patterns were circular insofar as their repeated frequency is concerned. Albanian migration, particularly around the border regions of Greece and Albania, presented features of repeated, seasonal migration (Markova 2005). At the same time, the mass deportations of irregular Albanian migrants by the Greek state indeed constituted a peculiar variant of the return (forced) strategy (Reyneri 2001:37) However, the forced nature of the return to Albania did not qualify these circular movements of Albanians to Greece as circular migration.

Albanian migrants were generally employed on a seasonal or temporary basis in labour intensive sectors noted for informal activity: agriculture,

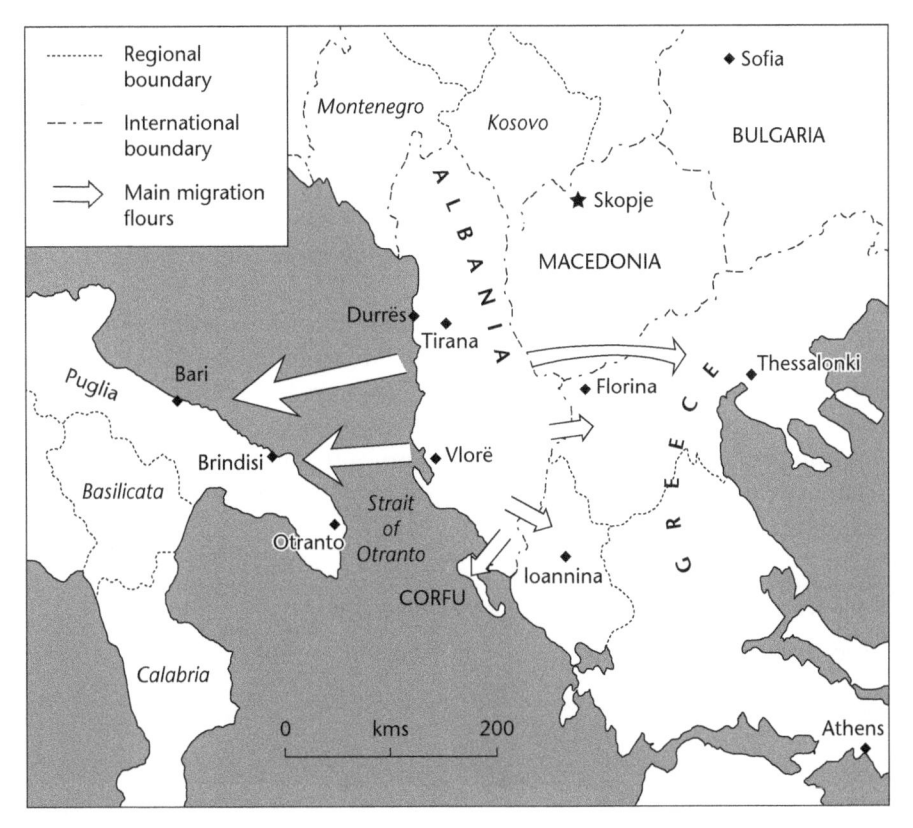

Figure 4.1 Albania and its neighbours: main migration routes
Source: King and Vullnetari, 2003.

construction, tourism, small scale family factories, and housekeeping. These 'circular' movements kept the migrants in irregularity for a long time, owing to the restrictive immigration policies of Greece. It is estimated that over 550,000 unauthorized migrants were working in Greece by the late 1990s. Most of them were employed in seasonal work and returned home in the off-season (Reyneri 2001).

However, in the early 2000s, most of these back and forth irregular movements evolved into permanent settlement (or gaining legality became easier). This was mainly due to the legalization procedures which were first introduced in 1998, setting the Greek state's requirements for social insurance contribution in order to prove legal work and obtain/renew one's residence permit. Indeed, the successive regularization programmes in Greece (1998, 2001, and 2005) gave Albanian migrants the opportunity to settle down and travel in a legal manner.

On the other hand, migrants without a stay permit could only move legally between the two countries if they were invited by employers for seasonal or temporary labour. This invitation system is called *metaklisi* (in Greek), and was introduced by the Greek government in 2001 under a system of annual quotas (Maroukis and Gemi 2011). In the case of Albanian workers this system of seasonal invitation (L.3386/05) took into account the bilateral agreement of 1997 between Greece and Albania, and, in theory, involved all seasonal professions. In practice, though, it has only worked for seasonal jobs in Greek agriculture (Maroukis and Gemi 2011).

The stay permits granted to Albanian nationals for seasonal and/or temporary reasons are presented in Table 4.1.

After the introduction of the six month window of the seasonal *metaklisi* system in 2001, formerly irregular circular migrants followed a more fixed pattern of circularity. Those who came to Greece under seasonal *metaklisi* did not overstay because they did not want to lose the opportunity to come the following year.[2] Since the option of legal entry and stay was finally available to migrants, they did not want to risk losing their legality, as they were illegal for many years (Maroukis and Gemi 2011).

Table 4.1 Stay permits for seasonal and temporary employment

NATIONALITY	CATEGORY	2007	2008	2009	Total
ALBANIA	FISHERMEN (L.3386/05, article 16A)		1	1	2
	SEASONAL WORK (L.3386/05, article 16)	13,416	13,731	13,696	40,843
ALBANIA TOTAL		13,416	13,732	13,697	40,845
MIGRANT TOTAL		13,509	14,841	15,053	43,403

Source: Ministry of Interior, October 2010.

This chapter is based on research that aimed to identify the existing patterns of circular migrants between the two countries, to map out the respective trajectories that they have followed so far, and to understand the prospects of this circularity for the parties involved (the migrant, the employer, the host country. and the country of origin). Concretely, it investigates the factors that motivate or hinder circular movements from the perspective of stakeholders from either country, and also with a view to capturing the migrants' perception and experience at both sides of the border.

4.2 Methodology

This chapter builds on thirty-six interviews with circular migrants and nineteen interviews with stakeholders (state officials, NGOs, experts) in both countries. The main criterion employed for the selection of the sample has been the occurrence of a temporary, repeated, and cross-border migration for economic reasons. As regards access to interviewees, we followed snowball sampling in combination with targeted sampling based on key informant input. Fieldwork in Albania was conducted in several locations, including Shkodra (northern Albania), Tirana (capital), Berat (southern Albania), and Sarande (near the border with Greece). Conducting interviews with circular and return migrants in Albania exposed first-hand the social underpinnings that frame circular migrants' investments back home, and what drives them back to the immigration host country. Interviews with stakeholders in Albania revealed a holistic picture of the features of circular and return migrants deriving from different parts of Albania, as well as information on the implementation of existing relevant policies.

In Greece, field research was collected in three locations: Athens, the region of Central Macedonia, and the island of Sifnos in the Cyclades. The former was chosen since the majority of Albanians are concentrated in the Greek capital. Many Albanian and ethnic Greek Albanian businesses as well as highly skilled workers are concentrated there. The island of Sifnos, on the other hand, included features of a local labour market, combining a) construction, renovation, building maintenance, and other preparatory activities for the tourist season, b) the actual tourist industry, c) the all year long constructions sector industry, as well as a consolidated migrant community. The Central Macedonian agricultural prefectures of Imathia and Pella had, from 2007 to 2010, over 60 per cent of the total of seasonal work visa applications in Greece. In addition, the proximity of this rural region to the city of Thessaloniki offered an opportunity to investigate the geographical and labour market mobility of the circular migrants. The fieldwork was conducted from May to August 2010.

4.3 Types of circular migration between Greece and Albania

This case study identified four types of circular migrants, according to their level of skills, the legal or irregular nature of their movement, its regulated or spontaneous character, and the time length of each stay and return (see Table 4.2). We shall analyse the profiles of the circular migrants configured in the aforementioned typology, the factors that favour or stop each type of circular migration, and the scope of spontaneous versus state-managed forms of circularity, with a view to understanding the prospects of this circularity for the parties involved (the migrant, the employer, the host country, and the country of origin).

4.3.1 *Legal seasonal migration*

The first type of circular migration is a side effect that derives from the seasonal *metaklisi* procedure that is in place. The policy of seasonal invitation of a foreign worker has unintentionally set a framework in which circular migration patterns occur. How safe is it, though, to argue that Albanian migrants coming to Greece seasonally under the system of foreign worker invitation (as it is stipulated in article 16 of L.3386/2005 and its amendment of L.12311/2008) are circular migrants? There is statistical evidence that points in this direction: nearly half of the 65,462 registered individuals who applied for a seasonal work permit during the period 2001 to 2011 have applied for such a permit more than once in Greek municipalities. The rate of the repeated seasonal migration under the system of *metaklisi* might be much higher, considering the fact that applications' data before 2008 were not efficiently registered in the municipalities (Maroukis and Gemi 2011).

Most of the qualitative interviews with migrants conducted in the region of Central Macedonia and the island of Sifnos indicated that Albanian migrants working seasonally in Greece under the system of foreign worker invitation usually go back to Albania in order to be with their family, and to assist with the family business (in most cases it is a farm). The very fact that they have to leave after six months in Greece 'pushes' them to build a life and invest back home. They return to Greece every year usually at the beginning of May, and stay until October/November.

4.3.2 *Irregular seasonal migration*

The second type of circular migration (irregular circular) is generally characterized by longer cycles than the other types; yet the duration of stay

Table 4.2 Typology of circular migration between Greece and Albania

DIMENSIONS	Type 1 Legal seasonal migration	Type 2 Irregular seasonal migration	Type 3 Legal circular migration of low- and semi-skilled worker	Type 4 Legal circular migration of semi- and high-skilled worker
1) Demographic features	Single male migration, age 21–58	Single male migration, ages 15–23, 35–45	Single male migration, family migration, age 30–55	Diverse younger ones are usually Omogeneis (Greek decent)
2) Legal status in Greece	Short-term/seasonal stay permit	Undocumented	2-year to 10-year stay permits	Indefinite stay permit or Special Omogeneis Identity Card
3) Duration	6 months—usually from May to November	Longer cycles depending on age, arrival arrangement and sector of employment	Construction: winter season in Greece, Easter break and August in Albania. Services: more varied pattern	Frequent travels back and forth (almost every month)
4) Skill level of occupation in Greece	Low skilled	Low skilled	Low or semi skilled	Semi to high skilled
5) Employment in Albania	Agricultural work on family land	Agricultural work on family land, work on family house or no work	Low-skilled work or running a small business in Albania mainly in: agriculture, construction and tourism/service sectors.	Highly skilled work or running their own business in Albania
6) Employment in Greece	Work mainly in agriculture or other seasonal employment such as herding or tourism. They usually work for more than one employer	Work in agriculture and construction sector or tourism. They usually work for more than one employer, across sectors and in different regions of Greece	Mainly in construction but also in agriculture and service sectors	Either self-employed or working for businesses, that are either Greek or Omogeneis.
7) Country where migrants' families are permanently situated	Albania	Albania	Greece, Albania	Greece, Albania

depends on age, arrival arrangement, and sector of employment. There are two kinds of irregular migrants who present elements of circularity. The first involves young Albanians, often under twenty-one years old, arriving irregularly in Greece to work in the fields of Central Macedonia and other areas of northern Greece. There are also young Albanians over twenty-one years old who come to Greece for seasonal work in the fields, but lack the social networks that would assure them a *metaklisi* visa. By and large, there is no long-term plan behind their irregular movements between Albania and Greece. They come to work in Greece in order to get by without burdening their parents.

The second kind of irregular seasonal migrant has usually been coming to Greece for more than a decade, but cannot enter through a legal avenue. Some of these are people who were deported to Albania and were registered in the 'list of undesirables' to whom entry to the country is forbidden for a period of five years.

However, since it is expensive and risky for these migrants to travel back and forth, they are likely to spend longer cycles of stay in Greece than the other types of circular migrants identified by this case study. The number of times they move between countries within a year depends on how much work they find in a certain period of time. At the time of the interview, when jobs in the construction sector had become scarce owing to the economic crisis, an Albanian male migrant who has been coming irregularly to Greece since 2006 to work in the construction sector had not gone back home for nine months.[3] The combination of irregular residence status and less work in the host country increases the likelihood of staying put in the host or origin country and stopping circular migration.

4.3.3 Legal circular migration of low- to semi-skilled workers

The two-year and ten-year long migrant permit holders working in low-skilled jobs in Greece constitute spontaneous circular migration. Albanian circular migrants of this third type working in the construction sector usually stay in Albania from December to February/March, working until July in Greece, possibly with a break during Easter, then return to Albania in August, and finally come to work in Greece between September and November. Most Albanians of this category follow this cycle more or less because their main work is in Greece and their work back home (agricultural work) takes place during certain fixed times over the year. The case of G, a builder with a two-year long stay permit, is unique, since he does the same work in both countries, and he goes to Albania from three to six times per year:

I go when I don't have work here [in Greece]. Now for example I will leave again on the 26th of June. I will have the mobile phone open all the time I will be waiting phone calls to tell me to come for work. (Maroukis and Gemi 2011)

The cycles of Albanian migrant workers in the service sector in Greece are more varied. This is mainly owing to the different cycles that characterize their diverse entrepreneurial activities in Albania and their work in Greece.

The circular migrants working mainly in the construction sector are people who have lived or live with their families in Greece. They work in Greece in order to supplement the income earned in Albania and/or fund their investment there, and at the same time maintain the bonds that are formed from life in the host country. Their work often oscillates between the agricultural and the construction sector as a result, They also work informally (usually registered with OGA, Agricultural Insurance Organization, and work in the constructions sector).

The circular migrants working in the service sector in Greece take different entrepreneurial paths in Albania from the construction sector workers. They rely on family too, yet they tend to invest more in new businesses than existing ones. Apart from the different ways their families experienced migration (more family reunification than single male migration), the type of investment in Albania is also related to the specificities of their work in Greece.

These circular migrants are not temporary migrants, as they have made investments in Greece. The social insurance contributions they have paid towards their pension for at least ten years now is something that cannot be overlooked.[4] Stepping down from the stay permit system and using instead the visa-free regime in order to enter and work in Greece when the opportunity comes up is not an easy option that they would gladly switch to; since losing their legal residence status would result in losing their entitlement to a pension from the Greek state.

An EDTO permit holder was interviewed.[5] After thirteen years of living in Greece and working as a cleaner, she opened a restaurant and a rooms-to-rent business with her husband in an Albanian tourist destination, and returned to Albania in 2004. Her children could not adapt to the Albanian reality, and persistently begged her to return to Greece. In 2007, she returned to Greece with her children. Her husband lives permanently in Albania in order to run the restaurant, and she works as a cleaner in Greece in the winter, with regular visits to Albania; in the summer season, she returns to Albania with her children to run her tourist business. Family migration and reunification involves integration in the host society on more complex levels, and thus leads to more durable circular patterns compared with single male migration.

4.3.4 *Legal circular migration of semi- and high-skilled workers*

This type of circular migration concerns migrants with higher educational backgrounds coming from various parts of the country of origin. Higher education is either an import from Albania or pursued in Greece.

In the case of ethnic Greek Albanians, their ethnic origin and related privileged legal status has been a key factor in their entrepreneurial success and its circular character. Indicative is the fact that most of the circular movements of ethnic Greek Albanians identified in the case study commence almost at the same time as their settling down in the host country. It is no coincidence that many studies find that ethnic Greek Albanians have a high incidence of self-employment and entrepreneurship among the wider community of migrants from Albania (Lyberaki and Maroukis 2005; Maroukis 2009). Ethnic Albanians with a high level of skills usually find work in Greece from the onset of their arrival, or soon after going through a series of lower status jobs.

Circular migration is necessary for these highly skilled circular migrants in maintaining employment connections and keeping track of their investment made in Albania. An Albanian journalist and artist interviewed who work in Greece and Albania travel between eight to ten times per year to Albania for work purposes. Working in Greece and opening a small business with its own premises in Albania is a pattern that cannot be sustained for long, unless it entails a partnership with a relative, colleague, or friend who can run the business.

4.4 Legal, institutional, and social factors that favour or hinder circular migration between Greece and Albania

Albanian circular migration to Greece is a phenomenon that developed spontaneously and, to a certain extent, irrespectively of and independently from state policies on either side of the Greek-Albanian border.

Greece does not provide an appropriate legal framework that would favour a circular migration flow, as the existing law passed in 2005 (L.3386/2005) does not cater for the eventuality of circular migration.[6] Article 16 on seasonal invitation of a foreign worker treats this type of migration as a one-off activity not likely to be repeated, since there is no provision for the regular renewal of the relevant permit. Interestingly, in Italy employers could apply for three-year seasonal work permits for seasonal migrant workers who were employed on a quota-based seasonal work permit for two consecutive years under law no.40/1998. Research in the early 2000s indicated that this measure had little resonance among seasonal migrant workers (Censis 2002; Devitt 2011).

On the other hand, prospective migrants have to commit to the social and cultural capital both at home and in the host country in order to make use of the entry channel of seasonal foreign worker invitation. Access to the relevant seasonal visa has been conditioned on the one hand by the practices and structures of local labour markets and on the other by corruption in Greek consulates in Albania at the initial and final stages of the application process respectively.

For example, a common practice witnessed by key informants has been the payment of €250 to €500 to the employer (mostly via an Albanian middleman), so that he declares the name of the prospective seasonal migrant in his nominal request to the regional prefecture (Perifereia). The other option is to maintain strong social ties with immigrants and/or employers in Greece. Such is the case where the prospective seasonal worker has a family/friendship connection with a mediator Albanian worker, who in turn has a good reputation within the local rural community and is in a position to ask local employers to put another name down on the list sent to Perifereia as a favour (Maroukis and Gemi 2011). These informal arrangements in local labour markets find fertile ground, because there is no mechanism to check what part of the land property declared in the farmer's tax declaration is cultivated other than the farmer's affirmation and the OGA (Agricultural Insurance Organisation) official's limited controls.[7] Indeed, several of our key informants argued that the phenomenon of employers putting down the names of, say, ten workers when they actually needed three (on the second level of nominal requests to the Perifereia) is widespread in the Greek countryside.

These informal work arrangements between prospective migrants, immigrant residents, and employers that come into play for the acquisition of seasonal worker invitation visas indicate that the social capital accumulated between and within migrant groups and employers in local labour markets often bends external legal rules on employment and state policies, and controls the migrants' access to these markets.

Once in Greece, the seasonal invitation workers' rights are in fact curtailed to the minimum. The social contributions paid by the employer and the Greek state for each worker theoretically entitle the latter to health care. However, OGA is eligible to issue health booklets for the seasonally invited migrants only after the six months that they are supposed to be working in Greece (Maroukis and Gemi 2011). This means that these migrants cannot make use of their social security contributions in practice. Nevertheless, this has not really affected their decision to migrate again and again over the years in the same way. Opportunities for work and integration in local labour markets weigh more in their life plans than state-awarded rights.

Contributing towards one's pension is not an option in the case of the seasonal foreign worker invitation scheme, as social contributions only relate to health care. This is likely to pose problems in the future for the migrants involved, yet again it made no difference to their decision to move back and forth every year. This is related to the fact that many migrants have some private savings, and to the younger age of many migrants using the seasonal foreign worker invitation channel.

Albanian circular migration has benefited significantly from regularization programmes and other laws (such as the privileged treatment of the Albanian citizens with Greek ethnic origin) that *de facto* facilitate frequent circular movement.[8] After all, a significant segment of Albanian circular migration to Greece regards long-term stay permit holders; long-term stay permits offer not only long-term but also short-stay options to their holders. Having the option to move becomes particularly significant in times of economic depression and high unemployment, as we have been witnessing in Greece since late 2009. An unemployed construction sector worker interviewed said that it is easier to go back to Albania when you have assured the return to Greece: 'now I'm waiting to get the ten year long permit, then I will go back [to Albania] and will be coming here [Greece] whenever work comes up' (Maroukis and Gemi 2011).

Yet being attached to a two-year long permit makes circularity difficult to maintain in the long term. Up to 2009 migrant workers insured with OGA were supposed to bring in employer affirmations proving 150 days of work per year for the renewal of their permits. The resulting illegal market of working day affirmations from employers and certificates from OGA correspondents forced the authorities to change the procedure in 2009, and to get rid of the employer's involvement. Until then, many construction workers who were initially registered in their stay permits as agricultural workers found farmers who affirmed the working days required, either through actual work on the farm when necessary or by paying the Greek farmer a certain sum (Maroukis and Gemi 2011). Several Albanian circular migrant interviewees were looking for self-employment options in order to return to Albania at the time of the interview (Maroukis and Gemi 2011), after more than a decade of haggling with employers for working days (OGA) and social insurance stamps (IKA, Social Insurance Organisation) for the renewal of stay permits, and while being on the brink of losing their legal residence status.[9]

Journalist sources, citing data provided by the Ministry of the Interior, refer to about 130,000 to 140,000 immigrant workers losing their stay permits because they were not able to secure the required number of social insurance stamps (IKA) in order to renew their documents in Greece.[10]

The positive steps made in recent legislation with regard to legal migrants who settle on a more permanent basis in Greece are expected to have a positive spill-over effect on circularity in the long term. The mobility prospects of migrants with two-year long stay permits can benefit from the recent introduction of a transparent process of citizenship acquisition for immigrants and their children who have been born or finished their education in

Greece (L.3838/2010).[11] Crucially, through this legislation, parents of children who qualify for naturalization (being born in Greece or having attended Greek education for at least six years, with parents residing legally in Greece for five years) are able to obtain a renewable five-year stay and work permit as parents of Greek citizens.

Interestingly, the risk of lapsing into illegality for female holders of stay permits for family reunification whose husbands lose their jobs and therefore their chances to renew stay permits is largely moderated by the following three legal provisions. First, migrant holders of a family reunification permit may switch after five years to a self-contained (*aftotelous*) stay permit (art.60 L.3386/2005 modified by art.45 L.3731/2008). Second, persons who lapse into illegality and can prove a long presence and bonds developed in the country may exceptionally be awarded yearly stay permits for humanitarian reasons (art.42, L.3907/2011). And third, the introduction of the *ergosimo* under Art. 20 of L.3863/2010 as a single method for the payment of wages and social security contributions of occasionally employed workers in the domestic sector offered a pathway to legalize undeclared work retroactively.[12] These legal developments help maintain legality and, depending on the household strategies, open the option of circular migration at a difficult time. This is particularly important nowadays, when more migrant women become the breadwinners of their households, working mostly as undeclared carers and cleaners in private homes.

Nevertheless, in a Greece of austerity the fact remains that it is difficult for Albanian migrants to find work, to purchase the social security contributions required for stay permit renewals,[13] and thus secure their chances to circulate between Greece and Albania for work purposes (Maroukis and Gemi 2011: 24). According to Labour Force Survey data of Hellenic Statistical Authority (EL. STAT), the migrant population in Greece has been decreasing from early 2010 onwards for the first time in the last twenty years (Triandafyllidou and Maroufof 2011). In 2011, more than half a year after the completion of the field research, legality mainly serves to return to Albania, and leaves the option to return to Greece when there is work open.

A major immigrant return to Albania is a development of the last couple of years, and should not be interpreted as the result of a failed integration. Return flows of Albanian emigrants to Greece are recorded already during the period 2001–4, and what starts as a return migration may turn into circular as various literature (Labrianidis and Hatziprokopiou 2005; Labrianidis and Kazazi 2006; Vadean and Piracha 2009), including our case study, indicates.

Unemployment has affected a considerable share of Albanian migrant households since 2009, and the shrinking of the construction sector in Greece has been the main cause of emigration back to Albania.[14] Literature suggests, however, that returnees before the crisis tend to represent immigration stories of success rather than failure (Labrianidis and Hatziprokopiou 2005; Labrianidis and Kazazi 2006; Germenji and Milo 2009). Vadean and Piracha (2009) also find that failed migration may act as a deterrent for future migration movements, while past positive migration experience affects circular and return migration alike. In this study we found that the settlement of Albanians in Greece that opened the paths of return and/or circularity before the crisis neither followed a linear trajectory nor was necessarily positive. The social integration of Albanian migrants in Greece may nowadays be celebrated as a success (mostly in comparison with the nationally and religiously different migrant arrivals in Greece during the last five years), yet it has been carved through xenophobic reactions, discrimination, and rejection in all levels of encounters with Greek society (a similar development occurred in Italy, as explained in Chapter 3). The high self-employment patterns of Albanian returnees (Labrianidis and Hatziprokopiou 2005) and circular migrants, their commitment to build something of their own, and the work ethic acquired in Greece and experimented with in Albania are tinted by negative and positive immigration and emigration experiences alike.

The circular connections that migrants establish between their country of origin and the host country need infrastructures for the reintegration of people, ideas, and capital alike. An Albanian circular migrant who works for an insurance firm in Greece and runs an insurance office in Albania, explains.

> The truth is that Albania has a lot of development potential. However, the state produces red tape, the taxes are not paid, and in the end the state does not collect revenue in order to provide services and is obliged to borrow continuously. (Albanian male, 28)

There are no reintegration policies in place for circular migrants accounted for by the Greek side. Return migration (which often is the prelude to circular and repeat migration) has been traditionally viewed by Greece mainly in relation to forced return (Maroukis and Gemi 2011). When it comes to the opening of a business or trade between the two countries, indeed, a *laissez-passer* provided by the host country for the individual immigrant is only one condition among many. The free movement of goods, the taxation of businesses, and the banking system in the country of origin are equally if not more significant issues that affect the re-entry of the circular migrant as an economic actor back home. The main problem of the mainly small to medium-sized businesses of return and circular migrants is indeed the restricted access to bank loans, and corruption in Albanian customs offices when imports are involved (Maroukis and Gemi 2011).

The main conduit, however, that makes circular migration a reality is family. The maintenance of social and family networks at both ends seems to be a prerequisite for the successful return (Labrianidis and Kazazi 2006) and the circularity of the migrant. Being close to an ageing parent, to a partner and/or children, to extended family, and to friends is not only a pulling factor but also the main support infrastructure for people who both return and work between the two countries.

As is the case in Italy (Devitt 2011), Albanian immigrants in Greece have been obliged to be self-reliant, which often translates to family-reliant, owing to low wages (one of the lowest annual average wages, based on purchasing power parity, in Europe, according to an OECD 2011 report), and a weak welfare state with a traditional focus on pensions (Ferrera 2006; Sakellaropoulos 1999). The economic recession accelerated this process, and many people drew on family and social networks to pursue work opportunities back home while remaining formally resident in Greece. A builder who retained connections with friends and family in Albania while he was settled in Greece relates his experience:

> It is the last two years that I go back and forth for work. The times before that, I used to go only to see the family. Here work started to dry up and I needed to get prepared for there as well. So that we are not out of work there too. (Maroukis and Gemi 2011)

When it comes to the perpetuation of highly skilled university employment in both countries, the Albanian Ministry of Education has a scholarship named *fondi i ekselences* for graduates who wish to proceed with postgraduate courses abroad. There is also the Brain Gain Programme, which provides financial incentives to members of the Albanian diaspora who return to Albania and find employment in public administration after a competitive call.

Albanian reintegration policies need to pay even more attention to the other more numerous categories of low- and semi-skilled circular migrants rather than focus on the highly skilled. They are bearers of small-scale capital and skills, and should be supported in order to change Albania's neglected rural landscape, which is a key variable towards unlocking the country's development potential. What is needed, though, is for these migrants to be 'reached' by regional labour offices and NGOs working on reintegration of returnees on the local level. It is also important that the labour offices provide consultation that corresponds to the character and the needs of the Albanian market, broken down by locality and sector.

Albanian policy stakeholders need to realize that loans, basic infrastructure, consultation and information services, and vocational training are equally crucial to bigger and smaller migrant investors who return or go back and forth in urban and rural areas.

All in all, years after the bilateral agreement on seasonal labour between Greece and Albania, the two countries do not seem ready to benefit from the realities of the geographical mobility of labour that is observed on the ground.

Although circular migration does indeed take place, mainly through informal channels and outside labour inter-state agreements, the current migration policy in the two countries remains trapped in a dichotomy of temporary versus permanent migration.

4.5 Is circularity good, and for whom?

So far in our analysis, we have distinguished between groups of people who move between Greece and Albania, mapped out policies and legal rules that are difficult for local authorities to follow up, thus creating problems to circular migrants at times, and observed various profiteering groups in between. Is circularity good, though, and for whom? At this point, we shall analyse the effects of circular migration on the individual level of the circular migrant, and on the level of the host and source economy. As we shall see, the positive effects of circular migration are skewed.

The main benefit for low-skilled circular migrants working in the construction, agricultural, or service sectors is that they have earned a living for a number of years and sustained their family back home (in many cases having built houses or invested in their family farm). Depending on their age, their immersion in local labour markets in Greece, and the legality of their circular movements, they build a viable way of earning a living that their family can rely on, and their return or retirement can be cushioned against.

The majority of circular migrants working under seasonal *metaklisi* in Greece come from rural areas of southern and central Albania. Some maintain long-term investment plans when in Albania, involving the purchase of agricultural equipment, like tractors, or other infrastructure for their landholdings, while others just do enough to get by. The problem is that they cannot make use of their health insurance payments in the host country, even though positive steps have been made in this direction by the OGA. Second, they do not have the option to pay into pension contributions for the part of their working life spent in Greece.

Young Albanians, aged between sixteen and twenty years old, who come irregularly to northern Greece to work in the fields, or other Albanian youths aged up to twenty-five years old, who use the seasonal worker invitation channel following in the steps of their fathers, are other sub-categories identified in our research. For them, moving between Albania and Greece is an easy way to make some money without burdening their parents, and most of these youths do not have any particular investment plans. This survival strategy leads them deeper into the trap of inertia, since it neither pushes them forward to migrate permanently nor forces them to invest in economic activity at home. On the other hand, there are middle-aged Albanian migrants circulating irregularly from Albania to Greece who could not get a stay permit during the past regularization programmes, and still need to cover their families' pressing financial needs. When in Albania they work on the family farm or are unemployed, as we hear from such an Albanian circular migrant:

> Now if I work five, six or seven months here, I will go back to Albania. If I find work there [in his village next to Berat] OK, if not I will go to the village up above in order to plant olive trees, raisins. But this requires money now. If I need money, again back to Greece. (Maroukis and Gemi 2011)

Circularity has helped Albanian migrants who are in possession of a two- or ten-year stay permit in the host country (mainly construction and service sector workers) to adapt their work around the demands of family life, and possible periods of unemployment in either country.

Several legal migrants who had been living with their families in Greece returned or were about to return to Albania at the time of the interview, either because of family obligations, an opportunity to run a business of their own back home, and either unemployment or a slowing down of work activities in the host country. Our case study indicated that having worked in Greece helps to build prospects for work in Albania, as we see from the circular migrant who recounts his experiences here:

> In Abania I have friends that tell me 'come so that we make a group' and work there in constructions with 20–25,000 lek daily earnings. There I'm god. First, they ask you if you have worked in Greece. If you say yes, they employ you at that very moment without anyone intervening and vouching for you. (Maroukis and Gemi 2011)

Maintaining an employment relationship in Greece while concurrently running a business in Albania is crucial in order to better support the business venture. Indicative is the case of an Albanian circular migrant who runs an internet café in the premises of the University of Tirana from Monday to Thursday. He spends Fridays and weekends in the Athens suburbs, working as a waiter in a fish-tavern:

> I don't know if I will keep going back and forth. It depends on work. If work goes really well in Tirana I will not be able to come as I do now. Now though that work is less [the interview was conducted in late June at the end of the academic year] the money I earn in the fish-tavern is essential. (Maroukis and Gemi 2011)

Retaining a stay permit in Greece and going back to Albania, while keeping in touch with local and co-national employers and colleagues in Greece, seems to be the desired strategy of Albanian immigrants today who cannot afford to live in the host country. Apparently circular migration patterns may not only help ameliorate economic prospects in the country of origin but also offer an alternative to hardships encountered in the host country.

Of course, the significance of circularity depends on the type of work involved. As Julie Vullnetari argues, 'There are types of employment which can allow for, and even benefit from, circularity, whereas there are others for which a constant physical presence at work throughout is a must' (Maroukis and Gemi 2011).

Nevertheless, circular migrants with stay permits face difficulties in renewing their stay permits owing to unemployment and financial problems in Greece. They will not be able to move as often as they need for their work between the two countries, as new legislation is not in their favour. The new visa liberalization between the EU and Albania, which has been in force since January 2011, will only help short-term and seasonal informal work, but does not cover any other employment areas (Maroukis and Gemi 2011). Any obstacles to the legal circularity of Albanian migrants, such as the loss of stay permits, are not in the interests of Greek insurance funds, since they will lose revenue from the reduction of the Albanians' social security contributions. One needs to keep in mind that Albanians compose more than half of Greece's total legal immigrant population, and that a certain number of migrants have already moved or are expected to move back to Albania in the coming years. Greece will lose social security contributions from an important segment of its workforce should these persons maintain contact with the Greek labour market and engage in undeclared work.

The social and economic integration of Albanian migrant workers in Greek local labour markets would be another loss for the Greek economy. The just-in-time availability of trustworthy labour hands has been the competitive advantage of Albanian circular workers, compared with other less settled and less numerous nationalities in Greek agriculture, for years. Albanian construction and agricultural sector workers, under seasonal or long-term permits, have always been workers whom Greek employers have relied upon, and can employ with little or no prior notice.

Circular migration has so far had a limited effect on the economic development of the country of origin. Circular migration has helped the majority of migrants to sustain their families, maintain and at times expand their agricultural activities, and/or open a small business. Overall, our study shows that when situated in Albania the majority of (low- and medium-skilled) circular migrants generally do not disentangle from a survival-led consumption feeding construction and import, and move towards an export-oriented production pattern.

The circular migrants who are likely to bring more capital and skills back to their country of origin are legal migrants who spontaneously circulate between the two countries (types 3 and 4). The legal seasonal migrants who come to work through the relevant bilateral labour agreement for six months every year and then return home (type 1) tend to bring some capital often invested in their agricultural landholdings, or building or renovating a family house/flat, or merely fund their living expenses in Albania through their labour in Greece. Compensation for irregular circular migrants' (Type 2 in Table 4.2) work in Greece is usually just enough to make ends meet in Albania.

Not working or investing in some entrepreneurial activity when 'back home' can have devastating effects on local societies in the country of origin. Circular migrants from rural areas in Albania tend to introduce what is thought of as a higher standard of living to their peers. Other villagers in turn desire these comforts, and see immigration as a means to attaining the same lifestyle as the circular migrants. This tendency to migrate is also witnessed in the younger generations from rural Albania, who follow in the footsteps of their circulatory parents.

4.6 Conclusion

There are several questions that one should keep in mind when studying circular migration between Greece and Albania. Is circular migration after all a matter of migration policy and geography? What is the impact of circular migration for the destination and origin country? Is it primarily a product of legal regulations and geographical limitations that influence control over flows of people? Or is it the social process and policy through which migrant (transnational) households integrate and reintegrate in local labour markets?

To be sure, geography plays a certain role. As Albanians in Greece indicate, the proximity of the host country affords them more options for circular migration patterns. On the other hand, distance sets the tone in the case of Moroccan migrants living with their families in Italy, as they find it more difficult to save, and thus travel back home less often (Devitt 2011).

Legality provides the option to move. The stronger the legal status and the fewer restrictions there are on the duration of time spent abroad, the more likely immigrants are to engage in circularity. However, migration policy and legal restrictions to movement do not suffice in explaining why some migrants move back and forth rather than establish themselves in the country of immigration. We have seen that the system of seasonal invitation of foreign workers in agriculture may oblige the workers it involves to build their life back home, but it is the social dynamics developed in local labour markets that assure their return to Greece every year. The role of migration policy is even more limited when called to explain the shaping of other more spontaneous forms of circular migration that are encountered. We have seen that the integration trajectories of Albanians in the immigration country, the social and technical skills obtained through immersion in labour markets and localities with different characteristics, the family ties maintained in the place of origin and developed in the host context all set different patterns of return and circularity when juxtaposed with the objective realities of a host and origin country with weak welfare states, traditionally characterized by informal economic activity and corruption, and lately, in the case of Greece, high unemployment.

Whether a new labour agreement or legislation aiming to regulate the circular flow between the two countries would offer added value in the above-described flow of people and capital is debatable. Maybe policy efforts would be more effective if they addressed the de facto circular flows of people as opportunities for transferring skills, and social and economic capital. Policy should not fall under an overarching target of controlling how many migrants come in and leave, but rather what they bring in or take out, and how.

References

Barjaba, K. and King, R. (2005). 'Introducing and Theorising Albanian Migration', in R. King, N. Mai and S. Schwandner-Sievers (eds), *The New Albanian Migration*. Brighton: Sussex Academic Press, 1–28.

Carletto, G. et al. (2006). 'A country on the move: International migration in post-communist Albania', *International Migration Review*, 40(4): 767–85.

Censis (2002). *I lavoratori stagionali immigrati in Italia*. Rome: Censis.

Continuous Reporting System on Migration (SOPEMI). (2010). *International Migration Outlook—SOPEMI 2010*, OECD. http://www.oecd.org/migration/internationalmigrationpoliciesanddata/45627967.pdf (accessed 28 July 2012).

Devitt, C. (2011). 'Circular migration between Morocco and Italy: A case study', *Metoikos Project,* European University Institute. http://www.eui.eu/Projects/METOIKOS/Documents/CaseStudies/METOIKOScasestudyItalyMorocco.pdf (accessed 28 July 2012).

Ferrera, M. (2006). *Le Politiche Sociali*. Bologna: Il Mulino.

Germenji, E. and Milo, L. (2009). 'Return and labour status at home: Evidence from returnees in Albania', *Journal of Southeast European and Black Sea Studies*, 9(4): 497–517.

IOM International Organization for Migration (2008), *Migration in Albania: A Country Profile*. http://publications.iom.int/bookstore/free/Albania_Profile2008.pdf

King, R. and Vullnetari, J. (2003). 'Migration and Development in Albania'. Brighton: University of Sussex, Development Research Centre on Migration, Globalisation and Poverty, *Working Paper C5*. http://www.migrationdrc.org/publications/working_papers/WP-C5.pdf

King, R. and Vullnetari, J. (2009). 'Remittances, return, diaspora: Framing the debate in the context of Albania and Kosova', *Southeast European and Black Sea Studies*, 9(4): 385–406.

Labrianidis, L. and Hatziprokopiou, P. (2005). 'The Albanian migration cycle: Migrants tend to return to their country of origin after all', in R. King, N. Mai and S. Schwandner-Sievers (eds), *The New Albanian Migration*. Brighton: Sussex Academic Press, 93–117.

Labrianidis, L. and Kazazi, B. (2006). 'Albanian Return-migrants from Greece and Italy. Their impact upon spatial disparities within Albania', *European Urban and Regional Studies*, 13(1): 59–74.

Lyberaki, A. and Maroukis, T. (2005). 'Albanian Immigrants in Athens: New survey evidence on employment and integration', *Journal on Southeast European and Black Sea Studies*, 5(1): 21–48.

Markova, E. (2006). 'Migration in SEE: A development opportunity', *The Bridge*, 04/2006, issue 3. http://www.bridge-mag.com/index.php?option=com_content&view=article&id=100:themes-16-2006&catid=4:themes-2006&Itemid=6

Maroukis, T. and Gemi, E. (2011). 'Circular Migration between Albanian and Greece: A case study', *Metoikos Project*, European University Institute. http://www.eui.eu/Projects/METOIKOS/Documents/BackgroundReports/BackgrounReportGreeceAlbania.pdf

Maroukis, Th. (2009), Economic Migration to Greece: Labour Market and Social Integration (Οικονομική Μετανάστευση στην Ελλάδα: Αγορά Εργασίας και Κοινωνική Ένταξη), Athens: Papazisi (in Greek).

Orozco, M. (2010). *'Country Profile: Albania'*, *Migrant Remittances*, 7(2), 7–8.

Piracha, M. and Vadean, F. (2010). 'Return Migration and Occupational Choice', *World Development*, 38(8), 1141–55.

Reyneri, E. (2001). Migrants in Irregular Employment in the Mediterranean Countries of the European Union, *International Migration Papers* (IMP) 41:37. http://www.ilo.int/public/english/protection/migrant/download/imp/imp41.pdf

Sakellaropoulos, T. (1999). *The Reform of the Welfare State: Volume A* (Η Μεταρρύθμιση του Κοινωνικού Κράτους: Τόμος Α). Athens: Êritiki (in Greek).

Triandafyllidou, A. and Maroufof, M. (2011). GREECE—Report prepared for the SOPEMI Meeting Paris, 1–3 December 2010. http://www.eliamep.gr/en/eliamepnews/εκθέσεις-sopemi-για-την-ελλάδα/(accessed 28 July 2012).

Annexes

Annex 4.1 Socio-demographic characteristics of the sample

	Total	Gender		Age			Marital Status		
		M	F	25–35	36–45	46–55	Married	Single	Children
Circular Migrant	31	24	7	11	14	6	21	10	22
Return Migrant	5	1	4	3	2		4	1	4
TOTAL	36	25	11	14	16	6	24	11	26

Annex 4.2 Sector and type of occupation

	Total	Sector & Type of Occupation						
		Agriculture	Construction	Tourism	Greece Domestic service	Own Business	High status job	Other
Circular Migrant	31	8	7	4	2	3	4	3
Return Migrant	5							
TOTAL	36							

	Total	Sector & Type of Occupation						
		Agriculture	Construction	Tourism	Albania Domestic service	Own Business	High status job	Other
Circular Migrant	31	3	2	2		15	5	4
Return Migrant	5					3	2	
TOTAL	36							

Annex 4.3 Interviews with key informants in Greece and Albania

Institution	Country
Brain Gain Programme, PNUD	Albania
Ministry of Justice	Albania
Non Governmental Organisations (2)	Albania
Ministry of Labour	Albania
National Employment Agency	Albania
University of Tirana, Faculty of Economics	Albania
University of Tirana, Faculty of Law	Albania
Ministry of Interior	Albania
Ministry of Foreign Affairs, Institute of Diaspora	Albania
Municipality of Tirana	Albania
IOM	Albania
European Commission Delegation	Albania
Researcher, Sussex University	Albania
Ministry of Interior (3)	Greece
Police Officer	Greece
Agricultural Insurance Organisation	Greece
Total	19

Notes

1. The government of Albania estimates that the number of Albanians abroad in 2005 was over one million, representing 30 per cent of the total population. A 2008 report by the International Organization for Migration (IOM) estimates that about 860,485 Albanian migrants, more than a quarter of the population, lived abroad at some point in 2005.

2. During the last couple of years seasonal migrants needed to have their passport stamped before the end of the six-month period in order to reapply the following year (Maroukis and Gemi 2011). This seems to be an efficient control mechanism for the detection and, therefore, the prevention of seasonal visa overstays.
3. In pre-crisis time, he usually stayed from three to six months.
4. For more information on social insurance contribution of migrants, see Triandafyllidou and Maroufof 2011:29.
5. Special Omogeneis Identity Card.
6. This is the latest law in force.
7. The OGA correspondent is a civil servant working in the municipality, an inspector for employment in agriculture on top of every other job relevant to his position in the municipality. The number of OGA correspondents is also small since they are appointed by the regional (Perifereia) and not by the prefecture municipalities (Nomo). These structural features of the correspondent limit their availability and capacity to properly inspect violations (Maroukis and Gemi 2011).
8. The main legislation regulating Greek immigration policy is the L. 3386/05, which in 2009 was amended by L. 3801/09. This law introduced more favourable provisions for family reunification of immigrants, long-term residents, etc.
9. Construction sector workers are officially insured in IKA. Similar negotiations with (sub-) contractors took place in the construction sector (see Maroukis 2009).
10. *Ελευθεροτυπία*, 2 January 2010 '*Δικαίωμα στη ζωή μ' ανοιχτά χαρτιά*' by Ioanna Sotirchou, available at: http://www.enet.gr/?i=news.el.article&id=117071. See also '*Η οικονομική κρίση οδηγεί τους μετανάστες . . . στη μετανάστευση*', 23 August 2010.
11. The number of foreign students studying in Greek schools is estimated to reach 120,000 or 10 per cent of the entire school population (more information available at: http://secondgeneration07.blogspot.com/). Yet, 250,000 is estimated to be the number of children who have been born in Greece to migrant parents (http://archive.ekathimerini.com/4dcgi/_w_articles_politics_100002_23/12/2009_113525).
12. When it comes to highly skilled migrants, the existing legal framework clearly becomes more open and inviting. Already there are simplified and short admission procedures in favour of highly skilled third country nationals.
13. Substantial delays of Greek state authorities to issue stay permits on time have put a strain on Albanian migrants' mobility between Greece and their country of origin in the recent past, and might do so again in the near future, given the shrinking and reorganization of civil servants that has been taking place in Greece during the past few years of economic crisis and austerity measures.
14. In 2009, the number of unemployed Greeks rose about 30 per cent over the previous year, while the number of unemployed foreigners doubled, with foreigners comprising 9.8 per cent of employment and 10.5 per cent of unemployment (SOPEMI 2010). In the first quarter of 2011 the unemployment rate of foreigners registered by the Greek Labour Force Survey was 19.8 per cent.

5

Circular Economic Migration between Italy and Morocco

Camilla Devitt

5.1 Introduction: framing migration between Morocco and Italy

In this chapter I examine circular economic migratory movements between Italy and Morocco. This exploratory study, largely based on qualitative interviews with Moroccan circular migrants, as well as Italian and Moroccan policymakers and stakeholders, identifies the main institutional and legal constraints on circularity, and presents a typology of circular economic migration currently taking place between the two states. Importantly, the chapter also investigates to what extent circular migration is of benefit to the migrants themselves, and the sending and receiving states.

Morocco is the country of origin of one of the largest communities of non-Europeans resident in Western Europe. Moroccan migration to Italy began in the mid-1970s as a form of free movement before the introduction of visa requirements to enter Italian territory. This movement commenced in a context of economic and political instability in Morocco and the closure to labour immigration in traditional destinations for migration in Northern Europe in the early 1970s. While Moroccans still migrated to France, Germany, Belgium, and the Netherlands, notably via family reunification and family formation channels, Italy and Spain represented alternative destinations. Moroccans could move to the latter countries relatively easily and find informal work, initially in street-selling and agriculture. Levels of migration to Italy remained marginal until the 1980s and grew significantly in the 1990s; indeed, Moroccans were the largest foreign community in the country, before being overtaken by the Albanian and Romanian communities in recent years (Mghari and Fassi Fihri 2010).

Since Italy's adhesion to the Schengen visa regime in 1990, irregular migration from Morocco (and other migrant source countries) has been significant. The activation of a system of annual quotas for the entry of non-EU workers in 1995 did not succeed in reducing irregularity, partly because of delays in approving quota decrees, a mismatch between the size of quotas and the demand for and supply of foreign workers, and bureaucratic delays in issuing authorisations for work permits.[1] The number of non-EU citizens admitted into Italy for work purposes is defined by the government every year with the Flow Decree (*Decreto Flussi*). The prospective employer applies to employ a particular non-European Economic Area (EEA) worker, technically resident abroad, at a specific time of the year defined by the Decree, and applications are accepted for evaluation until the quota is reached. Since 1998, the quotas have contained country-specific sub-quotas, with the aim of providing an incentive for sending countries to collaborate in combating irregular migration. However, the quota reserved for Morocco has never been higher than 4,500 persons per year, and was only 500 in 2003 (Sciortino 2009).

Entering the country by land or sea, Moroccans often obtain residence permits as a result of one of the regular amnesties for undocumented migrants that are granted by Italian governments, or, paradoxically, within the system of annual quotas for the entry of foreign workers (Colombo 2009). This system of *ex-post* regularization is a reflection of the general functioning of the Italian state and labour market. The state administration's difficulties in planning and enforcement have resulted in a reliance on regularizing irregular *fait accompli* (other examples include regularizing illegal buildings and undeclared work). The main recruitment channels in the Italian labour market are informal (i.e., via personal and face-to-face contacts, rather than an anonymous, meritocratic system), and there is, moreover, a large informal economy by Western European standards, which provides employment for irregular migrants. The quota system is also the object of fraudulent applications; in the absence of a genuine job offer, employers request work permits for foreign workers, often following payment by an intermediary in Italy (Devitt 2011).

By 2010, the Moroccan community in Italy, the third largest foreign community in the country, had a population of 431,529. The Moroccan region of Chaouia Ouardigha in the centre north of the country (see Figure 5.1) has retained its position as the main region of origin of Moroccans residing in Italy. Indeed, according to consular data from 2008, over a quarter of the Moroccan community in Italy hails from that region (25.3 per cent). The region of Grand-Casablanca, a source of Moroccan immigrants in Italy since the 1990s, comes a close second (22 per cent), and is followed by Tadla-Azilal (16.1 per cent). Other regions, which are much less significant, include Rabat-Salé-Zemmour-Zaer (10.1 per cent), Marrakech-Tensift-El Haouz (8 per cent) and Souss-Massa-Draa (4.6 per cent).

Figure 5.1 Map of Moroccan regions
Source: Drawmeagraph.com

According to the Italian national statistics institute, ISTAT, in January 2010, over half of the Moroccans residing in Italy were living in four northern regions: Lombardy (104,606), Emilia Romagna (67,262), Piedmont (62,366), and Veneto (56,704). In southern Italy, the majority of Moroccans reside in Campania (12,267), Sicily (11,468), and Calabria (10,737) (ISTAT 2010; Mghari and Fassi Fihri 2010). Just over half (59 per cent) of Moroccans resident in Italy are men. The average age is thirty-five years and the average length of time spent in the country is just under five years (4.9). Most have secondary school education (57 per cent). Nearly a fifth have primary school education (18.8 per cent), while over a fifth are literate but do not have any qualifications.

A little under 73 per cent of Moroccans are actively engaged in the Italian labour market, this proportion rising to 86.1 per cent among men and falling to 43.3 per cent among women. The average annual wage is €11,437, which is slightly higher than the average for immigrants in Italy in general (€10,343). Moroccans are also more likely to be employed with fixed-term contracts than other large foreign communities—19.9 per cent compared with the average of

15.6 per cent. The first Moroccan migrants worked in agriculture, or sold Moroccan carpets and artisanal products. They then moved into other sectors, such as construction, small industry, and cleaning services. Today, just under 7 per cent of them are employed in agriculture, 48.9 per cent in industry (including 19 per cent in construction), and 42.5 per cent in services. By 2008, 78.5 per cent of active Moroccans were employed, while 19 per cent were self-employed, and a little over 2 per cent were searching for work. Moroccans are the immigrant group with the largest number of businesses in ownership; there were 35,308 Moroccan business owners in 2010 (out of a total of 213,267 foreign business owners). Two-thirds of Moroccan-owned businesses are in the trade sector, under a fifth in construction, 5 per cent in transport, and little over 1 per cent in the manufacturing industry (Caritas 2010; Mghari and Fassi Fihri 2010).

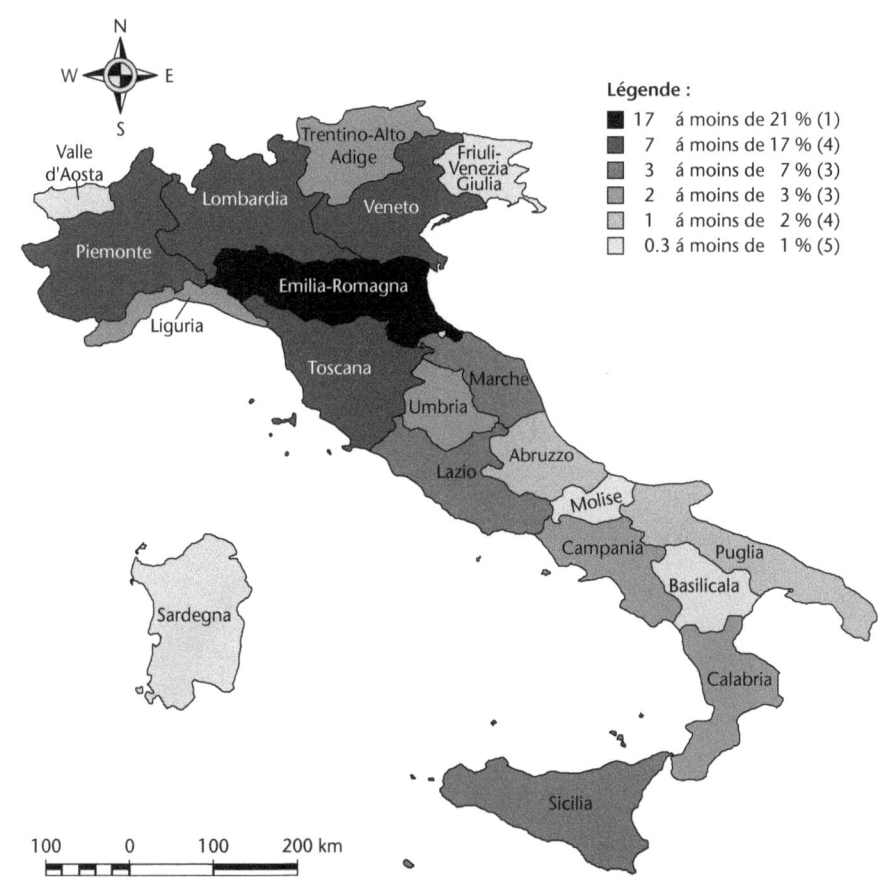

Figure 5.2 Distribution of Moroccans resident in Italy based on regions of residency
Source: Mghari and Fassi Fihri, 2010: 69.

The most significant economic gulf within any one state in Europe is between north and south Italy. Northern Italy is one of the most industrialized regions, while southern Italy is one of the least developed. Moroccans are concentrated in the north (see Figure 5.2), owing to the existence of regular employment opportunities in industry and services. In the south, informal, precarious work is more common, and most Moroccans are employed in commerce and agriculture. Self-employment among Moroccans is higher in the south (see Figure 5.3). For example, while 16 per cent of them are self-employed in Milan, 52 per cent are in Bari. Self-employment in the south generally reflects difficulties in finding regular employment, and a way of supplementing income derived from seasonal or occasional employment. In the north, self-employment often represents a form of social mobility (Paterno et al. 2008).

Figure 5.3 Regional distribution of self-employed Moroccans in Italy
Source: Mghari and Fassi Fihri, 2010: 72.

Moroccan settlement in Italy is reflected in relatively high levels of family reunification and naturalization. For example, in 2003, Moroccan citizens constituted 6 per cent of all visas issued to foreign nationals for employment, and 13 per cent of those issued for family reunification. Moroccans are the immigrant group with the highest number of cases of naturalization; in 2006, 3,295 Moroccans became Italian citizens, followed by 795 Albanians. Furthermore, Moroccan men have the highest rate of intermarriage with Italian women of all foreign groups.

5.2 Methodology

A quantitative estimate of circular economic migration between the two states is precluded by the absence of administrative and survey data on back and forth movements and their motivations. This is partly explained by the fact that the concept of circular migration is a new one, which has not yet entered the vocabulary of most administrations.

This analysis of circular economic migration between Italy and Morocco is based on existing, rather scarce, theoretical and empirical research on circular migration, and interviews with thirty Moroccan circular economic migrants and twenty-one Italian and Moroccan policymakers, stakeholders, key informants, and researchers, conducted during the period June to November 2010. The interviews with twenty Moroccan circular migrants in Italy were conducted in Emilia-Romagna (twelve) and Campania (eight), in order to take into account the socio-economic differences between northern and southern Italy. While Emilia-Romagna is the region with the second largest population of Moroccans in Italy, and interviewee identification was aided by the researcher's personal knowledge of the area, Campania is the southern Italian region with the largest Moroccan community.

The ten interviews with circular migrants in Morocco were carried out in the town of Khouribga, in the region of Chaouia Ouardigha. This region was selected because it is the most significant region of origin of Moroccans living in Italy. The interviews with circular migrants in Italy and Morocco were mainly conducted in Italian. Moroccans circulating between the two countries have generally been living in or coming to Italy regularly for at least five years, and consequently are fluent in Italian. It can also come naturally to speak of experiences in Italy in Italian. A small number were carried out in Arabic in both countries, with the use of an interpreter. The interviews with policymakers, stakeholders, key informants, and researchers (see Annex 1 for a list) were conducted in Italian in Italy and French in Morocco. The interviews were taped when possible, and transcribed in Italian and French. Circular migrants were identified by means of snowballing in Italy. The main gatekeepers included the Emilia Romagna regional administration and cultural mediators based in Naples. The circular migrants interviewed in Morocco were selected with the help of a local association in Khouribga, and a researcher in Rabat. While the number of interviews with Moroccan circular migrants was limited, and snowballing results tend to focus on a particular social network (in this case, traders and transporters), interviews with policy-makers, stakeholders, key informants, and researchers confirmed the significance of the types of circular migration identified.

5.3 Institutional and legal constraints which favour/hinder circular migration

It is important to underline that Moroccan migration to Italy has been sedentary rather than circular over the past two decades. Indeed, there are four main factors which have obstructed circularity: visa requirements; employee status and employment-based work permits; low earnings; and the absence of a livelihood in Morocco. Before the establishment of a visa regime in 1990, Moroccans could freely come and go between the two countries. Today, their movements are restricted by immigration rules. While permits for employment/self-employment allow back and forth movements under certain conditions, undocumented status prohibits circularity between the two countries, as the trials and fees involved in gaining entry to Italy make return unlikely before a migrant has regularized his/her position there. The majority of active Moroccans in Italy are employees, and their presence in the country depends on remaining in employment. Italian employers generally need stable, dependable, foreign workers, and do not appreciate frequent or long absences from work; and immigrants are focused on renewing their work permits in order to remain legally resident. Low income levels mean that Moroccan immigrants, particularly those with families in Italy, find it difficult to save money and are generally not in a position to travel home often. Finally, most Moroccans in Italy do not have businesses or land in Morocco, which would stimulate circularity.

A low level of circularity is particularly the case in northern Italy, where the vast majority of Moroccans are resident. In northern Italy, Moroccan immigrants generally have work permits, rather than self-employment permits, and they have been in relatively stable employment. They appear to circulate less than the majority of Moroccans in Campania, Calabria, and Sicily, who have self-employment permits and more precarious employment.

However, the current economic downturn, fall in consumption, and rise in unemployment in Italy, as well as economic development in Morocco, has led many Moroccans in the north and south of Italy to engage in circular trade. In fact, economic circularity between Morocco and Italy is in part a reflection of the inadequacy of the Italian social welfare system. Eligibility for social benefits is particularly circumscribed in Italy, with large swathes of the labour force receiving little or no public support when unemployed (Ferrera 2006). Immigrants employed regularly may not be eligible for unemployment benefits owing to short-term or discontinuous employment. The minority of migrant workers who are employed in medium to large firms, and are eligible for primary labour market benefits, may still be obliged to work irregularly in order to supplement these benefits, as they will in general receive less financial support from their families than Italians. Informal circular economic activity is often a substitute for adequate public social assistance in Italy; in fact, the informal economy in Italy traditionally plays this role.

5.4 Typology of circular economic migration between Morocco and Italy

There are two main forms of circular economic migration: first, a person normally resident in his/her country of origin may decide to spend a few months abroad in order to earn some money; and second, a person principally resident abroad may go to his/her country of origin on a regular basis in order to set up and oversee an economic project. The following classification is divided into two typologies according to the main country of residence of the migrants. These two typologies are based on eight dimensions: the legal or irregular nature of the movement; the level of skills of the people involved (low/semi-skilled/high-skilled); the time length of each stay and return (short-term, medium-term, and long-term circularity); residency in north or south Italy; work status in the main country of residence (employed/self-employed/unemployed); number of years living in or migrating to Italy (more or less than ten years); the country of residence of the migrant's nuclear family; and the economic activity which circular migrants engage in.

As regards the legal nature of the movement, I distinguish between circular mobility taking place under the framework of bilateral agreements, circular migrants who hold permits/identity documents that allow them to engage in circular mobility, and circular migrants who cross borders illegally (see chapter 1 of this volume). In the case of migrants holding permits or identity documents permitting circularity, the main legal statuses identified in the interviews are specified, including dual citizenship, long-term resident status, and work permits for employment or self-employment. Regarding skills, I distinguish between unskilled workers (elementary occupations), semi-skilled workers (clerks, service workers, skilled agri-fish workers, craft and trade workers, plant/machine operators and assemblers), and skilled workers (legislators, senior officials, professionals, managers, technicians).[2] In terms of duration of stays and returns, I distinguish between repeated short stays taking place within less than a year; short stays of between two months and a year that follow an annual cycle; and long-term circular migration that involves stays of a couple of years in each country.

The fourth dimension allows us to evaluate the role of the socio-economic context in the receiving country in incentivizing or obliging circularity.

Table 5.1 Typology of Moroccan economic circular migrants circulating between Morocco-Italy with main residence in Italy

Dimensions	Type 1 Circular trade and transport	Type 2 Economizing in Morocco	Type 3 Seasonal agricultural work in Morocco	Type 4 Brain circulation/ cross-border investment
1. Legal status in Italy	Permits/ID documents allowing them to circulate: Dual citizenship LT residency Work permit for employment or self-employment	Permits/ID documents allowing them to circulate: Mainly work permit for self-employment	Permits/IDdocuments allowing them to circulate: Work permit for employment or self-employment LT residency	Permits/ID documents allowing them to circulate: Dual citizenship LT residency Work permit for self-employment
2. Skill level of occupation in Italy	Semi-skilled	Semi- & unskilled	Semi- & unskilled	Skilled
3. Time length of each stay and return	Repeated short stays or annual stays of a few months	Two month stays annually	Three to six month stays annually	Repeated short stays
4. Residence in north or south Italy	North & South	South	North & South	North
5. Work status in Italy	Mainly self-employed and unemployed	Unemployed & employed	Employed	Mainly self-employed
6. Number of years living in Italy (more or less than 10 years)	Mainly more than 10 years	Both more & less than 10 years	More than 10 years	More than 10 years
7. Nuclear family country of residence	Mainly Italy	Morocco	Morocco or Italy	Italy
8. Circular economic activity	Transport & trade	Save money	Work in family farm	Business/ development project

Circular Economic Migration between Italy and Morocco

Table 5.2 Typology of Moroccan economic circular migrants circulating between Morocco and Italy with main residence in Morocco

Dimensions	Type 1 Seasonal street-selling in Italy	Type 2 Seasonal agriculture in Italy
1. Legal status in Italy	Permits/ID documents allowing them to circulate: Work permit for self-employment	Permits/ID documents allowing them to circulate: Dual citizenship LT residency
2. Skill level of occupation in Morocco	Semi-unskilled	Semi-unskilled
3. Time length of each stay and return	3 months annually	6 months annually
4. Socio-economic context in Italy (north or south Italy)	South	North
5. Employment status in Morocco	Self-employed	Self-employed or unemployed
6. Number of years living or migrating to Italy (more or less than 10 years)	Mainly more than 10 years	More than 10 years
7. Nuclear family residence	Morocco	Morocco
8. Circular economic activity	Street-selling	Agriculture

This variable is of particular importance in the case of Italy, where socio-economic conditions vary significantly between the north and the south. The fifth considers the more specific factor of work status, with the assumption that owing to lower levels of autonomy, employment is less conducive to circularity than self-employment and short-term unemployment. Regarding the number of years living in or migrating to Italy (more or less than ten years), it is expected that those in Italy for longer will be more likely to circulate. Finally, it is assumed that if the nuclear family is not present in the same state as the migrant, the latter will be more stimulated to move back and forth between country of destination and origin.

The typologies are also ordered in terms of significance, with the most common form of circularity in the first row in Tables 5.1 and 5.2. The estimated significance of each category in terms of numbers involved in different types of circularity is based on interviews with circular migrants and policymakers, stakeholders, key informants, and researchers in the two states.

Four types of economic circularity involving Moroccans principally resident in Italy were constructed based on these eight characteristics (see Table 5.2). The second typology of Moroccan circular migrants mainly resident in Morocco contains two types of circular economic migration (see Table 5.3).

5.4.1 *Moroccan circular economic migrants based in Italy*

TYPE 1 'CIRCULAR TRADE AND TRANSPORT'

The most common type of economic circularity involving Moroccans who are principally resident in Italy is circular trade and cross-border transport. Reflecting the gender profile of most Moroccans working in commerce in Italy, this is a largely male activity and encompasses an age group ranging from the mid-twenties to the mid-sixties. These Moroccans buy goods in Italy and sell them in Morocco, returning with Moroccan goods to sell in Italy, mainly to the Moroccan community. They also transport other Moroccans' belongings to Morocco, an enterprise that is particularly profitable in the summer.

While they used to sell Chinese goods acquired in Italy in Morocco, Chinese settlement in Morocco has made this commercial channel redundant; and this is argued to have led to a reduction in cross-border trade involving Moroccan traders based in Naples. Moroccans now mainly sell second-hand Italian goods, from electronics to furniture, shoes, and clothes in the weekend markets of the north-central region of Chaouia-Ouardigha and in the Central Region (Casablanca). This phenomenon is symbolized by the Turin Market, an open-air market in the town of Khouribga, in Chaouia-Ouardigha, named after the northern Italian city with the largest Moroccan population in Italy. The more professional traders travel all over Morocco; selling better quality goods in the richer areas of the country and poorer quality goods in less economically developed zones. These items are mainly bought in second-hand markets in Italy. Some Moroccans specialize in buying new products from businesses which are closing down.

The vast majority circulate via road and ferry. In order to maximize earnings the vans are packed past the legal limit of 3,500 kg. This increases the risk of accidents, as well as being fined €400 by the Italian police. Another problem lies in transporting other Moroccans' belongings; as the transporters do not have receipts for these goods, the police have no proof that they are not stolen. However, in general the Italian police are deemed to be elastic and rarely create problems for the migrants. Some send containers of products to Morocco and travel there themselves by air in order to sell the products. The latter is more expensive than transporting goods by van, and is generally a collaborative effort involving a few people. These circular migrants travel back and forth from once a year to every month and spend from one week to three months in Morocco each time. Clearly, those who travel more frequently are more professionally engaged in this activity, while those coming once a year do so primarily to see their families but also to cover the costs of their trip home and/or make a profit.

Cross-border auto trade and transport between Italy and Morocco is an informal activity. This informality is determined by the difficulty to make a profit within the current legal and administrative framework as well as earnings maximization. As noted above, transporters and traders tend to pack their vans over the legal limit. Moreover, all of the interviewees maintained that the customs tariffs were too high to make regular transport possible. Consequently, in a win-win situation, the circular traders pay Moroccan customs officials under the table in order to pass through. With informal customs fees of about €1,000 to €1,500 per van, this is by no means cheap, and is a source of much frustration among circular transporters and traders. Furthermore, the Moroccan police also request bribes in order to pass from Tangiers to Casablanca. Circular migrants also assert that, unlike container transport, there are no existing administrative regulations for cross-border transport involving vans filled with hundreds of disparate items. A circular migrant trader tells us of his difficulties:

> It's not a regular job. How can it be regular? Difficult. Because if you go to the Italian administration, they don't know how to manage it. I went to three or four accountants. One said to do this, another said something else. They know how to manage containers but not vans full of hundreds of objects. (circular trader/transporter, Bologna)

The motivations of circular traders and transporters vary; however, it is mainly a case of economic necessity. A minority of these entrepreneurs choose to engage in this job rather than work for an employer. Circular traders and transporters have work permits for employment or self-employment, long-term residency status, or dual citizenship and have been living in Italy for at least five years, with many of them in the country for more than a decade ('People who are here for a long time know how things work' (Moroccan circular trader, Faenza)).

Circular trade and transport has been a feature of Moroccan migration to Italy for the past decade at least. While the transport of other Moroccans' belongings was more profitable before the crisis, when people had more money to send material remittances, cross-border commerce has increased substantially over the past two years. The current economic downturn and rise in unemployment in Italy, as well as concomitant economic development in Morocco, has led many Moroccans in the north and south of Italy to engage in circular trade. For example, a circular trader based in Bologna maintained that 'Before there were only three people doing this job in the whole of Bologna. Now there are lots of us, hundreds of people are doing this work now.'

In general, those hailing from southern (and central) Italy—in particular, Naples—work in commerce all year round in Italy, and supplement their income by going to Morocco to sell Italian products between once every two years to four times a year. Those based in northern Italy are carpenters, electricians, builders, and mechanics, who have lost their jobs and started working in commerce over the past two years in order to support them and their families. A Moroccan circular trader explains:

> I worked as an electronic technician, repairing video recorders and other machines, here in Bologna. Then I became a partner of the firm where I worked in 2000 and I opened my own workshop near the train station. But things started going badly with the crisis, the price for repairs went down dramatically, I had to change my job. I began transporting and selling things in Morocco. (circular trader, Bologna)

Most of these individuals are middle-aged and are unlikely to be hired again in the event of an economic upturn. Furthermore, the Italian social welfare system is maintained to provide very limited financial support to those who have lost their jobs. These people all declare that they would not be doing this job if there were work in Italy.

> The firm where my father worked closed two years ago. He had worked for twenty years in fibreglass production. Now he does this job as he is fifty-five years old and nobody will hire him. He got some support from the state when he lost his job; he was on 'cassa integrazione'. The state gives financial support for two or three years when a firm has difficulties, you get €800 and €500 for the last year, but it's not enough. (circular trader, Faenza)

> In 2007, there were 300–400 vans entering Morocco from Italy, now there are about 2,000. People lose their jobs, they may get unemployment benefit, but they say 'what will I do?'... It's boring sitting at home. At least I will earn enough to get by, it's not like you get rich. There is nothing else. Now, the economic situation in Italy is terrible. People are ripping up their documents and leaving. And no more are arriving. (circular trader, Bologna)

Two other categories of circular traders resident in northern Italy were identified: those supplementing their income from employment or self-employment in Italy, and those who began working in cross-border trade full-time with the aim of social mobility. In the first category, migrants have retained their jobs and businesses during the crisis, but have decided to make some extra money on the side and finance their trips home by selling Italian goods in Morocco. This is easier for self-employed individuals; in general, Italian employers require full-time, year-round workers, and circular migrants find that the formal holiday periods do not provide them with sufficient time in Morocco. Indeed, one interviewee had lost jobs three or four times because he took too much time off work in order to go to Morocco.

> They [Italian employers] make you work all year round, also on Sundays, if you do it, you're good, if not, you are looked upon very badly. But I come to Morocco

anyway, if I lose a job I don't care, it's happened three or four times. Because there is a summer of twenty days and two weeks for New Year. For me these are not enough. You need six days for the return trip home, not even a month is enough. (circular trader, Khouribga)

The second category were previously employed in various activities in northern Italy but chose to work in cross-border trade and transport owing to an improvement in income, a preference for self-employment, and the perceived lack of skilled jobs available for foreigners in Italy.

While the economic crisis is the main stimulus for growth in this form of economic circularity between Italy and Morocco, it has been aided by the recent development of a ferry service from Genoa to Tangiers. Previously, Moroccans resident in Italy who wanted to transport goods to Morocco themselves had to drive to Sète in southern France, from where they could take a ferry to Morocco. Some people drive all the way from Naples to the Spanish border.

Interviewees generally maintain that the job is tiring and stressful, and they complain about the cost of the ferry (c.€800) and passing through customs and police blocks in Morocco. As one interviewee maintained, 'There are no problems from the Italian state. Only from Morocco. The Morocco customs, we have problems with them. They ask for money.' One interviewee asserted that people are forced to do this job, as they generally prefer to be in one place, not suspended across the Mediterranean Sea: 'We do this because of the crisis, because, come on, you are either here or there. It's tiring, six and a half days on the ship there and back, sometimes there are delays.'

Nevertheless, apart from permitting people to make a livelihood, particularly in times of rising unemployment in Europe, this economic circular activity has one important advantage; it permits people to see their families (nuclear/extended) more often than most Moroccans in Italy are able to.

Policymakers, researchers and key informants in both states maintain that this is the most common form of economic circularity between Morocco and Italy. However, it is a surprisingly understudied phenomenon, as a circular trader/transporter declared: 'Nobody thinks of those who do this job. We work and help two states but nobody thinks of these people.' Circular trade and transport is difficult to quantify in terms of the numbers engaged in it owing to its informal and transnational nature. To some extent, its high visibility may explain why people perceive it to be the most significant form of circular economic migration between the two states.

TYPE 2 'ECONOMIZING IN MOROCCO'
Spending a few months in Morocco every year in order to relax, spend time with family members, and save money is common among young Moroccans

in Campania. These young men are legally resident in Italy, generally in possession of permits for self-employment, and are often employed in short-term, casual jobs.

Owing to the lack of regular work in southern Italy, when renewing their permits, migrant workers often get business licences and then work permits for self-employment. They can go back and forth regularly with these permits. In reality, they are often intermittently employed rather than working for themselves. Precarious employment incentivizes young, unmarried Moroccans to go to Morocco for a few months a year. They do not have to consider employer needs as they go when unemployed. Moreover, they save money by going to Morocco, since they stay with their families there, and do not have to pay expenses in Italy for a couple of months. As a young Moroccan resident in Naples maintained, 'I go to Morocco because I don't have work here and with a thousand euros you can live in Morocco for five months as I live with my parents there.'

Most of this category of circular economic migrants does not work while in Morocco. They do not feel that it is worth their while, as the wages are much lower than in Italy. One of the interviewees asserted that the people who work in Morocco when on their holidays are married and have families to look after. This category of circular economic migration between Italy and Morocco is significant among young Moroccans in Campania. A cultural mediator based in Naples maintained that as a general rule, 'The older generation spend most of their time in Morocco and three months in Italy. The younger ones are mainly in Italy and spend two months in Morocco drinking tea.' Further interviews in other regions would be necessary in order to understand if it is a common form of circularity in other parts of the country. Owing to the higher significance of work permits for self-employment in the south of the country, it seems likely that this form of circularity is more common there.

TYPE 3 'SEASONAL WORK IN MOROCCO'

The third type of circular migrant based in Italy is resident in northern and southern Italy, and returns to Morocco every year for three to six months to work on the family farm.

> I go to Morocco for three months a year. I work on our land with my father, he is eighty years old while my mother is seventy, so when I go there it's my duty to help them. My wife and children live in Morocco. I want to get them papers so that they can come here on holiday, if they come to live here, it would be too expensive. (circular migrant, Naples)

This type of circular migrant is mainly male and is legally resident in Italy. They are often employed in agriculture and live in a rural environment in Italy, but some of them live in urban contexts and are employed in other sectors, like construction, or engage in street selling. Reflecting the employment situation of the majority of Moroccans in Italy, these migrants are generally employed in unskilled and semi-skilled work in Italy. Their families are variably based in Italy and Morocco, and this partly determines the frequency of trips to Morocco. It is difficult to ascertain the significance of this type of circularity. It does not appear to be common, and is clearly limited to migrants originating from rural areas whose families own land.

TYPE 4 'BRAIN CIRCULATION/CROSS-BORDER INVESTMENT'
Brain circulation/cross-border investment between Italy and Morocco involves Moroccans resident in Italy for over twenty years who are either dual citizens or long-term residents. This category mainly consists of males, some of whom have university degrees. Their families are generally with them in Italy, and of the five interviewees two are married to Italians. These immigrants have worked in various jobs, generally working their way up the career ladder from manual labour to business ownership, directing non-governmental organizations and public sector employment. They have achieved the legal and economic stability from which they can create an economic project in their country of origin. Some of them have opened businesses in Morocco; others buy, build, and sell property, or assist Italians investing in Morocco. Some of them bring small groups of Italian tourists to Morocco; others manage development projects, including sustainable tourism and rural development projects. They go to Morocco between once a month and four times a year, and stay for between five days and three months at a time. One such migrant explains his situation:'

> We have a small packaging business here in Italy, we work with another big business. I have nearly forty employees. It's a sector which hasn't been hard hit by the crisis because we work with perfumed products for the bathroom. We also work in Morocco so that when my brother is here, I am there and vice versa. There we work on the land, we bought machines here to produce wheat and a tractor. We also build houses and sell them. I worked in construction here for nearly ten years so I have the experience to do things in Morocco. Because at one time it cost nothing there, not like now. (circular migrant, Imola)

These people are generally not forced to circulate in order to make ends meet. The advantages are financial and social, or sentimental. This category of circular migrants make a profit from circulating, and some of them feel that they are helping their families or co-nationals in Morocco through creating employment or improving local infrastructure. There are various incentives to invest in Morocco. For example, a representative of the Moroccan Chamber of Commerce in Italy asserts that previously it took about a year to set up a business there because of bureaucratic requirements and delays, but that now it can be done in fifteen days. Moreover, in the agricultural sector, the government provides significant financial support for investors. The Italian regions also provide funding for development projects in countries of significant out-migration to Italy, which Moroccan non-governmental organizations in Italy can apply for.

Over the past decades, remittance transfers from Moroccans resident in Italy have continuously increased, at least until the global economic downturn of 2008 (ICMPD and IOM 2010). In 2004, Morocco was the world's largest remittances receiver in per capita terms (de Haas 2007). A survey of Moroccans resident in Europe visiting Morocco during the summer of 2005 provides us with general information regarding the investments in Morocco of Moroccans resident in Italy. Moroccans resident in Italy mainly invest in property (86.7 per cent), agriculture (4.4 per cent), commerce (3 per cent), tourism (1 per cent), and industry (1 per cent).This investment structure mirrors that of Moroccans resident in other European countries, such as Spain and France. The better off, that is employers and self-employed, invest the most; however, counter-intuitively, the better educated are less inclined to invest in Morocco. The longer the duration of stay in Europe, the more likely it is that Moroccans invest in Morocco. Furthermore, those who feel integrated in Europe invest more in Morocco (CERED 2007).

The traditional focus of investments in real estate is explained by various socio-economic factors, including the fact that it is a low risk investment and status symbol (de Haas 2007). However, it also reflects the fact that only a minority of Moroccan immigrants resident in Italy are in the position to open a business in Morocco. A representative of the Moroccan Chamber of Commerce in Italy maintains that as the majority of Moroccan immigrants are employed in manual jobs, they do not earn enough to save for significant investment in Morocco. Furthermore, there can be difficulties in managing businesses from afar; it is necessary to have a trusted person in Morocco or to be able to spend considerable time there in order to manage a business. An circular migrant entrepreneur recounts:

> They [most Moroccans in Italy] don't have the money to carry out a project in Morocco as the majority are manual workers. They have developed skills at work in Italy but don't have enough finance to invest. A manual worker can't have the money for an investment like the one I am making, a project of €700,000, and you have to live in Morocco in order to know the reality there and to have contacts. I have contacts with businesses in Morocco and with the Moroccan business assocation. I also know the Italian administrative system. (circular migrant, Reggio Emilia)

Circular migrants interviewed maintained that they only knew a couple of other Moroccans resident in Italy who owned businesses in Morocco. Involvement in development projects is also rare, perhaps because Moroccan associations in Italy are still largely embryonic, and mainly focus on questions of local community and religious and cultural maintenance (Consiglio Nazionale Dell'Economia e del Lavoro 2001).

5.4.2 *Moroccan circular economic migrants based in Morocco*

TYPE 1 'SEASONAL STREET SELLING IN ITALY'
This category appears to be the most significant type of economic circularity between Morocco and Italy involving Moroccans who are principally resident in Morocco. It is primarily a southern Italian phenomenon, and is an historic form of circular economic migration between the two countries. Rates of settlement among Moroccan street-vendors increased over the past decade. While in the mid-1990s many Moroccans returned to Morocco twice a year, by the early 2000s many of them were staying in Italy all year round, either engaged in commerce or employed in other sectors during the winter months (Censis 2002). Seasonal street-selling involving returns to Morocco thus probably concerns a minority of street-sellers. While many Moroccan street-vendors in southern Italy are undocumented, those who spend just a few months a year in Italy are necessarily legally present.

These circular migrants are generally male, and are most often of the first generation of Moroccans in Italy; however, some more recent arrivals also engage in this form of circularity. They come to Italy for the Italian holiday periods in order to sell. During the summer, between May and October, they sell by the seaside, then they go home to Morocco. Some of them come back for Christmas and Easter. These migrants are generally from rural areas in Morocco, the majority from Chaouia-Ouardigha in north central Morocco, and they often cultivate wheat on their farms during the rest of the year. As such, they have two lives: one as a farmer in Morocco and another as a hawker in Italy. A circular migrant explains:

> I first came to Italy twenty-six years ago. I spend three months here every year selling T-shirts and other things on my cart. I live most of the year in Morocco with my family. I have an Italian residence permit, which I got in 1987. I prefer living in Morocco as it costs less and here in Italy things are bad. I have two sons working in Italy ... I will stop this work when I reach retirement age. I went to the accountant and I am OK, I pay my contributions. (circular migrant, San Marcellino)

These migrants tend to buy their merchandise—mainly clothing and small objects—from Chinese stockists in Naples. Their families are in Morocco, and when in Italy, they generally stay in provincial settings where they feel more at home and where the rent costs less. It is not a problem to leave the farm in Morocco for a few months, as other family members will look after it for them. A key informant, whose uncle drives a bus from Naples to Morocco and back every week, maintains that these circular migrants come to make money and bring it back to Morocco. They have no wish to settle or integrate in Italy, and do not trust the Italian authorities.

TYPE TWO: 'SEASONAL AGRICULTURE IN ITALY'
Before the introduction of visa requirements, Moroccans used to go back and forth between Italy and Morocco for seasonal work in agriculture. For example, many interviewees spoke of how Moroccan teachers used to come to pick tomatoes in Italy during their summer holidays. Now, most foreign seasonal farm workers in Italy live in Italy all year round. Very few migrants employed in seasonal agriculture in Italy have permits for seasonal work. For example, according to the Ministry of Labour and Social Affairs, in 2009, while 34,668 permissions to request visas for seasonal work in agriculture and tourism were issued to non-EU nationals, only 11,719 seasonal work permits were effectively requested across Italy. In fact, it appears that the seasonal work permit system is of negligible use to employers who have a choice of readily available migrant workers to hire; including migrants who enter the country with tourist visas, migrants with resident permits for non-seasonal employment or other motives, students, and undocumented migrants.

Circular Moroccan migrants employed in Italian agriculture have lived in Italy for many years, and are either long-term residents or dual citizens. They prefer to be based in Morocco as it is less costly and they have their families there. Some of them are employed in Morocco in agricultural work on their own land, while others do not work in Morocco. Some work for some months in Italy and then receive agricultural unemployment benefit for the rest of the year, while living in Morocco. This category of circular economic migrant was mentioned by interviewees in northern Italy, and it was asserted to be an uncommon lifestyle.

5.5 Is circularity good, and for whom?

Circular migration has been proposed by the European Commission as a new approach in responding to member states' needs for foreign workers and providing an alternative to undocumented migration. This back and forth movement is also presented as a form of migration, which will be particularly beneficial to sending states, by means of reducing brain drain and facilitating socio-economic development.

The Commission defines circular migration as a form of managed migration allowing some degree of legal mobility back and forth between two countries (for detailed analysis see Chapter 2). Two forms of circular migration are considered most relevant in the EU context: business people and professionals resident in the EU engaging in an activity in their country of origin, and people resident in a third country who come to the EU temporarily for work, study, or training, notably seasonal workers (CEC 2007).

Responding to public concerns regarding undocumented immigration, the integration of foreigners provides Italian governments with an incentive to organize circular migration programmes. The Italian Ministry of Labour and Social Affairs aims to establish circular migration schemes similar to the Spanish-Moroccan initiative in Huelva. On 1 April 2010, a circular from the Ministry of Labour and Social Policies reserved 4,000 admissions within the 80,000 quota for seasonal worker entries, for circular migration projects (EMN 2010). However, many Italian policymakers and stakeholders are sceptical about the usefulness of the concept, particularly in the Italian context. An official of the Interior Ministry maintained that, in order to be considered circular migration, a scheme had to include some form of training or upskilling; otherwise, the added value for migrants and sending countries would be limited. Nevertheless, he saw this form of migration as ill-fitted to the reality of migrant work in Italy; 'temporary migration in Italy is mainly seasonal and above all extremely low-skilled so there is very little professional enrichment, for example picking apples in Trentino, when you return to Egypt, Tunisia or Morocco, "yes I can pick apples but nobody taught me how to cultivate apples," so it's a very limited concept'.

In theory, circular migration can be a triple-win situation if the migrant has a preference for 'part-time' migration, if his employer needs temporary workers (if he is employed), and finally if the migrant is able to bring something back (money, skills) to his country of origin.

For most circular migrants interviewed within the context of this study, circulation represents a means of economic survival, but for some it is a form of socio-economic mobility. As a representative of the Italian trade union CGIL maintained, if voluntary and facilitated by legislation, circular migration could be seen as a maturation of the phenomenon of migration, in the sense that leaving one's country does not have to be seen as emigration ('migration from one country to another does not have to be seen as the last beach'). Indeed, the success of circular migration schemes, which necessarily oblige returns to the country of origin, partly depends on whether the migrants involved have a preference for short-term work abroad as opposed to settlement abroad.

While fixed-term and atypical contractual employment arrangements have been on the rise over the past decade, most Italian employers require stable long-term workers. For them, circularity represents an insecure investment in terms of employee training. For employers of seasonal workers, the question of whether seasonal workers stay in the country or go back to their country of origin after the season is of negligible interest, as long as the workers are there when needed. Labour demand in the Italian tourism sector is currently satiated by Eastern European, in particular Romanian, workers. The latter are

European citizens who can move back and forth freely. Furthermore, informal recruitment channels dominate across the Italian labour market, partly owing to low demand for skilled workers—which reduces the importance of curriculum-based anonymous recruitment—and the dominance of small family firms. As a representative of the Italian Hotels Federation maintained,

> Italian hotels are generally very small, the average has thirty rooms, and often they are the hoteliers' houses so when you want to hire someone and have them sleeping in your house, you need to have met them or for somebody you trust to recommend someone, and the Ministry can never do that. (Italian Hotels Federation representative)

Free-moving Romanians are also employed in northern Italian agriculture. The southern Italian citrus fruit sector is suffering from a structural crisis in which the possibility of paying decent wages and providing decent conditions to seasonal workers does not appear to be seriously considered. In fact, with falling international prices for citrus fruit, last year many farmers chose to leave their oranges on the trees rather than pay a worker below the minimum wage to pick them (Devitt 2011).

Moroccan policymakers also find the concept of circular migration to be of limited usefulness in terms of responding to the needs of migrants and countries of origin and destination. An official from the Hassan II Foundation highlighted the fact that the Spanish circular migration programme with the Moroccan employment agency ANAPEC involves a small proportion of total Moroccan presence in Spain (c.12,000 out of a total of 600,000 Moroccans in Spain), and that the 'real migration' between Morocco and Spain and Italy is an often permanent migration of individuals, facilitated by migrant networks (see Chapter 6 on Morocco-Spain in this volume). Finally, because the majority of immigrants in Italy are employed in low- to medium-skilled work, Italian and Moroccan policymakers and stakeholders do not emphasize the benefits of 'brain circulation/cross-border investment' when discussing circular migration between the two states.

5.6 Conclusion

The case of Moroccans circulating between Morocco and Italy for economic motives is one of spontaneous or individual initiatives, which is not regulated by any bilateral or multilateral agreement between states. Six types of circular economic migratory movements between Italy and Morocco were identified in this study. Four of these involved Moroccans mainly resident in Italy, while two were engaged in by Moroccans with principal residence in Morocco. The most significant forms of circular economic migration between the two states involve cross-border trade; in particular the selling of products purchased in Italy in Moroccan markets.

Circular economic migration between Italy and Morocco is, however, limited by visa requirements, the prevalence of employee status, low earnings among Moroccans in Italy, and the absence of livelihoods in Morocco. Moreover, as there is no social security agreement between Italy and Morocco, Moroccans cannot aggregate pension entitlements from the two states, which creates a further disincentive to circularity (Avato 2008).

As more Moroccans gain long-term residency status and dual citizenship, we can expect an increase in circularity; however, in the context of a 'no policy change' scenario, economic circularity between the two states is likely to remain marginal. This is the case for brain circulation/cross-border investment and regulated seasonal circular migration; the two forms of circulation promoted by the European Commission.

As regards brain circulation and cross-border investment, Moroccans in Italy have relatively low potential, as they are concentrated in low-skilled, low-paid jobs. Moreover, while the Moroccan government provides incentives for investment, they do not specifically target Moroccans resident abroad. Effective regulated circular seasonal migration schemes are difficult to envisage in Italy, owing to the structural and administrative factors outlined above, which obstruct the existing seasonal labour migration system. These schemes necessitate a high level of coordination between employers, employment services, and the public administration, incentives for employers to work through the system, the enforcement of immigration and labour market regulations, and protection of migrant workers' rights. Furthermore, contrasting the large informal economy is a *sine qua non* of effective circular migration schemes.

References

Avato, Johanna (2008). *Portability of Social Security and Health Care Benefits in Italy*. Washington, DC: World Bank.
Beguy, D., Philippe, B., and Msiyaphazi Zulu, E. (2010). 'Circular Migration Patterns and Determinants in Nairobi Slum Settlements', *Demographic Research*, 23(20): 549–86.
Caritas (2010). *Immigrazione Dossier Statistico 2010 XX Rapporto*. Rome: Caritas.
CEC (2007). *Communication from the Commission to the European Parliament, the Council, the European Economic and Social Committee and the Committee of the Regions on Circular Migration and Mobility Partnerships between the European Union and Third Countries*. Brussels: CEC.
Censis (2002). *I lavoratori stagionali immigrati in Italia*. Rome: Censis.
CERED (2007). *Les Marocains résident à l'étranger: analyse des résultats de l'enquête de 2005 sur l'insertion socio-économique dans les pays d'accueil*. Rabat: HCP.

Colombo, A. (2009). *La sanatoria per le badanti e le colf del 2009: fallimento o esaurimento di un modello?* Turin: Fieri.
Consiglio Nazionale Dell'Economia e del Lavoro (2001). *Le associazioni dei cittadini stranieri in Italia.* Rome: CNEL.
Constant, Amelie F. and Zimmerman, Klaus F. (2011). 'Circular and Repeat Migration: Counts of Exits and Years Away from the Host Country', *Population Research and Policy Review*, 30 (4), 495–515.
De Haas, H. (2007). The Impact of International Migration on Social and Economic Development in Sending Regions: A Review of the Empirical Literature. *IMI Working Papers*, paper 3. Oxford: IMI.
Devitt, C. (2011). 'La rivolta di Rosarno: gli immigrati si mobilitano?' in Elisabetta Gualmini and Eleonora Pasotti (eds), *Politica in Italia. I fatti dell'anno e le interpretazioni. Edizione.* Bologna: Il Mulino.
Einaudi, Luca (2007). *Le Politiche dell'immigrazione in Italia dall'Unità a oggi.* Roma: Gius. Laterza and Figli.
EMN (2010). 'Temporary and Circular Migration: Empirical Evidence, Current Policy Practice and Future Options in Italy', in European Migration Network (ed.), *Third EMN Italy Report Labour Market and Immigration.* Rome: IDOS.
Ferrera, Maurizio (2006). *Le Politiche Sociali.* Bologna: Il Mulino.
Fincati, Veronica (2007). *Gli immigrati marocchini in Italia e nel Veneto.* Venice: Regione Veneto.
Hugo, G. (2009). *Circular migration and development. An Asia-Pacific Perspective.* Prague: Multicultural Centre Prague.
ICMPD and IOM (2010). 'The Moroccan Experience', in ICMPD-IOM (eds), *Linking Emigrant Communities for More Development Inventory of Institutional Capacities and Practices.* Geneva: IOM.
ISTAT (2010a). *Populazione straniera residente per sesso e paese di cittidinanza—primi 16 paesi al 1 gennaio 2009 e 2010.* Rome: ISTAT.
ISTAT (2010b). *Stranieri residenti appartenenti alle prime 12 communita piu numerose, per regione.* Rome: ISTAT.
Khachani, M. (2008). *La migration circulaire: Cas du Maroc.* In CARIM notes d'analyse et de synthèse 2008/07. Florence: EUI.
MCMRE and IOM (2009). *Etude sur la contribution des Marocains Résidant a l'Etranger au développement économique et social du Maroc.* Rabat: Ministère charge de la Communauté Marocaine Résidant à l'Etranger.
Mghari, Mohamed (2008). *La Migration Circulaire: Quelques Eléments d'Approche au Maroc.* In CARIM notes d'analyse et de synthèse 2008/38. Florence: EUI.
Mghari, Mohamed and Fassi Fihri, Mohamed (2010). *Cartographie des flux migratoires des Marocains en Italie.* Geneva: IOM.
MIDA. *Moroccan investment development agency investment opportunities 2010 [online report].* http://www.invest.gov.ma/?Id=26&lang=en&RefCat=4&Ref=147 (accessed 27 July 2012).
Newland, K., Rannveig Agunias, D. and Terrazas, A. (2008). *Learning by Doing: Experiences of Circular Migration.* Washington, DC: MPI.
OECD (2008). *Education at a Glance 2008.* Paris: OECD.

Paterno, A., Strozza, S. and Terzera, L. (2008). *Sospesi tra due rive Migrazioni e insediamenti di albanesi e marocchini*. Milan: FrancoAngeli.

Schmoll, C. (2003). 'Mobilita e Organizzazione delle Commercianti Tunisine', in A. Colombo and G. Sciortino (eds), *Stranieri in Italia. Un'Immigrazione normale*. Bologna: Il Mulino, 195–221.

Sciortino, G. (2009). *Fortunes and Miseries of Italian Labour Migration Policy*. Rome: CeSPI.

Vertovec, S. (2007). *Circular Migration: The Way Forward in Global Policy?* In *IMI Working Papers*. Paper 4. Oxford: IMI.

Annex 5.1 List of interviews with policymakers, stakeholders, key informants, and researchers

No. of interview	Date	Organization	Place of interview
1	9/6/2010	Interior Ministry, Immigration Dept	Rome
2	17/11/2010	Labour and Social Affairs Ministry, Immigration Dept	Rome
3	7/6/2010	Emilia Romagna Region, Immigration Dept	Rome
4	9/6/2010	CGIL trade union	Rome
5	9/11/2010	Confindustria	Florence
6	17/11/2010	Federalberghi	Rome
7	9/6/2010	IOM	Rome
8	5/9/2010	Foreign Counselors Bologna Province	Porretta
9	6/9/2010	Association of cultural mediators	Naples
10	8/6/2010	Fieri	Turin
11	8/6/2010	Department of statistics, Università di Napoli Federico II	Naples
12	11/10/2010	Hassan II Foundation	Rabat
13	14/10/2010	Council of the Moroccan Community Resident Abroad	Rabat
14	14/10/2010	Ministry of the Moroccan Community Resident Abroad	Rabat
15	12/10/2010	Consular and Social Affairs Directorate of the Foreign Affairs Ministry	Rabat
16	13/10/2010	National Agency for the Promotion of Employment and Skills (ANAPEC)	Casablanca
17	13/10/2010	International Chamber of Commerce	Casablanca
18	12/10/2010	Regional Centre for Investments	Rabat
19	15/10/2010	Centre of Demographic Studies and Research (CERED)	Rabat
20	11/10/2010	Moroccan Association for the Study of Migration (AMERM)	Rabat
21	17/10/2010	Migration and Development Association	Khouribga

Notes

1. The quota system was established in 1990 (Einaudi 2007).
2. This categorization is based on the OECD's occupational skill classification: OECD 2008.

6

Circularity in a Restrictive Framework: Mobility between Morocco and Spain

Carmen González Enríquez[1]

6.1 Introduction

The international mobility of workers and their entry to the European Union is highly regulated by both Community-wide and national laws primarily aimed to restrict immigration. These laws either ease or restrict migrants' ability to maintain their economic activity and residence in their country of origin while retaining their legal status in the country of destination. During the years 1997–2007, Spain was the leading recipient of immigrants in the EU; most of them arrived as false tourists, leaving a legacy of deep concern with the phenomenon of irregularity. In this context, Spanish rules and their implementation have obstructed potential circular migration by restricting it in practice to those who obtain citizenship, or to only temporary agricultural migrants. The latter have been subject to strict regulations and surveillance, giving rise to a mutually satisfactory scheme to the countries of origin and to the intensive Spanish agricultural sector.

This chapter describes circular migration between Morocco and Spain in the framework of cooperation and conflict between both countries, analyses the main features of Moroccan migration to Spain, the manpower needs of the Spanish agricultural sector, and the regulatory structure which hinders other forms of potential circular migration between the two countries. The opinions and expectations of Moroccan workers and both Spanish and Moroccan stakeholders in relation to circular migration are also analysed. Finally, the conclusion looks at the sustainability of current temporary agricultural migration schemes while unemployment among Spaniards and resident immigrants curtails their social legitimacy.

6.2 Framing migration between Morocco and Spain

The frontier between Spain and Morocco—the Mediterranean Sea, the Straits of Gibraltar, and the fences which surround Ceuta and Melilla—separates two very different social and economic worlds. Spain's per capita GDP in 2010 was ten times that of Morocco, a difference much greater than that separating the US and Mexico (five times). When labour migration became a visible phenomenon in Spain during the 1990s, Moroccan workers comprised the largest single national group of migrants, while images of small boats arriving at the Andalusian coast full of young Moroccan males, irregular migrants, were frequent in the media. Although during the following decade Moroccans were outnumbered by Latin Americans and Eastern Europeans, for years afterwards they continued to dominate the Spanish public's image of immigration.

Morocco is also a stepping stone for Sub-Saharan immigrants on their way to Spain and Europe. They arrive in Morocco from Algeria, and attempt to cross the Mediterranean Sea or to enter Ceuta or Melilla by climbing the fences which surround both cities, and which were built in 1995 to prevent such entry. Since 2003, EU conditionality in its relations with Morocco has led to the effective involvement of Moroccan police forces in the surveillance of its coasts to prevent the irregular migrants using them as a point of departure. The persistence of this Moroccan cooperation in the prevention of irregular departures from its coasts is of vital importance for Spain and for the whole Schengen Area. Morocco, however, suffers from migratory pressure from the south, while it lacks financial incentives and human resources to control the flow.

Although the presence of 750,000 Moroccans in Spain is the most visible face of the relationship between the two countries, both historical and present-day factors create a dense and complex network of shared interests, economic rivalry, political cooperation, territorial conflict, and mistrust. Among the elements of conflict, the Moroccan claim on Ceuta and Melilla stands out. These two small cities on the North-African coast, bounded by Moroccan territory and the Mediterranean Sea, form the only EU territory on mainland Africa (however, they are not part of the Schengen Area). The Kingdom of Morocco has claimed sovereignty over the 'enclaves' since its independence in 1956, but the United Nations does not consider the cities colonies, as they have been inhabited by Spaniards since well before Morocco became a kingdom. Their population, 76,000 in Ceuta and 65,000 in Melilla, is increasingly being made up of Muslims of Moroccan origin and Spanish citizenship, who as a result are altering the social and political life of the cities (Planet 1998; González Enríquez 2007).[2]

Competition in the European market of agricultural products, the use of Moroccan waters by Spanish fishermen, and Spanish support for Western Saharan claims for independence are also a continual source of confrontation. These tensions between Morocco and Spain have given rise to a climate of mutual distrust and rivalry. On the other hand, counteracting these tensions, in recent years a growing economic and political mutual dependence has developed: Spain is Morocco's second-largest investor and trade partner after France,[3] Ceuta and Melilla are indirectly promoting economic growth in the neighbouring Moroccan areas, and the Kingdom of Morocco needs Spanish cooperation, or at least neutrality, in its approach to the European Union. Spain has been one of the main supporters of Morocco's inclusion in the EU's European Neighbourhood Policy, and was also the main European promoter of the Euro-Mediterranean Partnership (known as the Barcelona Process), designed in 1995 to foster relations between the southern members of the European Union and North African countries. Political and police cooperation against Islamic terrorism is also significant, and of great importance for both countries since the Casablanca terrorist attack of 2003 and the Madrid one of 2004.

In this context of conflict, cooperation, and mutual dependence, immigration is something more than a demographic movement with an impact on the labour market, the welfare state, and cultural life: it is also a tool in the arena of international relations.

6.3 Methodology

Information provided in this chapter has been produced through empirical research carried out in two areas: the first was devoted to the institutional, demographic, and economic framework of circular labour movements between Morocco and Spain, and the second to the analysis of the experience of circular migrant workers.

During the first phase, the analysis of documents and compilation of the bibliography was complemented by interviews in Morocco and Spain with stakeholders directly or indirectly involved with migration between the two countries. All in all, twenty-nine persons have been interviewed in Madrid, Huelva, Cartaya, Almería, El Egido, Puebla de Vícar, Lleida, Barcelona, Rabat, and Casablanca. Interviewees included officials of public institutions (Spanish and Moroccan ministries of Labour, the Moroccan State Employment Service, the Spanish Embassy in Rabat, Spanish local councils, government delegations in the provinces of Huelva and Almería, the Catalonian Labour Department, the Council of Moroccan Community and the Ministry of Moroccan Community), leaders of trade unions (Spanish UGT and Moroccan UGTM), leaders of Moroccan migrants' associations in Spain (Ibn Batuta and ASISI), members of NGOs devoted to the immigrants in Spain (Almería Acoge, ACCEM, CEPAIM, Huelva Acoge), leaders of agricultural employers' associations (ASAJA and COAG), individual employers in Huelva, and Moroccan experts from research or social foundations with experience on migration (CIREM, CERED, and La Fondation Orient-Occident).

The second phase of research, carried out in June 2010, focused on the province of Huelva, where around 8,000 Moroccan women were working seasonally in the harvesting of strawberries. Thirty interviews were conducted by a Moroccan interviewer in two different municipalities, Lepe and Cartaya, using an interview guide designed to gather the main features of their experience as circular migrants, and their opinions and expectations from their migratory experience. The contacts with the women snowballed, and interviews were held in their lodgings.

6.4 A low qualified and weakly integrated migration

The Moroccan community is the oldest of the contemporary and economically motivated migratory populations that have settled in Spain. It was in the mid-1980s that Moroccans began to inhabit certain areas of the Spanish Mediterranean coast, and from 1998 to 2008 they formed Spain's largest single national migratory community. In January 2010, there were 754,000 Moroccan citizens living in Spain (1.6 per cent of the entire population) (see Figure 6.1), although by then the Romanians already outnumbered them by around 80,000 (Padrón Municipal, INE).

As regards their socio-demographic traits, Spain's Moroccan-born population is mainly, and comparatively, young (between twenty-five and forty-five years of age), male, and married (64 per cent). The two latter factors indicate a pattern of migration that consists of the prior arrival of the husband, followed some time later by the wife and maybe children. Households are larger (4.03 people per household) than those of Moroccans living in other European countries, and fertility rates are comparatively high, at an average of 2.75 children. The educational level of Moroccan immigrants is low compared with other groups, whether other immigrants in Spain or Moroccans living in other European countries. Illiteracy rates and the percentage of people lacking a formal education are high (20 per cent and 21 per cent respectively), while those with a university education are few (10 per cent of those living in Spain) (Cebolla & Requena 2009).

The integration of Moroccans in the labour market is related to some of the socio-demographic traits just described. The activity rates of men are high, while those of women are very low (only one in three women is active in the workforce). During the past years of economic growth (1996–2007), Moroccan men were mainly employed in the construction sector, followed by agriculture, and services. In 2006, still during the expansive period of the Spanish economy, Moroccans' concentration in agriculture in the general regime of the Social Security was triplicating that of the whole migrant population and it was thirty times bigger than that of Spaniards. Also in the construction sector, Moroccan concentration is more pronounced than that of the whole foreign population and Spaniards. Twenty-nine per cent of Moroccan affiliated in the general regime of the SS were working in the construction sector, seven points above the rest of foreign workers and twelve points above Spanish workers. Accordingly, few Moroccans hold skilled or highly skilled professional positions in Spain.

The international economic crisis which began in 2008 has seriously hit the Spanish labour market. In 2011, unemployment reached 20 per cent for the country's Spanish population and 33 per cent for foreigners, but Moroccan-born migrants are affected by unemployment to an even greater extent than the average migrant population (Arango and González 2009). From 2007 to 2010, Moroccan male unemployment increased from 11.7 per cent to 41.7 per cent, while that of women rose from 22.1 per cent to 51.2 per cent. Total unemployment among Moroccans was 44.5 per cent in 2010, and particularly affected young adults aged between sixteen and twenty-four, with a rate of 62.5 per cent. The high rate of unemployment has reduced the entry of Moroccan migrants, and affected return and exit rates. In 2010 and 2011 the number of Moroccan-born persons who left Spain was higher than that of Moroccan-born migrants to Spain. Very few of those who left (less than 10 per cent) returned to Morocco. (INE, Estadística de Variaciones Residenciales). However, statistical sources are inconsistent on this issue, as they register simultaneously a slow but steady increase of the whole Moroccan population in Spain during the years 2010, 2011, and 2012 (INE, Padrón Municipal).

Some authors suggest that temporary displacements—not statistically registered—may be occurring, whether to Morocco or to other European countries (Colectivo IOÉ, 2010). Most probably many unemployed migrants without children in the Spanish school system would opt to return to their country, if they did not risk losing their stay permit in Spain by leaving temporarily (if a TNC immigrant spends more than six months outside the country in a single year, his or her stay permit could be revoked).

The legal status of Moroccan migrants has changed greatly over the years. In an attempt to reduce the irregular migration of false tourists, in 1991 Spanish authorities imposed a visa requirement for Moroccan citizens. However, irregularity continued to be the most common type of migration because of the inadequacy of legal channels of migration, the demand for workers in the agriculture sector of the Mediterranean coast, the lack of surveillance of

Circularity in a Restrictive Framework

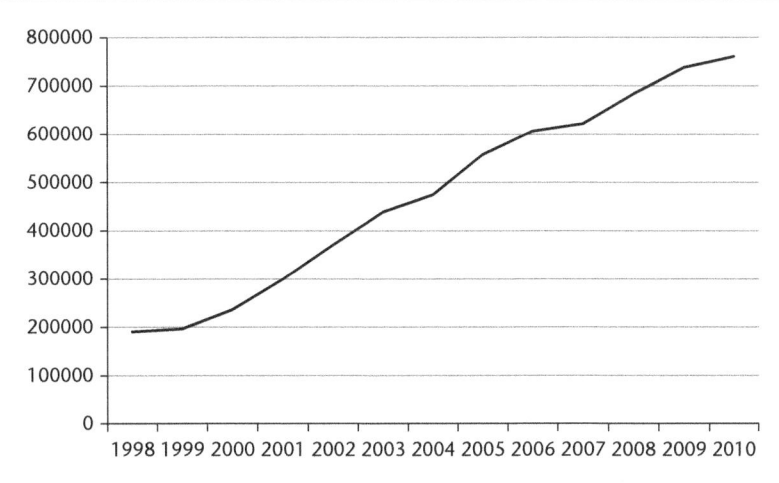

Figure 6.1 Moroccan immigrants in Spain
Source: Instituto Nacional de Estadística (Spanish National Institute of Statistics).

maritime frontiers, and the weakness of labour and police control over irregular migration (González Enríquez 2010). As a result, during the 1990s thousands of young Moroccans crossed the Gibraltar Straits on *pateras* (small boats) to find irregular jobs in either agriculture or construction. Irregularity has been a common feature of Moroccan immigration up to the extraordinary regularizations of 2000–1, which provided legal status to the irregular community formed during the 1990s.

The deployment of SIVE (Integrated System of Exterior Surveillance, *Sistema Integrado de Vigilancia Exterior*) in 2002, in the area of the Gibraltar Straits and then at other points of the southern Spanish coast and the Canary Islands, led to the capture of most boats carrying irregular migrants, who were immediately sent back to Morocco. As a consequence, the arrival of new irregular migrants from Morocco declined significantly, while successive regularizations legalized the status of the irregular migrants who were already in the country. In the last extraordinary regularization process, held in 2005, the percentage of Moroccans who applied was very low (16 per cent compared with 50 per cent among most other national groups), as most Moroccan immigrants were already regular. Since then, the percentage of irregularly staying Moroccan migrants is the lowest in comparison with other national groups.

Leaving aside the structural aspects of migrant integration (occupation or legal status), the social integration of Moroccan migrants in Spain, in its cultural elements, is weak. The average low level of education, the illiteracy of many women, their rural origins, and the traditional and patriarchal culture among most Moroccan migrants have been obstacles in the way of integration. In spite of their decades-old presence in Spain, 29 per cent of Moroccan immigrants recognize that they do not speak Spanish well enough, a percentage only exceeded by the Chinese. The lack of Spanish fluency is much stronger among Moroccan women, two thirds of whom cannot use the language (Cebolla and Requena 2009).

There is already an important amount of literature dealing with the opinions, attitudes, and perceptions of Moroccans and Spaniards regarding their mutual coexistence, which consistently states the lack of empathy between both groups. Public opinion polls conducted by the Spanish CIS (Centro de Investigaciones Sociológicas) show that since the late 1990s Moroccans form the less valued collective of immigrants, below the Sub-Saharan Africans. This negative public opinion existed already before 9/11 and has been reinforced since then, especially by the 11 March 2004 attack in the Madrid metro, which caused 191 deaths and whose perpetrators were Moroccan immigrants. After this terrorist incident, the social environment deteriorated for Moroccans. Media reports in 2004 showed that Moroccan immigrants were finding it more difficult to rent a flat or to get a job. A poll conducted by the Real Instituto Elcano shortly after the attack revealed that 19 per cent of those polled favoured a mass expulsion of all Moroccans from Spanish soil.[4] This very negative attitude has been tempered since then, but nevertheless Moroccans continue to form the less appreciated immigrant group. Moroccans are conscious of their low ranking in public opinion, and have complained about acts of discrimination. According to an opinion poll conducted in 2009 by the Conseil de la Communauté Marrocain à l'Etranger, 53 per cent of Moroccans living in Spain think that Spaniards hold a bad or very bad image of them, while 80 per cent state that it is more difficult for Moroccans to find a job, and 67 per cent think that they face more difficulties to rent a flat.

6.5 The legal framework of circularity

After several years of a massive influx of irregular migration, which made Spain the largest receiver of immigrants in the EU, the Spanish normative and administrative practices evolved towards much more cautious and restrictive approaches. In its effort to close the doors to irregular migration, ways to spontaneous circularity were severely curtailed. Until 2001 the movement of circular migrants was possible due to a lack of immigration policies or their non-enforcement. However, since 9/11 the climate changed, as irregular migration was rendered gradually more costly for the immigrants, who now faced a greater risk of detention and forceful repatriation. As the requisites to migrate legally were toughened, and surveillance against irregular migration increased, room for circularity was narrowed.

Circularity in a Restrictive Framework

Even for regular migrants, spontaneous circular migration has been severely restricted by the Law on Foreigners (2000) and its implementation. According to this law, renewal of residence permits to migrants who spend more than six months out of the country during the course of one year would not be issued. Also, long-term residents, a status that can be obtained after five years of continuous legal stay, now face restrictions to their mobility, since EU norms prevent them from spending more than twelve months out of EU territory. This clause in the 'Council Directive concerning the status of third-country nationals who are long-term residents' (2003/109) was incorporated into the Spanish law during the reform of the Law on Foreigners that was drafted in 2009.

Entrepreneurs, self-employed workers, or freelance professionals, who form a good part of circular migrants in other European countries, face a restrictive framework which prevents their migration into Spain. Although the Law on Foreigners and its Implementation Rules allow labour permits for self-employed workers or investors, granting them is discretionary, and the permits are usually denied (Trinidad 2003). Petitions are rejected owing to a policy which is based on the suspicion that applicants would more than likely fail as self-employed workers or entrepreneurs, and hence become a burden on the welfare system. This discretionary policy towards those wishing to set up their own business in Spain has rendered this kind of immigration negligible. The possibility of obtaining legal residence based on self-employment was not included in the scenarios for the 2005 amnesty either, as the scope for fraud was considered too high by the Ministry that was in charge of implementing the regularisation. Only in the Spanish-African towns of Ceuta and Melilla can a noticeable presence of Moroccan entrepreneurs and self-employed workers be found, owing to the proximity of both cities to Morocco, and the freedom of entry for Moroccan citizens living in the bordering provinces. As mentioned, Ceuta and Melilla do not belong to the Schengen Area; hence Moroccan citizens can enter into them, but are not allowed to cross freely from there to any other Spanish soil, be it in the Iberian Peninsula or the islands.

Access to Spanish citizenship has been remarkably low among Moroccan migrants in Spain. In 2010, only 15 per cent of Moroccan immigrants were Spanish citizens, a percentage similar to that of the much more recently arrived Ecuadorians, but lower than that of Argentineans or Colombians, also newcomers when compared with Moroccans. The Spanish Civil Code which regulates access to citizenship requires a legal stay of ten years before the application for citizenship, but only requires a two-year stay for nationals of Latin-American countries, Portugal, the Philippines, and Andorra, or for Sephardic Jews. As Latin-Americans form more than half of TNC immigrants (58 per cent in 2010), the two-year exception becomes the rule, whereby the ten-year stay requirement becomes a specific discriminatory measure against

Moroccans (who comprise 18 per cent of TNCs, the biggest single national non-EU group). This resultant discrimination affects decisively any opportunities Moroccans have to migrate back and forth freely, since such free flow of people is only permitted to Spanish or EU citizens. On the other hand, Moroccan administrative practices hamper the naturalization of Moroccan migrants, forcing them to choose between their nationality and any new one.

The Spanish legal framework does not favour the migration of highly qualified professionals from third countries, as they face important difficulties to validate their degrees. Spain has not developed any efforts to attract Moroccan students to its universities, in spite of the fact that the Spanish language continues to be understood in some areas of Morocco (especially those in the north and west which belonged to the Spanish Protectorate from 1912 until 1956). In 2009, only 2,590 Moroccan university students were attending Spanish universities, most of them in the town of Granada, in Andalusia. Finally, when foreign students finish their degrees or post-graduate studies in Spanish universities, they encounter the same difficulties as any other immigrant does to enter the Spanish labour market and get a residence permit.

The economic crisis and the growth of unemployment among immigrants have provoked a minor normative change devoted to promote the return of unemployed foreigners, by opening a 'special door' for them to immigrate again. This measure was initially presented in 2008 as a Voluntary Return Plan, which allowed TNC immigrants to receive their unemployment benefits in two instalments (instead of on a monthly basis) under the condition that they leave the country and do not return for three years. This Return Plan did not achieve the expected results, since the requisite of not returning to Spain for three years was too harsh a prospect for most migrants. Indeed, many of these migrants had endured long periods of irregular stay before obtaining their permit, a permit they would have to give up if they wanted to take advantage of the Return Plan. Only 13 per cent of unemployed immigrants were eligible to this Return Plan (80,000 in 2008), since only regular migrants who had paid social security fees during at least one year could take part, and only 10 per cent of them (8,000) applied for the plan. In 2010, this measure was included in the Implementation Rules of the Law on Foreigners, and it can be deemed as the only norm which promotes circularity among immigrants, allowing them to go back and forth. However, the three year requisite remained, counteracting the incentives provided by the norm.

If spontaneous circular migration is severely curtailed by the legal and institutional framework, a small space is opened for a highly regulated form of circular mobility in the seasonal agricultural work sector. In this sector, Spain has developed specific programmes, has gained experience after several mistakes, and has finally achieved some success. Circular migration between Morocco and Spain is currently restricted to this very narrow labour niche, the temporary agricultural work being concentrated in the south-western province of Huelva, with a minor presence in the south-eastern province of Almería, and in the north-eastern province of Lleida.

6.6 Potential and real circular migrants

The proximity between Morocco and Spain, separated by the 14 kilometres of the Gibraltar Straits, constitutes a strong basis for circularity, a potential for circular migration that could be developed if the institutional framework would favour it. Several informative polls conducted through the latter part of the 2000s provide information about the frequency, intensity, and nature of contacts between Moroccan immigrants in Spain and their native country: the Spanish *'Encuesta Nacional de Inmigrantes'* (ENI) conducted during the last weeks of 2006, the Moroccan 'Poll to Moroccan Citizens living in Spain' developed in 2009, the Moroccan survey *'Les Marocains Residant à l'Etranger'* whose fieldwork was conducted in 2005, and the also Moroccan report *'La reinsertion des migrants de retour au Maroc'* based on a survey conducted during the years 2003–4. According to the most recent of these studies (Poll to Moroccan Citizens living in Spain 2009), 32 per cent of Moroccan citizens living in Spain visit Morocco several times at year, while 44 per cent visit once a year (a total of 76 per cent of Moroccans visit their country at least once a year). This percentage is higher than the corresponding number among Moroccan immigrants in other European countries (69 per cent). Most first generation immigrants in Spain plan to spend their retirement years in Morocco (69 per cent), in contrast with immigrants in other European countries (52 per cent) with a longer history of Moroccan migration. However, of the second generation of Moroccan immigrants in Spain only a small percentage (5 per cent) plan to move to Morocco on a permanent basis. These results are congruent with the accumulated knowledge about the progressive decline of relations with the origin country among successive generations of migrants.

Fifty per cent of immigrants in Spain economically support relatives in Morocco. The Spanish Central Bank estimated the total amount of remittances at €528 million in 2007, but according to other sources such as the Moroccan *Office des Changes* which takes into account informal remittance channels, a much larger amount of around €800 million is calculated (Moré 2009). About 45 per cent of Moroccan immigrants in Spain own a house or flat in Morocco, and 31 per cent own an agricultural plot, but only 15 per cent maintain any kind of economic activity in Morocco. This percentage coincides with that of Moroccan-born migrants who have achieved Spanish citizenship.

Despite this potential for circularity which proximity and social practices reveal, in the context of a restrictive legal framework which curtails mobility and hence circularity, circular migration is only possible in the following cases:

1) When migration is free because no visa is required. This is the case of Ceuta and Melilla.
2) When migrants have achieved citizenship, and hence are Spanish for all legal purposes.
3) When circularity is organized by state agents.

A large number of people (around 30,000, mostly women) cross the frontiers of Ceuta and Melilla on a daily basis to carry goods for trans-frontier traders, who buy in the two cities and sell in Morocco. These Moroccans live in the neighbouring provinces of Nador and Tangier, and are granted a special permit from the Spanish authorities to enter Ceuta and Melilla on the condition that they leave before midnight. Many of these female porters cross the frontier several times a day. Aside from the above-mentioned group, several hundred women and a smaller number of men use this special permit system to work in the cities, either as domestic help or in the agricultural or construction sectors. They do not spend the night in the cities (or are at least not meant to), but rather in their villages on the Moroccan side of the border. For this reason, they are considered commuters and not immigrants for this study.

Around 128,000 Moroccan born persons are Spanish citizens in 2012, and this naturalization allows them to freely travel between the two countries. At least half of these naturalized citizens live in Ceuta or Melilla. In the rest of the Spanish territory there is no significant number of Moroccan migrants with Spanish citizenship who maintain economic activity also in Morocco. Moroccan traders with Spanish citizenship usually travel to other European countries, mostly the Netherlands, to buy the Arab goods they sell in Spain. A large number of Moroccan products are traded indirectly in Spain through agents settled in Northern or Central Europe, and travel throughout the continent.

In contrast with Italy, the research has not found regular Moroccan immigrants working as vendors or street pedlars, a subsector which in Spain is almost fully covered by Sub-Saharan migrants. Also, in contrast with the typology of circular migrants found in other European countries, where qualified workers form a relevant part of circular migrants, qualified immigration from Morocco to Spain is very scarce, and not noticeable in qualified labour posts.

6.6.1 *Agricultural seasonal migration*

Spain's intensive agricultural sector became increasingly dependent on foreign manpower in a process that began in the mid-1980s and consolidated during the 1990s. As fertility rates decreased among Spaniards, educational levels of the new generations improved, and more attractive labour opportunities opened up, partly because of economic growth generated by entry into the European Union in 1986, farmers found it increasingly difficult to employ local manpower. In order to fill this urgent need for manpower, farmers had to turn to immigrants to sustain the spectacular development experienced by intensive agriculture over the past few decades with the introduction of new farming techniques, most noticeably in the former quasi-desert areas of Almeria.

In fact, irregular migration filled this gap from the very beginning, and intensive agriculture became the main labour niche for irregular immigrants. During the ensuing years, the most typical path followed by male irregular migrants was their integration into the labour market through agriculture and a posteriori regularization from the extraordinary regularization processes that took place from 2000 to 2005, or through ordinary regularization channels. An additional problem related to this phenomenon was the flight of migrants. Once they became regularized, they tended to look for less physically demanding jobs, causing a continuous demand for new immigrants in the agricultural sector. The improvements throughout the decade of the 2000s in the control of migrant inflows with the sharp increase in labour inspections, the signing of accords between Spain and several migrant-sending countries (Morocco among them), the regularizations and the restriction of first labour and residence permits to specific sectors and provinces, finally achieved a noticeable normalization of migrant labour in the agricultural sector.

The so called *contingente* has been the main institutional tool to regulate the entry of seasonal agricultural workers, who arrive in Spain with a contract that has already been signed in the country of origin.[5] Through the *contingente*, collective contracts are signed, usually in countries which have previously established migration accords with Spain (Colombia, Ecuador, Morocco, Dominican Republic, Mauritania, Ukraine, Romania, and Bulgaria). The agricultural provinces of Huelva and Almería account for most of these contracts.

Some agricultural regions had developed a tradition of recruiting workers in several Eastern European countries with which they had established fluid and stable relations. In Huelva, for instance, from 2002 to 2007, workers recruited in Bulgaria, Romania, and Poland made up more than 90 per cent of the *contingente*. In 2009, however, Moroccan workers constituted almost 75 per cent of this *contingente*, since most East Europeans did not need to use this legal channel any more, although they continued working in the temporary agricultural works.

Some relevant differences among provinces, related to the nature of agricultural work, appear, regarding length of the stay, and gender and family conditions of workers. To sum up, in Huelva and Lleida almost all circular migrants are women, and their average stay is three months. In Almería most circular migrants are married couples, who stay for longer (nine months on average), because of the different harvest times of crops they tend.

From 2008, the high level of unemployment among Spaniards and immigrants already in Spain caused a return of job seekers from the construction industry (the sector most affected by the economic crisis) to agriculture. As a result, the number of seasonal contracts offered to temporary migrants decreased.

6.6.2 Moroccan agricultural seasonal migration in Huelva

Moroccan seasonal migrants are concentrated in the province of Huelva, where 16,271 Moroccan workers were recruited using the circular framework in the 2009 agricultural campaign. Only 519 were contracted in Almería in 2008 (the peak year, according to available data), and less than 200 took part as circular migrants in the province of Lleida (Catalonia). It must be stressed that these data refer only to circular migrants, i.e. to those contracted through the *contingente* while residing in their origin country, who usually return in successive years. It should be noted that the number of Moroccans residing in Spain and working seasonally in agriculture, and combining this job with others in agriculture or in other sectors, is clearly much higher, although statistics are not available to substantiate this.

The south-eastern area of the province of Huelva is well known for its strawberries and other red-fruit farms, whose crops require a large amount of manpower during planting and harvest. It has been a flourishing sector, whose growth has been paralleled (during the 2000s) to that of the construction sector, to which many Spanish workers fled, leaving agriculture. Table 6.1 shows the evolution in the number of authorized temporary work and residence permits related to this sector in the province.

Table 6.1 Temporary work and residence permits assigned to the agricultural sector of Huelva, by countries of origin

Year	BUL	COL	ECU	PHI	MOR	POL	ROM	SEN	UKR	Total
2000						600				600
2001					198	540				738
2002		149			336	4,954	970			6,409
2003		177	15		95	7,535	4,178			12,000
2004	508	105	8		620	8,506	10,589			20,336
2005	604	82	64		1,094	7,361	13,186			22,391
2006	941	8	26		2,330	9,796	19,153			32,254
2007	3021	22	12		5,277	0	20,710			29,042
2008	4656	11	14	270	13,600	0	20,634	749	557	40,491
2009	373	0	11	0	16,271	0	3,743	40	183	20,621
2010	0	0	0	0	6,153	0	0	0	0	6,153

Source: Sub-delegation of the Government in Huelva.

Circularity in a Restrictive Framework

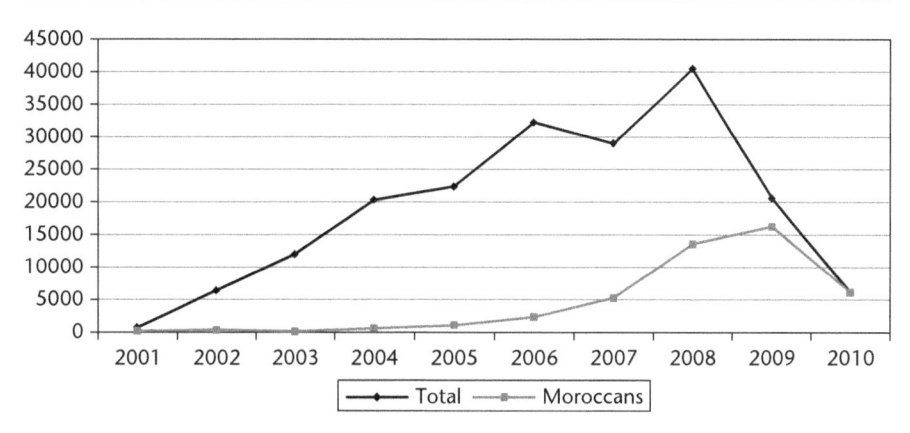

Figure 6.2 Seasonal work permits in Huelva for foreign workers
Source: Sub-delegation of the Government in Huelva.

Figure 6.2 reflects the steady increase that peaked in 2008 at almost 40,500 temporary workers, and the steep decline since 2009. It should be highlighted that Moroccans have been the only non-EU citizens who have continued taking part in the campaigns. As already mentioned, workers migrating from Eastern European countries belonging to the EU do not need a work permit, and hence are not included in the data, although they have continued to work in the campaigns. It is not easy to calculate the percentage that immigrant temporary workers make of the whole manpower employed during planting and harvest, as there are no official global data on the remaining groups. The size of the entire workforce employed in the campaigns includes those shown in the table above, plus the following categories: irregular immigrants (employed in a significant number up to 2005), regular migrants already living in Spain, and native workers. According to the Cartaya Town Council, around 110,000 people are directly employed in the agricultural sector during the campaigns. Hence, immigrants arriving with a temporary work permit accounted for 40 per cent of the workforce at the peak reached in 2008.

This mobility is regulated by the Labour Accord signed between Morocco and Spain in 2001, which came into effect in 2004.[6] It sets parameters for labour migration in aspects such as the communication of labour offers, information on selection procedures, training, salaries, workers' social rights, provision of visas, travel and accommodation. The Moroccan *Agence Nationale de Promotion de l'Emploi et des Competénces* (ANAPEC), belonging to the Ministry of Labour, is the main Moroccan institutional agent in the process, while in Spain a broader range of stakeholders intervene, from local authorities to territorial government delegations, trade unions, and employers' associations.

Moroccan seasonal workers have participated in successive campaigns since 2001, but the first recruitment cycle (from 2001 to 2003) failed in its attempt to yield a stable source of temporary workers. As stated by both Moroccan and Spanish stakeholders, the lack of transparency and corruption in the preselection procedure in Morocco during those years resulted in a high rate of non-compliance and non-returns. Most of the women who received a temporary residence permit came from cities, had no agricultural experience, and, above all, had no intention of returning to Morocco. Many of these women did not even turn up at the strawberry farms, and 60 per cent of those recruited did not return to Morocco. This percentage rendered the plan of having a stable source of Moroccan workers for the subsequent seasons unsustainable. As shown in Table 6.1, recruitment shifted to Eastern and Central European countries such as Poland, Romania, and, to a lesser degree, Bulgaria. During 2004, 2005, and 2006, between 20,000 and 30,000 workers from these countries took part in the campaigns. However, the entry of these countries into the EU and/or the end of the moratorium period for the free movement of their workers gave their nationals free access to jobs in all economic sectors. This openness of all labour markets aroused fears among agricultural employers about the flight of migrants to less demanding job sectors and the eventual scarcity of manpower. For this reason, both employers and the regional authorities turned to the Moroccan labour source once again.

In 2005, ANAPEC and the Spanish authorities adopted an agreement to revise the criteria used in the selection of temporary workers; in future, only rural women with farming experience and dependent children would be chosen. Also in that year, ANAPEC received sizeable European aid via the MEDA funds for its institutional development, which enhanced the agency's capacities and boosted the transparency of its selection processes.[7] The result of the new selection criteria and the greater involvement of Spanish entrepreneurs in the selection was a fall in cases of non-returners (the percentage of non-returns was 22.7 per cent in 2006, falling to 9 per cent in 2007, and 5.7 per cent in 2008), which has made it possible to maintain the programme, and increase the number of women hired to a peak of 16,000 in 2009.

The fact that recruitment was restricted to women with family in Morocco to encourage their return has brought about criticisms among observers, some of them claiming that such a discriminatory selection is 'in breach of basic human rights' (Fargues 2008: 11). The requirement of the husband's acceptance of his wife's participation in the programme (as stipulated by ANAPEC to ensure that someone in the family would be taking care of the children) has also been criticized by Moroccan women's associations, who consider it contrary to female freedom and independence.[8]

Women have traditionally been employed in the delicate culture of strawberries, as they seem to have the proper skills for it. The strawberry harvesters from Poland, Bulgaria, Romania, and even Senegal are also women. But the skill set is not the only reason that women are preferred, as employers have admitted that women are more compliant and less likely to cause disturbances. In the case of Moroccan women, interviewed employers perceived their traditional cultural habits as a very positive factor, as an employer recounts:

> There is another advantage. I have not created their culture. It is what it is and I am not going to change it. But we are favoured by it: they do not smoke, do not drink, do not go out. All Europeans love that they do not do these things. (agricultural employer, Cartaya)

Criticisms in the media suggest that women are in a weak position, and that this can give rise to labour and even sexual abuse.[9] The concentration of tens of thousands of young women in villages and in the countryside, and the predominance of men among employers and foremen, create the conditions for sexual harassment to exist and go unpunished. Nonetheless, associations, trade unions, and NGOs working in Huelva underline the broad picture of respect towards immigrants' rights, both as workers and individuals, although they report on some cases of abuse from employers (less than 5 per cent fail to comply with labour agreements, according to the trade unions).

In this context, the town council of Cartaya—in partnership with employers' associations, trade unions, NGOs, other associations, and Spanish public administration officials—applied for and received financial aid from the European Union's AENEAS programme, devoted to the financial and technical assistance of third countries on migration issues.[10] The project, known as Comprehensive and Ethical Management of Circular Migration between Morocco and Huelva (AENEAS-Cartaya), lasted for thirty months between the end of 2005 and mid-2008; it exceeded local expectations of managing the flow of some 2,000 Moroccan workers yearly. During the 2006, 2007, and 2008 campaigns (within the project's duration), more than 21,000 work and residence permits were issued in the area covered by the project.

The goal of AENEAS-Cartaya—according to its founding documents—was to create an institutional structure and protocol in order to improve recruitment in Morocco.[11] The project aimed to coordinate the different steps of recruitment, and distribute the activities of different institutions that intervene in the movement of seasonal workers from Morocco to Spain. It also aimed to ensure the compliance of social agreements, contribute to the integration of foreign workers in the community, and offer supplementary training. As part of the project, a local institution entitled the Foundation for Foreign Workers in Huelva (FUTEH, *Fundación para trabajadores extranjeros en Huelva*) was created. The organization of the Foundation included three advisory commissions, one formed by local councils of the strawberry area

(COMI), the second including trade unions and immigrants' associations (COSTE), and the last one devoted to farmers' associations (COPA).

The project was developed through agreements between Spanish consulates, the frontier police, and port authorities, to facilitate travel from Morocco to Huelva, and the return of seasonal migrants to Morocco. An agreement was signed between AENEAS-Cartaya and the Moroccan ANAPEC in 2006, which established the competences or activities that were assumed by each institution and the cooperation between them. The agreement lasted until 2010 and, according to it, immigrants had the guarantee that their contracts would be renewed in subsequent years, provided that they returned to Morocco once their contracts came to end.[12] According to the agreement, AENEAS-Cartaya was expected to provide information, management of the selection process, formation on security and health aspects related with the work, visas, contracts, accommodation, travels, and two information centres, where workers could communicate with relatives using the Internet, placed in the Moroccan village of Benslimane and in Cartaya. Another important set of activities involved those related to the training of seasonal workers, which included language courses organized by the town councils.

6.7 Is circularity good, and for whom? The opinion of stakeholders and immigrants about seasonal agricultural migration

6.7.1 Stakeholders

The impact of circular migration from Morocco on the Spanish economy is very high locally, especially in the area of Huelva, while its importance in Almeria and Catalonia is limited and negligible in the rest of the country. Huelva's farmers—at least those who have large properties and are heavily dependent on hired manpower—are deeply concerned about the reliable supply of labour. It is common to hear statements such as 'circular migration from Morocco has meant "salvation" for my business' and 'promoting seasonal migration from Morocco has been one of the best things we have done'. Circular legal migration ensures the provision of an experienced workforce throughout the campaign. For this reason, employers and political authorities are deeply concerned about return. If there is no massive return to Morocco once each campaign finishes, the whole system or procedure of circular migration will lose social and political legitimacy, and the supply of experienced workers can be lost, while the cost of recruiting, hiring, and training new labourers is too high for the sector.

Interviews with local, regional, and national Spanish authorities show a broad consensus about the advantages of circular migration, to the extent that local economies largely depend on the seasonal provision of workforce in the agricultural sector, and the procedures guarantee that migration is conducted legally, while providing social rights and equal treatment to immigrants, and reducing uncertainties among workers and employers. Spanish associations, NGOs, and trade unions that deal with seasonal migrants remark that circular migration allows Moroccan women to obtain a considerable income (compared with what they could gain in Morocco) over a brief period of time.

On the other hand, some observers refer to the low level of social integration in Spain as a negative aspect of the seasonal migratory work of Moroccan women. Owing to their lack of fluency in (or complete ignorance of) the Spanish language, their short period of stay, and their residence in collective accommodations scattered in the countryside, interaction with local people is very scant. Town councils and associations offer training and language courses and intercultural activities, in order to promote interaction, but these initiatives seem not to be enough to achieve social integration. This weak integration does not appear to provoke social conflicts among Moroccan immigrants and the local population: tensions, although scarce, appear more frequently in the relations between Moroccan and East European migrants.

The generally positive mood towards seasonal Moroccan migration in agricultural areas is falling victim to the economic crisis: the growth of unemployment among the local population has caused tension towards migrants, as unemployed Spaniards seek temporary jobs in the sector.

On the Moroccan side, among stakeholders the evaluation of circular migration is very similar and broadly positive, while their main demand is that such programmes are enlarged to include other geographical areas and for longer periods of stay.[13] However, few of the interviewed stakeholders in Morocco had accurate information concerning circular migration to Spain, as circularity is a feature of only a minor part of Moroccan migration. Only those directly involved in the management of circular migration or in research on it have enough information and the criteria for evaluating the experience. They share the evaluation of present circularity as having a positive but too limited effect, owing to the small number of workers involved and to the short periods they spend in Spain. The indirect impact on professional training or cultural change is also small.[14] Hence, circular migration is relevant and positive in the lives of those women who take part in it, but it is hardly a tool for local or even family development. It may help children's schooling, and even allow for the beginning of some small businesses, but most women lack the skills required for initiating an autonomous economic activity. According to a survey conducted by ANAPEC (2009), only 6 per cent of the women involved in circular migration start an investment project. On the other hand, the effect of the circularity of mothers on the children's wellbeing and family stability is not well known, owing to the lack of empirical research in this field. Several stakeholders pointed out that this type of migration may threaten family life, since many husbands reject their wives' participation in seasonal work in Spain. In fact, the unease of husbands seems to pose a greater challenge to the circular experience than the care of children. Many Moroccan villages are still traditional and patriarchal, and the departure of a married woman to work in a foreign country can be seen as a sign of the husband's incompetence, or even as unfaithful female behaviour. Sources also relate cases of husbands who marry other women while their wives are in Spain.

6.7.2 Immigrants

This section is based on the analysis of thirty interviews conducted with Moroccan female temporary workers employed in strawberry harvesting in Cartaya and Lepe (Huelva) during June 2010. Interviewees were aged between twenty-five and forty-four, mostly married, divorced, or widowed mothers, and with a very low level of education—two-thirds were illiterate. Sixty per cent usually worked in Morocco in the irregular economy as temporary agricultural workers, pedlars, or as domestic help. They came from all areas of rural Morocco, and for almost all interviewees Huelva was the only foreign place they had ever visited. All workers had participated previously in the programme, 50 per cent of them since 2008. Their stay period in Huelva spanned from a few weeks to nine months, the maximum allowed by Spanish law; the average was three months.

When asked about the reasons of their decision to migrate, the most frequent responses were:

1) Job insecurity in Morocco: the women spoke of long working days that could last for twelve hours, labour instability and very low salaries. Although the legal minimum wage in Morocco is 55 dirhams a day (around €5), day labourers claim they usually earn smaller wages. As one of the interviewees said, 'There [in her village] I always live hand to mouth.'

2) Lack of economic resources: all workers come from rural and deprived areas. Many of them support single-parent families, dependent on the mother's income.

3) The need to save to build a house, open a business, or pay health or education expenses.

4) The family vetoing female work in Morocco: in some cases, women can work only abroad, away from their villages, as tradition disapproves of them working outside the family plot.

5) Curiosity about Spain and Europe: this reason was mentioned by the two most highly educated women, who in turn were in the best labour positions in Morocco.

Wages are mentioned as the best aspect of their seasonal migration to Huelva. All workers answered to a direct question on this issue that they were satisfied with regard to the wages they obtained in Huelva. Wages totalled €37.80 per day for harvesters and €39.42 for planters, as established by the provincial collective agreement on agriculture. The average income for those staying three months was thus €2,722 (harvesters) or €2,838 (planters), amounts that can make a difference in the consumption level of a family in rural Morocco.

The Spanish language is, however, the main obstacle for these migrants. Almost all women, 97 per cent of them, said they had suffered on occasions from their lack of knowledge of Spanish. They are always accompanied at work by a translator, and all the formalities and procedures needed to organize their stay and work are prepared and made by others. But difficulties arise when the women use their free time to walk around the villages, buy something, or engage with the locals. In these cases, communication is based on sign language, and socializing with locals is almost impossible, as one migrant explains:

> After buying something or using the phone at the Internet café, when I finish I open my hand and they take the money. I do not understand anything of what they say. I smile and leave. They speak to you and you do not know if they are praising or insulting you. (circular migrant, Cartaya)

Half of the women had signed up for the Spanish courses offered by the programme organizers. Others were unable to do so because of the lack of spaces available, thus illustrating the demand for the courses and their shortage. Labour conditions were qualified as good by 40 per cent of the workers, while another 40 per cent said they were tough. The women worked six and a half hours per day six days a week (Monday to Saturday) in a physically demanding job. As for accommodation conditions, 87 per cent of the workers said they were 'good' or 'very good'. They especially valued the use of electrical appliances, showers, and hot water, as many of them came from houses where some of these facilities were lacking. One female migrant tells us, 'We have all kind of things. We are not lacking anything. We have more than in Morocco: hot water, fridge, everything.' They also valued security, the feeling of being protected. Women who expressed dissatisfaction as regards their accommodation (13 per cent) mentioned distance as the main problem, as the collective houses where they were living were located outside the village. A minority of the women who were staying in the municipal hostel at Cartaya claimed

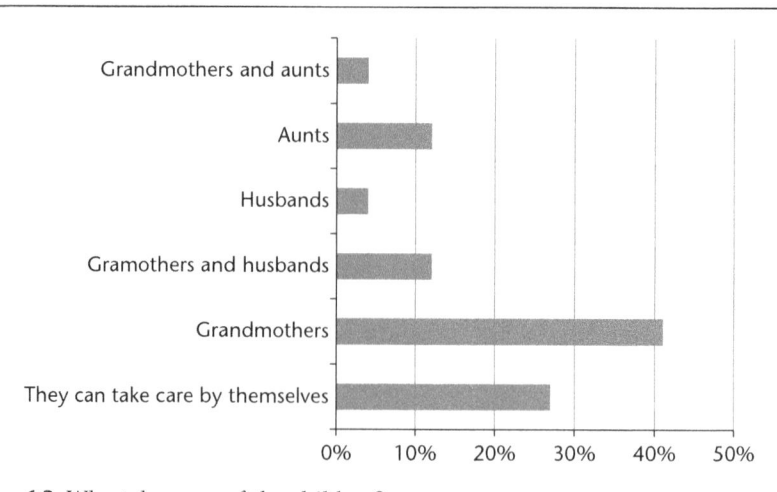

Category	Percentage
Grandmothers and aunts	~3%
Aunts	~10%
Husbands	~3%
Gramothers and husbands	~10%
Grandmothers	~42%
They can take care by themselves	~27%

Figure 6.3 Who takes care of the children?
Source: Interviews with Moroccan temporary workers. Huelva. June 2010

discrimination against them, as Romanian temporary workers were staying in brick and cement houses, which were better insulated than their building. Coexistence with other groups of workers was good—as 93 per cent said they had not experienced any unpleasant situations in their relations with their co-workers. The 7 per cent who mention a problem complained about discrimination against Moroccan women by Romanian women.

Care of children during their mothers' stay in Huelva was left to relatives, in most cases to grandmothers, followed by aunts, back in Morocco (see Figure 6.3). It should be highlighted that only one of the married women in the sample answered that it was the father who remained in charge of the children's care during her absence. When asked about the effect of their absence on family life, there were a variety of answers: the most frequent was 'they have missed me', followed by 'they are used to it' or 'they accept it'. Several women admitted that their husbands accepted reluctantly their temporary migration, whether for affective causes or for traditional cultural reasons.

Children are the main reason for women returning to Morocco, as they were previously the reason for travelling abroad. 'I am here for them' (the children) was the most often repeated sentence when asked about their motivation for working in Huelva and for returning to Morocco. Secondly, most women said they did not want to leave their country ('you always feel better in your own country'). And, finally, illegal immigration (the only alternative to returning once their stay legally ends) is contemplated as a bad experience: the image of irregular immigrants among these workers is one of lack of dignity, weakness in front of their employers, lack of a family and social support system, and humiliation.

Circularity in a Restrictive Framework

Income earned during the stay in Huelva (see Figure 6.4) is devoted in Morocco to family expenses (90 per cent), followed by savings (23 per cent), the buying of property (27 per cent), travel, including the trip to Mecca (10 per cent), paying back creditors (7 per cent) or to a child's wedding (7 per cent). Almost all the women (97 per cent) planned to invest in either a house (44 per cent) or a small business (41 per cent), such as a grocery store, a hairdresser, or a farm. Contrasting with this wish is the scarce 6 per cent of workers who finally can create some kind of business, as already mentioned.

Reintegration into normal life after returning to Morocco seems not to be problematic. All interviewees said that they had not faced any integration difficulties once back with their family and in their village. The average stay of

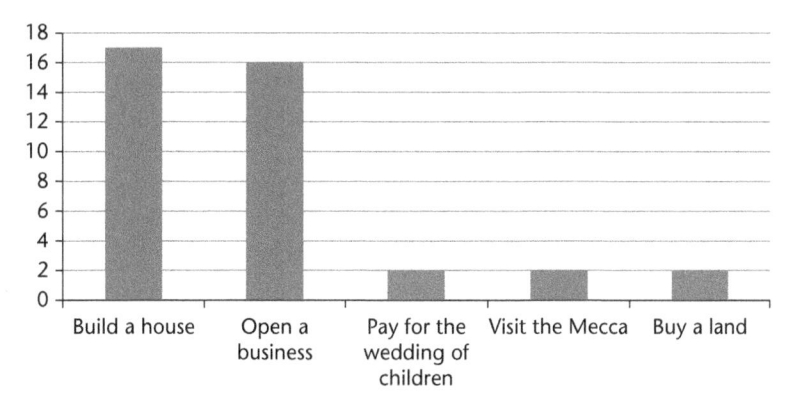

Figure 6.4 Plans for the investment of savings: absolute numbers
Source: Interviews with Moroccan temporary workers. Huelva. June 2010

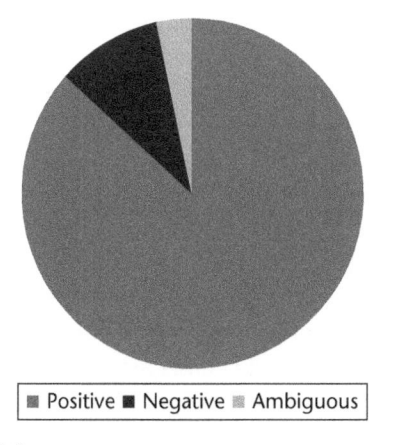

Figure 6.5 Evaluation of the programme
Source: Interviews with Moroccan temporary workers. Huelva. June 2010

135

three months allowed them to keep communications and links with relatives alive. All in all, the outstanding majority of women (87 per cent) felt satisfied with their temporal migratory experience (see Figure 6.5), and with the functioning of the programme. Only 13 per cent expressed an ambiguity or negative feelings, and most of them were concerned about the short period of time they would be working in Huelva. Consequently, when asked about their proposals to improve the programme, the most frequent answer was the demand for longer stays (57 per cent), followed by a wish to obtain residence permits (23 per cent).

6.8 Conclusion

The lack of open channels to circular migration between Spain and Morocco (or between Spain and any other non-EU country) is the result of an already long history of irregular immigration. The weakness of internal controls (whether labour or police) during the period of greatest influx of immigrants (1998–2007) pushed the legislators to strengthen the defensive aspects of external controls and procedures. When irregular migration between Morocco and Spain was relatively easy (during the 1980s, becoming more difficult in the 1990s), circular behaviour was also common, but the fight against irregularity has had the collateral effect of practically eliminating the conditions for mobility. As this mobility was restricted, circular migration became a marginal aspect in Moroccan migration. At the peak in 2009, only 16,271 Moroccans could be labelled as circular migrants in Spain, a very small figure compared with the 750,000 Moroccan migrants living in the country.

Among regular migrants spontaneous circular migration is severely curtailed by the existing legal framework, as the Implementation Rules of the Law on Foreigners do not allow for the renewal of a residence permit to those who spend more than six months out of Spain, either on a single trip or several during the course of a year. On the other hand, even those who access the status of long-term residents risk losing their status if they spend more than twelve months outside EU territory, according to the European Directive on third country nationals who are long-term residents (transposed into Spanish law in 2009). Circularity is restricted in Spain to highly organized circular migration in just one type of labour sector, and it is nothing more than temporary agricultural migration repeated throughout the years. Only those who gain Spanish or any other EU citizenship can migrate in a circular way freely. But only 15 per cent of Moroccans living in Spain have gained Spanish citizenship, a percentage identical to that of Moroccan migrants who maintain any economic activity in Morocco.

Comparing the Morocco-Spain circular migration experience with the objectives stated by the European Commission in its Communication on circular migration (2007, 248 final) the first aspect that stands out is the irrelevance in this case of the brain drain issue. Qualified migrants form a scarce minority in the whole of Moroccan migration to Spain, and are absent in the regulated forms of circularity. Also noteworthy is the virtual non-existence of all but two (seasonal workers and students) of the types of circular migrants listed by the Commission in that Communication. On the other hand, the Morocco-Spain circular migration experience has become a successful example of circularity as a means to fight irregular migration (one of the objectives of the European Commission when promoting circularity, as signalled in the Communication). The schemes developed under these programmes have put an end to the arrival at the farms of large numbers of irregular Moroccan and other national migrants looking for a job, a common event in the past in intensive agriculture areas.

The impact of the only relevant form of circularity (seasonal and regular) is locally important in several agricultural Spanish areas, notably in the strawberry fields of Huelva, where farmers feared the disappearance of their businesses because of the lack of manpower. An important conclusion can be drawn from these fears and the past experience of farmers: the combination of low salaries and harsh working conditions in the intensive agricultural sector make it attractive only to those foreigners who cannot migrate freely, and hence choose other sectors to work in. As Central and Eastern Europeans became EU citizens, and could move about and access freely the labour markets of Western member states, Spanish agricultural entrepreneurs began to fear their disappearance from the disposable labour force; and all eyes turned to Morocco. So, paradoxically, the success of the Spanish experience in its relation with Morocco in the field of seasonal migrant work has been made possible by the closure of doors to other forms of migration. The sustainability of this form of highly regulated circularity is therefore dependent on strict enforcement of rules governing migration, and on visa restriction.

The impact of the current circular migration in the development of Moroccan rural areas is very limited owing to the small number of workers involved, and to the short periods they spend in Spain. Although salaries paid in the agricultural sector in Spain are high in comparison with the average income of the rural population in Morocco, they are not high enough to cause a relevant effect in economic development. The low educational level which characterizes circular migrant women, most of them illiterate, renders more difficult the investment of earned income into new businesses. The indirect impact on professional training or cultural change also seems to be small.

In general, there is a global positive evaluation of the circular migration process among those concerned, although some minor criticisms are expressed by the workers interviewed, the entrepreneurs, trade unions, immigrant associations, and public institutions in Morocco and Spain. According to the Moroccan perspective, the enlargement of time and sectors of this kind of circular migration are of utmost importance. They would like to see similar programmes implemented in other Spanish geographical areas or other economic sectors, which would result in the contract of more workers for a wider stretch of time. From the Spanish perspective, the biggest threat to the sustainability of this mobility is the violent shock caused in the labour market by the economic crisis from 2008, and the pressure of local unemployed Spaniards and already staying immigrants, who are now willing to accept the labour and salary conditions which they rejected during years of prosperity. In effect this is an external condition that could diminish the social legitimacy of the circular scheme. Its future in the short run is therefore dependent on the evolution of the domestic labour market, and the overcoming of the economic crisis in Spain. In the long run, this form of circular mobility depends on the maintenance of a large income gap between Spain and Morocco, as only this gap would allow low-paid and harsh work to remain attractive for Moroccans.

References

AENEAS-Cartaya (2008). *Programme de gestion integrale de l'immigration saisonniere entre le Maroc et l'Espagne*. Rapport final descriptif, Cartaya Local Council.

ANAPEC (2009). *Migration et Développement*, La lettre d'Information de la Division Placement International, n. 7, December 2009.

Arango, J. and González Quiñones, F. (2009). *The Impacts of the Current Financial and Economic Crisis on Migration in the Spain-Morocco Corridor*, CARIM Analytic and Synthetic Notes 2009/39, Florence: European University Institute.

Cebolla, H. and Requena, M. (2009). 'Los inmigrantes marroquíes en España,' in D.S. Reher and M. Requena (eds), *Las múltiples caras de la inmigración en España*, Madrid: Alianza Editorial, 251–87.

CIREM (2011). *La migration cirulaire feminine, vecteur de developpement*. Barcelona-Rabat: Fondacion CIREM.

Colectivo IOE (2010). *El impacto de la crisis económica en la situación laboral de los inmigrantes marroquíes en España*, Notas Socioeconómicas de Casa Árabe 11/2010 [online]. http://www.casaarabe-ieam.es (accessed 27 July 2012).

Fargues, P. (2008). *Circular Migration: Is it Relevant for the South and East of the Mediterranean?*, CARIM Analytic and Synthetic Notes, 2008(40), Florence: European University Institute.

González Enríquez, C. (2007). 'Ceuta and Melilla. Clouds over the African Spanish Towns. Muslim Minorities, Spaniards's Fears and Morocco-Spain Mutual Dependence', *Journal of North African Studies*, 12(2), 219–34.

González Enríquez, C. (2010). 'Spain: Irregularity as a Rule,' in Anna Triandafyllidou (ed), *Irregular Migration in Europe*, London: Ashgate, 247–66.
González Enríquez, C. and Reynés, M. (2011) *Circular Migration between Spain and Morocco. Something Else than Agricultural Work?* [online report]. http://metoikos.eui.eu (accessed 27 July 2012).
Lmadani, F. (2010). 'Migrations féminines marocaines. Pour un regard genrée' [online report]. http://codesria.org/IMG/pdf/Fatima_Ait_Ben_Lmadani.pdf (accessed 27 July 2012).
L'Observateur, 4–10 February 2011, 'Le goût amere de la fraise espagnole' http://www.ccme.org.ma/fr/images/stories/YMD/LObservateur_du_Maroc.pdf.
Messaoudi, N. (2008). '12.000 mères marocaines pour la fraise espagnole' [online], http://www.rue89.com/2008/05/23/12-000-meres-marocaines-pour-la-fraise-espagnole (accessed 27 July 2012).
Moré, I. (2009). *Inmigración y remesas informales en España* [online], http://extranjeros.mtin.es/es/ObservatorioPermanenteInmigracion/ (accessed 27 July 2012).
Pajares, M. (2009). *Inmigración y mercado de trabajo.* [online], http://extranjeros.mtin.es/es/ObservatorioPermanenteInmigracion/ (accessed 27 July 2012).
Planet, A. (1998). *Melilla y Ceuta. Espacios-frontera hispano-marroquíes*. Ciudades Autónomas de Ceuta y Melilla and UNED.
Trinidad Garcia, L. (2003). 'El trabajo por cuenta propia de los extranjeros en España', *Migraciones*, 13, 61–106.

Other sources

Elmadmad, K. (2008). *Migration circulaire et droit des migrants. Le cas du Maroc*, CARIM notes d'analyse et de synthèse 2008/26. Florence: European University Institute.
Erzan, R. (2008): *Circular Migration: economic aspects*, CARIM Analytic and Synthetic Notes, 2008/31, Florence, European University Institute.
Haut-Commissariat au Plan (2005): *La reinsertion des migrants de retour au Maroc*, Rabat, Centre d'Etudes et de Recherches Démographiques.
Haut-Commissariat du Plan (2007): *Les Marocains Resident à l'Etranger*, Rabat, Centre d'Etudes et de Recherches Démographiques.
Khachani, M. (2008): *La migration circulaire: cas du Maroc*, CARIM Analytic and Synthetic Notes, 2008/07, Florence, European University Institute.
Mghari, M. (2008): *La migration circulaire: quelques éléments d'approche au Maroc*, CARIM Analytic and Synthetic Notes, 2008/38, Florence, European University Institute.

Notes

1. I am grateful to Miquel Reynés, who carried out a good part of the empirical research on which this chapter is based, and to Soufian Marouan, who conducted the interviews with Moroccan workers which consitute the basis for the analysis of their circular migration experience.
2. Spanish citizenship to Moroccan origin inhabitants of Ceuta and Melilla was first awarded in 1986, following a special proccess of naturalization held in both towns.

By then this population formed a small minority in the area, but its size has been increasing steadily during the last decades. Its bigger fertility rate (compared with that of Spanish origin couples) and the frequency among it of marriages with Moroccan citizens who move to live in Ceuta or Melila and who in turn can access Spanish nationality, forecast a near future of Muslim majority in both towns.
3. If irregular frontier trade through Ceuta and Melilla is also taken into account, Spain is Morocco's leading trading partner.
4. Poll conducted by the Real Instituto Elcano, June 2004, available at: http://www.realinstitutoelcano.org/.
5. The *contingente* is elaborated yearly by the Ministry of Labour Affairs and Immigration, and it defines the offer of employment for new and usually temporary migrant workers (i.e., it does not refer to those migrants already living in Spain). Those offers have been previously presented by big employers or a group of employers, as they must include at least 100 labour posts. Employers forecast their need of extra manpower that they expect will not be provided by Spaniards or by migrants already living in Spain.
6. 'Acuerdo sobre mano de obra entre el Reino de España y el Reino de Marruecos', 25 July 2001.
7. The MEDA Programme is the main EU financial tool of the European Neighbourhood Policy for Southern Mediterranean countries.
8. See Lmadani (2010).
9. See for instance the report published in *El País* (13 June 2010) entitled *'Abusos sexuales a inmigrantes'* (sexual abuse of immigrants).
10. More information on the programme is available at: http://ec.europa.eu/europeaid/what/migration-asylum/documents/aeneas_2004_2006_overview_en.pdf (accessed 22 November 2011).
11. During that period, other recruitment programmes took place in Senegal and the Philippines, but they had no continuity and, especially in the case of Senegal, were unsuccessful.
12. Information is available at: http://ayto-cartaya.com/inmigracion/images/inmigracion/Documentacion/Aeneas/Proyecto%20AENEAS%20Cartaya%20actualizado%2023-06-08.pdf (last accessed 1 March 2010).
13. This positive evaluation contrasts with the negative position of certain media and analysts in Morocco, who qualify the discrimination in favour of mothers with small children as unacceptable and immoral, and reject the Spanish insistence on ensuring the return to Morocco of seasonal workers. See, for instance, Messaoudi (2008).
14. The report conducted by CIREM among circular Moroccan women once they had returned to Morocco signals the increasing of self-confidence and autonomy as the main cultural impact of their experience (CIREM 2011).

7

Circular Migration between Hungary and Ukraine: Historical Legacies, the Economic Crisis, and the Multidirectionality of 'Circular' Migration

Ayşe Çağlar

7.1 Introduction[1]

Circular migration, both as a concept and as a policy tool, has been high up on the agenda of several institutions and agencies, like the World Bank and the European Commission, since the mid-2000s. Circular migration is defined as a temporary repetitive labour mobility between migrants' countries of origin and one of the countries of destination (Baltes-Löhr, C. et al. 2011). Coordinated circular migration—that is, repeated cross-border mobility administered by legal provisions and/or bilateral agreements—has been particularly fostered as a policy tool to regulate migratory flows from third countries to EU member states. Starting with a number of European Commission policy communications in 2005 (2005a; 2005b), which underlined the importance of circular migration for meeting the labour needs of EU member states, and for utilizing the benefits of migration on development, this form of migration increasingly became the preferred mode in the European Council, the European Commission, and the European Parliament policies and suggestions in the second half of the 2000s (Vertovec 2007; Baltes-Löhr et al. 2011).

Promoted as a triple-win policy tool for the sending and receiving countries, as well as for the migrants themselves, circular migration has been advocated as a (legal) alternative to undocumented and to permanent migration. It is cherished by several agencies as a solution to a number of challenges posed by labour markets, public opinion, and sentiments against migrant settlement processes, especially in Western Europe. Circular migration programmes interpellate migrants as development actors (on the basis of their remittances, investments, and transnational networks), who will also benefit from this form of migration in terms of their income, savings, and qualifications.

In 2006, the European Council invited the European Commission to explore the positive impacts of circular migration on development, and to propose schemes to channel and govern the flow of labour, capital, and know-how between EU member states and third countries via circular migration. In order to improve the management of temporary legal cross-border labour movements between the EU and Third Countries, the European Commission has come up with several mobility partnerships suggestions and agreements. A number of these incentives promote legal circularity of labour (like multiple entry/work permits) and the attractiveness of the EU for highly qualified workers, and also include programmes for the reintegration of returning migrants. On the basis of the 2008 Communication on Common Immigration Policy for Europe, the European Parliament adopted (in 2009) a resolution on such a common policy, complete with guidelines and tools to facilitate circular and temporary migration (Baltes-Löhr et al. 2011). The Stockholm Programme, adopted by the European Council at the very end of 2009, formulated circular migration as a policy.

All these incentives and legal provisions were meant to facilitate the circulation of human capital, including the transfer of skills to the 'developed' world; to ensure the flow of remittances; to solve sectorial labour shortages without bearing the 'social cost' of migration, and to accelerate economic growth in receiving countries on the basis of regulated, trained and cheap labour flows (Vertovec 2007; Glick Schiller and Faist 2010; Baltes-Löhr et al. 2011).

The World Bank's report on Europe and the former Soviet Union, which highlighted the benefits of a regulated circular migration, was important in putting circular migration in the agendas of policies pertaining to Eastern Europe. The proposed form of circular migration stood on a fine balance between the transfer of skills to Western Europe and the mitigation of a brain drain in Eastern Europe. Most importantly, it ensured a trained, reliable, and flexible pool of low-wage workers for the Western European economies, without bearing the costs of renewal of the labour force (Buroway 1976). However, the historical legacies and the regional specificities of Central and Eastern Europe, as well as the 2008 crisis which hit the economies of this region severely, complicated the nature of temporary and circular migratory flows in this region, and revealed the fault lines of this analytical lens.

In order to understand the migratory flows from Ukraine to Hungary, one has to focus on the regional specificities and historical ties that exist between these countries. The historical legacies between Hungary and

Ukraine shape the migratory dynamics between the two countries (Malynovska 2006a). Although only a small portion of migration from Ukraine is to Hungary (officially 2.4 per cent), almost all Ukrainian migrants to Hungary (up to 90 per cent of Ukrainian migrants) come from Transcarpathia (Transcarpathian District, in Ukraine, Zakarpattya), which shares a border with Hungary.[2]

Transcarpathia belonged to the Hungarian Crown within the Austro-Hungarian Empire between 1867 and 1918. However, the Treaty of Trianon in 1919, through which 60 per cent of the Hungarian population became part of neighbouring countries, granted Transcarpathia to Czechoslovakia (Kristóf 1999); though with the First Vienna Award (1938), southern Transcarpathia was ceded to Hungary, and after the Second World War Transcarpathia was incorporated into the Ukrainian Soviet Socialist Republic. It became the Transcarpathian District (*Zakarpatska Oblast in* Ukrainian). After the collapse of the USSR in 1991, it continued to be an integral part of Ukraine.

Though Transcarpathia has always been home to multiple ethnic groups (Ukrainians, Ruthenians, Hungarians, Roma, Germans, Jews, Romanians, and others), the large Hungarian minority in Transcarpathia (as well as in neighbouring Hungary) is the consequence of the Trianon Treaty. The legacy of the movement of borders in this region is present in today's cross-border movement of people. After 1989, indeed, 80 per cent of the migratory flows to Hungary were from the neighboring countries of Romania, Ukraine, and Serbia (Kristóf 1999), and were composed of ethnic Hungarians. Though not all migrants from Ukraine to Hungary come from the border region of Transcarpathia, this is the region where most of the Ukrainian citizens of ethnic Hungarian background live. They have been and still are embedded into social and cultural networks on the Hungarian side of the border.

The presence of Hungarian minorities in the neighbouring countries made the regulation of these borders and the migratory flows from there different from controlling any other migratory flows for the Hungarian state. As we have shown elsewhere, Hungary's border regulation regimes are situated at a fine balance between migration policies (mostly shaped under the EU pressures) and diaspora politics (Çağlar and Gereöffy 2008). In fact the new Hungarian Constitution adopted by the Hungarian Parliament on 18 August 2011 explicitly takes responsibility for all Hungarians abroad. Hungarian minorities abroad have a specific location within the state politics and the national imagination in Hungary. For this reason, the dynamics of border regulations in Hungary are entangled with Hungarian state's politics *vis-à-vis* Hungarian minorities in neighbouring countries. The Hungarian-Ukraine border and its varying regulations are a clear example of these entangled dynamics. Although cross-border mobility from Ukraine to Hungary intensified after 1989, and especially after 1991, these border crossings have a history going back to 1961. An official inter-state contract between the Soviet Union and the

Hungarian Republic regulated cross-border mobility until the collapse of the Soviet Republic.

The cross-border movement of people in Transcarpathia historically took several forms, such as expulsion, voluntary mobility, and population exchange. In the Soviet period, voluntary migration was largely restricted. Even getting a visa from a foreign country was easier than leaving the Soviet Union. After the collapse of the Soviet economy, voluntary migration (including its circulatory form) became the prominent cross-border movement in this region. Confronted with increasing economic hardship (especially with unemployment and failed salary payments for months), people from this region migrated in search of a better life and work.

Movement between Ukraine and Hungary started relatively early, already in 1991 and 1992, as a result of visa-free movement and the abolishment of passport restrictions. The migration patterns varied: they were seasonal, circular, and transit, as well as in the form of emigration. Although most of the migrants were from the Hungarian minority in Transcarpathia, there were and are also migrants from Ukraine without any ethnic attachment to Hungary. There were different regulations for the Hungarian and non-Hungarian origin Ukrainians. The Hungarian minority was subject to certain favourable procedures that eased their cross-border mobility. There was the local border traffic, which made cross-border mobility easier, and there existed some simplifying procedures for the Hungarian minority to have a Hungarian visa. Even after Hungary joined the Schengen Area in 2008, and the procedures became more complicated and fees were introduced, Hungary signed an agreement on local border traffic with Ukraine, to facilitate mobility within the border zone.

Despite several changes in the border crossings and visa regimes, migrations continued, and still continue with adjustments to the legal changes. Most of the labour and circular migrants from Transcarpathia come from Beregovo/Beregszasz *raion* bordering with Hungary.

In the context of these historical legacies and the altered border regime regulations between these two countries, which are strongly entangled with diaspora politics of Hungary, this chapter explores the migration patterns between Ukraine and Hungary, with a specific emphasis on different forms of circular migration. After a brief note on the methodology, I will focus on the changing border regimes, the plethora of visas and permits, and cross-border procedures that have been initiated to regulate the flows on the Ukrainian-Hungry border. Then I will concentrate on the changing volume and the composition of migratory flows from Ukraine and Hungary. The changing figures in the migratory flows from Ukraine to Hungary draw attention to the profound impact of the 2008 economic crisis, which was felt very severely in Hungary as well as in Ukraine. The migratory flows between these countries are now multi-directional rather than following a strict circulatory pattern.

The nature and the pattern of the current migratory flows between Ukraine and Hungary, which operate within a broader social field, urge us to put the concept of circularity of these flows under scrutiny. On the basis of some concrete migration paths, which either lost their circular character or their permanency, I conclude by raising some questions about the temporality in migration research, and especially in approaching circular migration flows, by underlining the impact of the global context of politics and the economy in understanding the changes in migration between Ukraine and Hungary.

7.2 A brief note on methodology

This chapter is based on data generated through ethnographic fieldwork on circular migration conducted between November 2010 and June 2011. The project combined quantitative and qualitative methods (in-depth interviews). However, one of the major challenges for this research was finding relevant and reliable statistics and survey data on the migrants in Hungary. Despite several surveys and work on the statistics on migrants from Ukraine to Hungary (OEP 2009, Hárs and Tóth 2010), finding reliable statistics on the number of Ukrainian migrants working in different sectors in Hungary proved to be a major difficulty.[3] Confronted with this problem, researchers of this topic use the existing statistics, like the OEP (National Health Insurance Fund—Orszagos Egeszsegbiztositasi Panztar) data to infer the volume and employment sectors of Ukrainian migrants in Hungary (Hárs and Tóth 2010). According to the Panta Rhei Social Research Group (2010), there are 20,000 Ukrainians working in Hungary. However the breakdown of this figure in terms of naturalization, settlement, and legal status is far from clear. In the absence of statistics some indirect indicators are being used. Self-employment statistics are one such for indirect inferences. As foreigners in Hungary are able to acquire residence permits by establishing a company, research about self-employed third country nationals in Hungary can be relevant to explore the migrancy from Ukraine to Hungary. According to the statistics, 10 per cent of all micro companies with one employee in 2005 were owned by foreigners (GKM—Ministry of Economy and Transport statistics).

Although agriculture is an important sector for immigrant work, it is an area where it is also difficult to get reliable data. Despite the increasing number of undocumented workers in the European Union in general, the lack of statistics for undocumented workers, which will allow us to go beyond equating illegal and migrant work, proves to be a major problem for researchers (Kubatov 2011; Hars and Sik 2008). In the absence of reliable statistics in several areas, the qualitative data with its advantages and disadvantages acquired priority in this research.

This research is based on fieldwork done in Hungary (Budapest and in the border region) and Ukraine (in the cities and villages of Transcarpathia). During the fieldwork, in addition to participant observation and interviews, researchers had the chance of discussing the existing data with stakeholders, policymakers, experts, and migrants in both Ukraine and Hungary. On their numerous trips on trains, buses, *mashrutkas* (a share taxi), and taxis between Budapest, East Hungary, and the different cities and villages in Transcarpathia, the researchers got to know the migrants, and engaged in lengthy conversations with them while waiting together at borders, in bus and train stations, in offices, embassies, and hospitals. The fieldwork included living in the same neighbourhood as migrants, both in their home and destination countries, sharing migrant situations, reconstructing migrants' paths and directionalities in different countries.[4] In fact, all the researchers have been involved with cross-border mobility and migration-related initiatives in Europe, including Hungary and Ukraine.

Furthermore, the language competencies (Russian, Ukrainian, Polish, Hungarian, Italian) of the fieldworkers allowed them to access migrants' own preferred language (which was not necessarily the state language), to express their migratory experiences.

The main fieldwork location was the town of Beregovo/Beregszasz (in addition to its surrounding villages), while most of the expert interviews (i.e., interviews with academics/researchers, journalists, and entrepreneurs who deal with Ukrainian-Hungarian migration at work, either in theory or practice) were conducted in Uzhgorod (and some in Beregszasz). These interviews were supported with some additional interviews conducted in Solotvyno/Aknaszlatina and the Chop/Zahony border crossing, and in the cars and buses travelling from Beregszasz to Budapest or Nyiregyhaza (through Luzhanka/Beregsurany border crossing). In Hungary, the interviews were conducted in Budapest. Moreover, one of the fieldworkers is herself a circular migrant (working in Ukraine and studying in Budapest), and her experiences and contacts provided an excellent entry point to the fieldwork.

7.3 Ukraine-Hungary border: changing border regimes and the plethora of visas, permits, and cross-border mobility procedures

7.3.1 *The regulation of the Ukraine-Hungary border and the Hungarian minority in Ukraine*

The Ukraine-Hungary borderland has been subject to a series of changing laws and border crossing procedures that aim to regulate cross-border mobility. To understand the complexities and constant alterations in the procedures of cross-border mobility, it is essential to have an overview of the laws and regulations, some of the trends in circular migration, and to highlight the legal and illegal employment opportunities. As the regulation of this border is closely related to the Hungarian minority in the neighbouring countries, with Hungary's accession to the EU and inclusion into the Schengen Area, the procedures for circular migrants from Ukraine have to be examined in the broader context of Hungary-EU relations and Hungarian diaspora politics. Thus, since 2003, the laws and procedures initiated to regulate the border have been entangled with EU policies to control the Schengen border, EU policies of enlargement, Hungary's candidacy, and later Hungary's membership to EU on the one hand, and with Hungarian national politics *vis-à-vis* Hungarian minorities in neighbouring countries on the other. In fact, the repeated changes in broader regimes and the plethora of visas, permits, and cross-border procedures take the character of a duet between the EU and the Hungarian state once we situate these changes in the entangled dynamics of EU enlargement and pressures on Hungary and Hungarian diaspora politics. Thus, the series of modifications in laws and regulations on border crossings between Ukraine and Hungary had been indexed to different domestic, international, and EU concerns, agendas, and politics. These ever-changing border regulation laws are good indicators of the tensions between diaspora politics and migration policies of Hungary that are strongly shaped by EU concerns of controlling and securitizing the Schengen borders.

7.3.2 *Cross-border mobility regulation from the Soviet period until 2003—simplified procedures*

Simplified procedures for crossing the border existed for the inhabitants of the border zone in the Soviet period, but it was only in the early 1990s that they were used intensively. The Transcarpathian border has been porous since 1961. There was a lively traffic of goods and people in this border zone, and most of the cross-border mobility was circular. There were cross-border commuters crossing the border daily, or even for shorter periods, for trade purposes. There were also seasonal migrants working in agriculture on the Hungarian side of the border. Cross-border work in agriculture without any work permits has been a practice for decades, until 2003. Until then, there were simplified procedures for border crossings. This possibility ended in 2003 with the prospect of Hungary joining the EU in 2004, but the mobility and circularity did not stop (Çağlar and Gereöffy 2008; Osztapec 2010). A simplified form of documentation was used, and it was attached to the identity card. Obtaining this document required much less financial contribution for Transcarpathian residents, and the document was issued within a shorter time for them. This document enabled limited access to the surrounding border zone, allowing Transcarpathian residents to stay ten days.

However, most importantly, people qualified to possess this simplified border crossing document were also permitted to apply for and acquire an international passport, which acted as a valid travelling document to all parts of Hungary for the duration of a month.

7.4 Cross-border mobility under the shadow of Hungary's EU accession

Hungary's EU accession and the negotiations during Hungary's candidacy loom large in the changes of the legal provisions of border crossing between Ukraine and Hungary. Visas to Hungary for Ukrainian citizens were established in 2003, owing to Hungary's further integration into EU structures. As in Poland, they were free of charge and relatively easy to obtain. With the conventions which came into force on 1 November 2003 between Ukraine and Hungary, Hungary and Serbia, and Hungary and Montenegro, the ethnic Hungarians living in Transcarpathia and in Vojvodina were required to apply for a visa when crossing Hungary's borders. It was referred to as the 'Polish model'. As a result, any Ukrainian citizen could obtain a visa free of charge, in exchange for Hungarian citizens entering Ukraine without any visa requirements. The Hungarian uniform Schengen visas issued by Hungarian embassies and the residence permits issued by Hungarian authorities applied to the entire Schengen Area.

However, some simplifying procedures existed for the Hungarian minority (for example, letters of recommendation from the cultural institutions accepted by the Hungarian consulate) so that they would have easier access to visas to go to Hungary. From 2008 onwards, because of Hungary becoming part of the Schengen Area, the procedure became complicated and fees were introduced (€35–50). However, Hungary was the first neighbouring country to sign an agreement addressing local border traffic (2007–8) through Ukraine.

Hungary joined the European Union on 1 May 2004, and the visa requirements introduced in 2003 were a prerequisite for membership to the EU.

7.5 The 'national' visa

The restrictions to cross-border mobility between Ukraine and Hungary by the introduction of visas in 2003 under EU pressures were modified for the Hungarian minority by Hungary's introduction of a 'national' visa in January 2006. This document entitled Hungarian nationals (in addition to the special travel allowances for the period of five years) to live within the borders of Hungary over those five years with intervals. The visa restricts its holder from travelling abroad into any other EU country (later this condition was amended). However, in order to acquire this visa, one had to produce documents which were very difficult to obtain, such as proving close family connections. Most importantly, the holder of this visa was not allowed to work in Hungary.

This type of visa was supposed to be an alternative form of travel for those living in Vojvodina and Transcarpathia who possessed Hungarian identity cards. The acquisition of this visa was almost impossible, and it was very rare for any applicant to be successful in their attempt.

However, when Hungary became a full member of the Schengen Area (at the very end of 2007), these options for the Hungarian minority changed significantly. Up to that stage, citizens of Ukraine and Serbia had the possibility of obtaining a visa to enter Hungary free of charge. From this point onwards, the citizens of both countries (ethnic Hungarian or not) were required to pay €35 in visa charges.[5] This was an important change, as visas were issued free of charge until then. Having joined the Schengen zone, Hungarian authorities obliged tourist visa applicants to obtain documents that could only be obtained from Hungary, for which the paper work could take up to five days and cost 25,000 Hungarian Forints (approximately €95).

7.6 Local border traffic agreement

On 18 September 2007, an agreement was signed regarding local border traffic. According to this agreement, people dwelling on Ukrainian soil, including nearly 90 per cent of the Transcarpathian Hungarians, were allowed to enter Hungary without significant administrative difficulties. These citizens were permitted to cross the border and go as far as a designated border strip of 35 to 50 kilometres. This special type of document was issued with a charge of €20, and what was essentially an equivalent of a visa seal was placed in the holder's passport. With this document, Ukrainian citizens of Hungarian nationality could enter Hungary without the so-called border-crossing stamps, but they were expected to live in a particular area of Ukraine, and were not permitted to go beyond certain Hungarian territories (i.e., the surrounding area of Nyíregyháza).

Another simplifying procedure for Transcarpathians of Hungarian ethnic origin is the institution of a liability statement, introduced by The Hungarian Foreign Ministry in 2008. It is a document in which an organization assumes responsibility for all activities of travellers in the Schengen Area (including all responsibility for illegal acts). Similarly, Hungarian ethnic applicants are entitled to visa fee refunds, which could be exercised through either body. This fee is financed by the Hungarian state; thus once again the Hungarian state gives support to the Hungarian minority in Ukraine. In comparison with the restricted travelling document, this obtained visa attached with a liability document allows its holders to stay in Hungary and in other Schengen Area states over the course of ninety days.

Here we see the significance of the Hungarian card, since it is the prerequisite for both the visa fee refunds and for the liability statement. Because of its benefits, a number of Ukrainians have also handed in their application for this identity card so that they can travel free of charge in the Schengen Area. The Hungarian card allows the holder neither to work nor access a residence permit, but it entitles the holder to insurance.

7.7 Venues for multidirectional migratory flows from Ukraine

7.7.1 Amendment of Hungarian citizenship

Another facilitator for the cross-border mobility of Hungarian minority from neighbouring countries proved to be the introduction of changes in Hungarian citizenship law.[6] The Amendment Act of Hungarian Citizenship was adopted by the Hungarian National Assembly on 26 May 2010; this simplified the procedures for gaining citizenship. The amendment states that to become a citizen of Hungary one does not need to be resident in Hungary or pass a citizenship test. It is perfectly sufficient to speak the language, and applicants are not required to provide a registered address or prove income in Hungary. This Amendment opened the way for mobility of the Hungarian minority living in neighbouring non-EU countries to the EU. On the basis of the Amendment, for example, the Hungarian minority from Ukraine can work in any member state without a work permit.

7.7.2 Changes in Hungarian citizenship

The most recent changes in Hungarian citizenship introduced an important layer of opportunities for circular migration to Hungary for the Hungarian minority in neighbouring countries, and most importantly to EU member states. According to the new law on citizenship, ethnic Hungarians in neighbouring countries can obtain a version of citizenship without voting rights and social benefits. These changes resemble the proliferation of membership regimes practised by several states (Mexico, Turkey, and India, to name a few) in order to tie their diasporas to homeland economies, and partly to domestic politics (Çağlar and Gereöffy 2008). The new Law on Citizenship in Hungary (2011) has already resulted in legal uncertainties and concerns for the neighbouring states, including the Ukrainian state. However, the acquisition of citizenship for Hungarians abroad seems to be a complicated and expensive procedure. The new law enables the Hungarian minority in Ukraine to trespass across the Schengen border between Hungary and Ukraine.

Both the Amendment Act of Hungarian citizenship and the new Law of Hungarian citizenship not only provide opportunities for cross-border mobility and access to labour markets for the Hungarian minority in neighbouring states, but also pave the way to break the bidirectionality of migratory flows from Ukraine. In that sense they are crucial legal and political interventions to the nature of migration flows. They facilitate multidirectional flows breaking the bidirectionality of most circular migration between Ukraine and Hungary.

7.8 Circular migration between Ukraine and Hungary

In the context of changing border regulations, the migratory flows between Ukraine and Hungary took varying forms. Even the pathways of the back and forth cross-border movements changed in light of the new regulatory constraints, but also in the context of new opportunities that came along, especially after the amendment and the changes in Hungarian citizenship. However, in addition to the changing border regulations and the legal provisions, which shaped the migration paths between Ukraine and Hungary, it was the social and the economic context of both countries and the economic crisis of 2008 which had a profound impact on the nature of migratory flows between the two countries, and in the region in general. Although different patterns of migration are always closely connected to the aspirations of individuals and households, it is the broader structural factors which shape the economic, social, and legal opportunities that influence the volume and the varying pathways of migration.

The European Commission defines circular migration as a form of migration that is managed in such a way that there is legal mobility back and forth between two countries (COM 2007; Baltes-Löhr et al. 2011). It involves repeated cross-border movements between two countries. In this definition, circular migration is closely related to temporary migration. Though it is different from temporary migration, temporariness is crucial to circular migration. The stay in circular migration is for a limited time. Furthermore, the mobility is bidirectional, meaning the movement is between the countries of origin and destination.

There are two basic types of circular migration: spontaneous and managed circular migration. Border zones are usually the areas where we find spontaneous circular migration. In most of the cases, these cross-border movements are not regulated through legal provisions. The recent interest in and enthusiasm about circular migration as a policy tool is, however, related to managed circular migration. In this kind of circular migration, cross-border mobility for a selected group of people is regulated through legal provisions that promote circularity, and ensure that the migration is temporary and repetitive. The legal provisions range from simplified procedures to bilateral agreements and dual citizenship.

However, as our case material illustrates, the distinctions between temporary, circular, and even permanent and return migration are far from being clear. As it has been repeatedly underlined by the critiques of circular migration (Glick Schiller and Faist 2010; de Haas 2010; Baltes-Löhr et al. 2011), they are fluid.

Our case material indicates that there are three dimensions that are important in exploring the nature of circular migration:

1) The legal or irregular nature of the movement, which is closely related to the regulated or unregulated character of the phenomenon.
2) The level of skills and education of the people involved (semi-/low-skilled versus high-skilled).
3) The length of time of each stay and return (short-term, medium-term, and long-term circularity).

On the bases of legal conditions, types of work, frequency of travelling, and the duration of the migrants' stay, our data indicate six main types of legal circular migration between Ukraine and Hungary.

7.8.1 Seasonal legal labour migration (the country of origin is used as a base)—spontaneous or regulated

In this form of circular migration, the migrants use Ukraine as their base: they travel to Hungary for seasonal work and back to Ukraine. It usually applies to agriculture, with its specific recruitment of a foreign seasonal workforce. The rules and procedures towards other EU member countries' citizens are the same as for Hungarian citizens, and simplified forms of employment (casual labour, agricultural seasonal work, tourist seasonal work) may be used. Third country nationals may be employed only in seasonal agricultural employment with the exception of those immigrated or settled in Hungary, who have a resident status. Any third country citizen may apply for seasonal work within a time limit of sixty days a year. Permits are issued by the job centre. A work permit is necessary, but no proof of the non-availability of members of the Hungarian/EU workforce (Kubatov 2011) is required (see Çağlar and Gereöffy 2008).

7.8.2 Circular legal labour migration (migrants based in the country of origin)—spontaneous

Ukrainians with Hungarian citizenship may travel and work in Hungary, Ukraine, and also in other EU member states. In most cases, skilled workers as well as businessmen and retired people are involved in such kinds of circular migration. However, as the case of a retired woman from Eger/Mukachevo illustrates, the boundaries between temporary, permanent, return, and circular migration are difficult to determine.

> After my husband died I decided to sell our house in Eger [Hungary] and buy a cheaper one in my home town Mukachevo. But you know, I'm still an active person even if I don't drive trucks any more, but I could work in Germany as a Hungarian in care work. (Ukranian female, 66)

This woman migrated from Ukraine to Hungary long ago, and her migration seemed to be a permanent one until her husband died. She has worked in Hungary, and retired from her job in Hungary. After her husband's death, she decided to go back to her hometown in Ukraine and settle there, because of the lower cost of living. However, she plans to embark on a circular migration between Ukraine and Germany in care work.

The case of a state employee in Ukraine, who is from the Hungarian minority, illustrates that what seemed to be a temporary migration could turn into a circular one, depending on legal opportunities in the context of economic hardship.

> I went to a car mechanic school in Debrecen [Hungary] for two years. Then I came back to Ukraine and was [legally] employed. My salary is incredibly low. Only with some extra irregular work I'm able to survive...I'm applying for Hungarian citizenship to work in the EU, according to the economic situation, in Hungary or other countries. (Ukranian male, 24)

7.8.3 Circular legal labour migration (country of destination becomes the base for circularity)—spontaneous

This refers to Ukrainians with low- or mid-level skills who are long-term migrants in Hungary, and have difficulties finding a job in this economic downturn, or are under-employed by having temporary or unstable jobs below their skills. These people start to circulate between the country they have settled in and to their countries of origin once they face economic hardship or stagnation. After a long-term stay in the country they have immigrated to, they go back to their country of origin to carry out household repair work, do temporary farm work, or other low-skilled labour. In all such cases the line between temporary (or permanent) migration and circular migration becomes blurred.

Although these migrants from Ukraine are settled (and legal) in Hungary, they show readiness to go to any place where there is employment and the possibility of a better income. Among those interviewed, some migrants from

Ukraine (who had the legal possibility) went to Germany, Russia, Slovakia and the Czech Republic.[7]

> I have been working since 1993 in Hungary. First with a tourist visa; every two months we went back home [Ukraine]. In the crisis of 1997, I stayed in Ukraine. We went to Siberia to work there for half a year with a contract, but were not paid well. Then we worked again in Hungary near Budapest. We decided to establish a company in 2008 in Hungary because this was the best and the only way to work legally. (Ukranian male, 40)

This construction worker's story indicates a kind of circular migration of mostly low-skilled long-term migrants.

7.8.4 Circular semi-legal labour migration (migrants use the country of origin as a basis for circularity)

In this form of migration, the migrant enters the country of destination on a legal basis, but work is informal, and it is without a work permit. Irregular and informal work in construction, domestic work, tourism, and catering are the sectors in which these kinds of circular migrants are employed. This type of migration may or may not follow a seasonal pattern, and is technically legal depending on the stay of the migrant. For example, the migrant enters with a Local Border Traffic Permit or, before Schengen, on a tourist visa, but her/his employment is irregular as her/his visa does not provide the right to work.

The people involved are semi-skilled or highly skilled people who are unemployed and/or cannot make ends meet in the country of origin, and for various reasons (e.g., family reasons) do not wish to migrate for longer periods. They take advantage of established social and ethnic networks, and engage in circular migration. Women migrants work in the care and cleaning sector, while men do construction and farm work. The following case of a twenty-three-year-old employee in Beregszasz is one variation of such a circular semi-legal labour migration. This group is very prone to conditions like the economic crisis.

> When I was a student I went to Budapest twice to work in the summer at the market. I had a tourist visa. It was no problem to get a job. They even promised to hire me. But I had no time any more. The third summer, by chance, I got the possibility to work seasonally in cucumber harvesting in Germany legally as a student. It was hard physical work but I earned a lot. (Ukranian male, 23)

There are also those who cross the border with a Local Border Traffic permit. The number of Ukrainians working in this way is decreasing, because of more controls and less availability of work. In addition, more unemployed Hungarians are willing to work. Moreover, in western Hungary the wages are higher, and for those who enter on such permits, this permit is valid only up to Nyiregyháza (a town 70 kilometres away from the border). This young state service and construction worker recounts:

> I was picking cucumbers in a village near the Austrian border. They said that you earn more in western Hungary. I even had permission to work... they tried to cheat me so I came back earlier than I had planned. Later I used to bring some stuff across the border in Vilok... Now I have no passport, so I'm not planning to go anywhere. (Ukranian male, 30)

7.8.5 Circular semi-legal labour migration (using the country of destination as the basis for circularity)

People involved in this kind of migration have low, medium or a high level of skills, they are long-term migrants in the destination country, but are having difficulties finding a job (e.g., owing to the current economic crisis) or are under-employed (have temporary or unstable jobs). These people are engaged in circular migration between the two countries to buy goods, usually from Hungary, and sell them in Ukraine. They engage in an informal trade without a licence.

Another form of such circular migration is seen among the students from Ukraine to Hungary. Their stay in Hungary is legal, and they work irregularly in offices or offer different services, as a former student who lives between Budapest and Kiev outlines:

> I studied in Budapest and worked in different offices... My experience was in a call centre, but at other work places as well we had to do all our legal work ourselves. They don't want to do anything regarding our insurance, tax or status. They prefer to pay a bit extra. So I often worked semi-legally. (Ukranian female, 24)

7.8.6 Irregular circular migration

In Ukraine to Hungary cross-border mobility, there are two basic types of irregular circular migration. In the first version, the migrant enters with legal documents, works legally, but then extends the period of legal stay (known as an overstayer). The second version is that the worker continues without the necessary documents, and finds employment in the informal labour market in seasonal or other temporary jobs (in agriculture, catering, tourism, cleaning, domestic care, and in other sectors), where native workers also often work informally. A young construction worker from Beregszász explains:

> In the early 1990s I was employed as a construction worker. Then I earned more by being self-employed and often we worked undeclared. Later I married in Ukraine and we now have two children. When our first child was born I still

worked as a tractor driver legally employed in eastern Hungary. In 2007, I decided to come back and now I work in Ukraine mostly undeclared in construction. (Ukranian male, 32)

This can also be the case with refugees who stay and work in Ukraine and try to enter Hungary to apply for asylum, but are not accepted by the Hungarian border guards, and are handed back to Ukrainian authorities. A Somali refugee in Budapest explains his plight:

> I lived in a town in Ukraine and tried to get to Hungary. Twice the Hungarian border guards caught me. They promised to bring me to an interview for refugees. But instead they brought me back. The Ukrainian border guards were angry. They had beaten me and arrested me. I was in the border guard prison in Chop twice for several months. Later I tried again to organize my way to Hungary. On the third time, I managed to arrive in Budapest. But then, I was arrested again. Finally, with the help of a lawyer of the Helsinki Committee I could apply for asylum. Now I am a recognized refugee in Hungary. (Somali male, 28)

7.9 Changing volume and composition of migratory flows from Ukraine to Hungary

It is noteworthy that the volume of migration flows from Ukraine to Hungary decreased in 2009. This decrease is even more significant once we consider that the Local Border Traffic, which was put into effect in 2007, and the Liability Statement Regulation, which would have encouraged and eased the migratory flows of the Hungarian minority from Ukraine to Hungary, was introduced in 2008.

Changes in migration from Ukraine are best illustrated by quoting some of the relevant statistics of the Office of Immigration and Nationality (OIN 2005-9: http://www.bmbah.hu/statisztikak_ENG_42.xls). The statistical data on 2008 and 2009 illustrate this decrease clearly (see Tables 7.1–7.6).

The decrease results from two factors: opening the border for Romanians and closing for it for Serbs, Montenegrins, and Ukrainians.

Number of applicants under Act l of 2007 (EEA) l.

Decrease for: Serbian, Ukrainian, Russian

Increase for: Romanian, German, Slovenian

Number of applicants under Act l. of 2007 (EEA) ll.

Numbers slightly rise during this period for all nationalities, except Serbians and Ukrainians.

The number of Ukrainians with a permanent residence permit decreased from 4,301 in 2008 to 3,920 in 2009. The number of Ukrainian applications for permanent residence cards decreased from 547 to 390 from 2008 to 2009,

Table 7.1 Number of foreigners holding a permanent residence permit

Nationality	2008	2009
Ukrainian	4,301	3,920
Total	28,52	23,475

Source: Office of Immigration and Nationality, OIN 2005–9: http://www.bmbah.hu/statisztikak_ENG_42.xls last accessed 30 August 2012.

Table 7.2 Number of foreigners holding a short-term residence permit

Nationality	2008	2009
Ukrainian	1,749	7,279
Total	15,305	33,682

Source: Office of Immigration and Nationality, OIN 2005–9: http://www.bmbah.hu/statisztikak_ENG_42.xls last accessed 30 August 2012.

Table 7.3 Number of applicants for permanent residence card

Nationality	2008	2009
Ukrainian	547	390
Total	4,364	4,656

Source: Office of Immigration and Nationality, OIN 2005–9: http://www.bmbah.hu/statisztikak_ENG_42.xls last accessed 30 August 2012.

Table 7.4 Third-country national family member of EEA citizen

Nationality	2008	2009
Ukrainian	35	19
Total	230	166

Source: Office of Immigration and Nationality, OIN 2005–9: http://www.bmbah.hu/statisztikak_ENG_42.xls last accessed 30 August 2012.

Table 7.5 Third-country national family member of Hungarian citizen

Nationality	2008	2009
Ukrainian	1,078	555
Total	3,379	2,110

Source: Office of Immigration and Nationality, OIN 2005–9: http://www.bmbah.hu/statisztikak_ENG_42.xls last accessed 30 August 2012.

Table 7.6 Cumulative number of applications for residence under Act II of 2007

Nationality	2008	2009
Ukrainian	8,399	5,524
Total	34,670	32,254

Source: Office of Immigration and Nationality, OIN 2005–9: http://www.bmbah.hu/statisztikak_ENG_42.xls last accessed 30 August 2012.

though this has increased for Romanians, Germans and Slovenians. The cumulative number of Ukrainian applications for residence dropped from 8,399 to 5,524 (this figure increased for the citizens of other countries) during the two year timeframe mentioned above.

These statistics draw attention to the fact that though changing border regulations shaped the migratory paths between Ukraine and Hungary, the changes in procedures and laws for cross-border mobility alone fail to explain the decrease in migration flows from Ukraine to Hungary. As the narratives of migrants in the former section indicate clearly, the social and economic context of both countries, and the broader economic and political context, had a profound impact on migratory flows from Ukraine to Hungary. The pathways and the duration of migration are closely related to the economic opportunities available at different localities.

If we locate economic reasons at the heart of circular migration, then we need to situate these mobility pathways within the economic and social context of this region in relation to the broader forces active on this region. We see that the migratory paths and people's decisions to migrate and embark on or move out of a circulatory pattern of migration are strongly shaped by the work and mobility opportunities available to them in their places of origin, destination, and elsewhere.

The Ukrainian and, in general, the post-Soviet economy started to decline in the years 1991 and 1992, owing to the political chaos that followed the collapse of the USSR. In the Soviet period, none of the republics were economically independent, which gave rise to shortages in goods and in some cases in labour. The early years of independence in Ukraine came with an economic crisis. In 1992, local cross-border movement was introduced between Ukraine and Hungary, as travel restrictions in Ukraine were abolished. It was possible to go up to Nyiregyhaza without a passport. This was the time when the shuttle trade boom between the two countries started, and the market in Nyiregyhaza became a popular destination for people from the Beregivskyi region. A former construction worker from Beregszász who is currently unemployed explains:

> I had a car, and those days you didn't need a visa or passport... I don't remember how far from the border you could go, but it was enough to go to the market in Nyiregyhaza. I used to go there almost every day in the morning and around lunch time I was back home. We were earning good money, those were very good days. (Unemployed Ukranian, 55)

It was also in the years 1992 and 1993 when people started going to Hungary to work illegally (to Budapest or to western Hungary). For most of them it was the first contact they had with Hungary, as a former miner tells us:

I can't remember when it was when I first went to work to Hungary, 1992 or 1993. A friend of mine had some relatives there, he went first and I joined him later. We worked at the construction site near Budapest for about two months, then we came back for some time and went back again...I remember, when I was going there for the first time on a train, a Hungarian ticket inspector took my ticket and then claimed I had no ticket and he wanted me to pay the fine. I told him it was my first time in Hungary and I didn't know the rules. Fortunately, some old lady confirmed that she saw me giving the ticket to the previous inspector...I was still employed in the mine in Solotvyno, but we earned almost nothing and there were big delays in receiving the salaries, we didn't earn much in Hungary, but it was better than here anyway. (Ukranian male, 41)

Migration from Transcarpathia to Hungary continued through the entire 1990s. Men mostly worked on construction sites and in industry, while women worked in light industry, like sewing. There were a few women from Transcarpathia in domestic work, but mostly this sector was dominated by women from Transylvania.

Introducing visas hardly changed the dynamics of mobility on the Ukrainian-Hungarian borders (Mitraeva et al. 2010; Mitraeva 2011), as visas were free of charge and relatively easy to obtain. This meant that people would continue to go to work and shuttle trading, carrying tourist visas. Moreover, there were some programmes for Transcarpathian Hungarian students to study in Hungary. What potentially might have discouraged Transcarpathians from going to Hungary was the introduction of fees in January 2008, and the new restrictions on amounts of cigarettes on entire borders of the EU.

A year after Hungary joined Schengen, both Hungary and Ukraine were struck with economical crises. According to many sources within European countries, Ukraine was the country which experienced the worst crisis and Hungary, together with Latvia, experienced the strongest crisis among EU countries. This had a dual impact on Ukraine and Transcarpathia. The level of unemployment increased, and at the same time wages decreased. These conditions gave people more incentive to leave the country. However, as Hungary, the common destination of circular migrants, faced similar problems to those in Ukraine, the destination country for Ukrainians changed.

The Ukrainian economy and labour market are characterized by low wages and often uncertain conditions. In 2008, the employment rate was as high as 53.5 per cent (60 per cent among men and 48.3 per cent among women). In October 2010, the average income in Transcarpathia was 2,353 UAH (€203), and the minimum wage was 907 UAH (€78). The monthly average was 418 UAH (€36), and an average wage per hour was 9.33 UAH (80 cents). The decline of the Ukrainian economy in 2009 was over 10 per cent, and production in Transcarpathia dropped by 50 per cent within a year. According to official figures, unemployment in 2009 was 9.9 per cent (6.4 per cent in 2008), although the actual numbers were even higher, as not all the unemployed were registered, landowners were not entitled to benefits, and migrants were not included in the statistics. Moreover, those who were employed often did not receive their wages on time, or were forced to take holidays or have their working hours decreased.

In Transcarpathia, the dominant industry is agriculture. The once active manufacturing sector included metal processing and engineering, the food industry, light industry, construction industry, mining, and energy. Despite the foreign investment in Transcarpathia, the construction sector diminished by 30 per cent in 2009 compared with 2008. In 2010, there were more bankruptcies and closures (50 per cent in all industries and 38 per cent in construction) than in 2009 (see http://www.karpatinfo.net/article116484.html). The crisis abroad and the resulting decline in the job market meant that Ukrainian construction workers stayed in the region (see http://karpatinfo.net/gazdasag/2010/09/19/csak-latszat-krizis-enyhulese-az-epitoiparban) rather than migrate.

In fact, the situation in Hungary during the economic downturn was not much different. The official employment rate in Hungary is around 57 per cent, mostly because of the relatively high performance of the irregular economy. Despite the government's efforts to increase the employment rate in recent years (Wetzel 2009), there has not been much success in this regard.

Economic crises in both countries resulted with the paradoxical 'small scale local construction boom' in 2009 and 2010 in Ukraine. People who worked in Portugal and Italy stayed there, as the labour market in those countries had not changed as dramatically as it did in Hungary. It was also too far to go back home or circulate sustainably. However, the situation for those who worked in Hungary was different, as they came back to Ukraine, and started to build and renovate their houses with their savings.

The lack of policies of integration of migrants in Hungary, and the general unwelcoming social context for the migrants, establish the context for the decreasing number of migrants from Ukraine to Hungary. With the deepening of the crisis and the increasingly difficult procedures to obtain visas after 2008, those circular migrants who used Ukraine as a basis for circular migration stayed in Ukraine. The high level of xenophobic attitudes in Hungarian society had also contributed to these dynamics (TARKI 2009). Despite the location of Hungarian minorities within official discourses and state policies, Hungarian minorities from neighbouring countries who come to work in Hungary are seen as foreigners who accept to work for lower wages and worse conditions.

7.10 Concluding remarks

Temporality is at the heart of circular migration, and its distinction from other forms of migration patterns. It is noteworthy that exactly these distinctions are blurred in the case of Ukraine-Hungary migration flows, especially after the crisis. Our case material on circular migration underlines the difficulties of operating with clear-cut distinctions as circular, temporary, permanent or return migration.[8] Furthermore, not only the boundaries between different forms of migration patterns are ambiguous and fluid in Ukraine-Hungary migration. Our fieldwork material indicates that in the case of migration from Ukraine to Hungary, the distinction between spontaneous and regulated circular migration is also blurred.

It is well known that in addition to the motives and aspirations of individuals, various external and structural factors play a crucial role in shaping migration pathways. Thus the blurring of different forms of migration from Ukraine to Hungary is the product of such broader conditions. The distinctions between circular, temporary, and permanent migration from Ukraine to Hungary, but also the dividing line between spontaneous and regulated circular migration, become blurred owing to a) unstable economic conditions both in Hungary and Ukraine; b) the repeated changes in legal provisions about the residence and work permits and cross-border mobility opportunities within the EU; c) the diaspora politics of the Hungarian state.

The duet between Hungarian politics on Hungarians abroad (especially those living in the neighbouring countries), and on migration and border management in line with the EU requirements, regulations, and pressures had an important impact on blurring the distinction between the two types of circular migration, namely, between spontaneous and regulated circular migration between Ukraine and Hungary.

The circular migration between Ukraine and Hungary has not been a formally administered circular migration but rather a spontaneous one, in its all forms. Other than the regulation of seasonal migration, especially on the border region, there are no regulated programmes to promote circular migration between Hungary and Ukraine. On the other hand, the Hungarian state's diaspora politics and its persistent efforts to trespass the closure of Schengen borders between Hungary and Ukraine, and the introduction of legal provisions to facilitate cross-border mobility in neighbouring countries function as a systematic and programmatic attempt to shape and manage circular migration between Ukraine and Hungary.

A closer look at the cases of circular migration from Ukraine to Hungary not only draw our attention to the blurred boundaries between different types and forms of (circular) migration but also to some changes in the bidirectionality of cross-border movements, which are depicted as the defining characteristics of circular migration in policy formulations. As seen from the aforementioned examples, some migratory movements that are thought to be permanent or temporary start following a circular pattern, or those which are thought to be a return migration start following a circular pattern (involving other countries of destination).

Three factors seem to lie behind these dynamics, which blur the distinctions between migratory forms: the economic crisis of 2008; the implementation of the Schengen border; and the complex dynamics of legal provisions, particularly targeting the Hungarian minority in Ukraine. As a result of the economic crisis which severely hit both countries, circular migrants from Ukraine changed the direction of their migration pathway to different countries, following a multidirectional migratory pattern rather than a bidirectional circular pattern. Thus the economic crisis broke the bidirectional nature of circular migration between Ukraine and Hungary.

Moreover, the legal provisions provided to the Hungarian minority open up the possibility of migrating to different countries within the EU. The diaspora who used to circulate between Ukraine and Hungary, or migrate to Hungary, appeared to be a permanent feature of migration for a long time. In most cases, both factors interact to give rise to unexpected mobility constellations, as the case of the aforementioned Ukrainian-origin woman who was settled in Hungary, and whose migration to Hungary seemed to be a permanent one, illustrates. Confronted with the crisis (with a very low pension in hand), she decides to return to Ukraine, where the living cost for her is much lower than it is in Hungary. However, this is a return in order to embark on a new kind of circular migration between Ukraine and Germany for care work, which is facilitated by her Hungarian citizenship.

Even this simple case raises the question of difficulties in determining the migration forms as temporary, circular, or permanent. In fact, this is one of the major criticisms raised against the concept of circular migration, which has been increasingly valorized as a policy tool since the mid-2000s (Vertovec 2007; Baltes-Löhr et al. 2011). The profound impact of the crisis on circular migration patterns and pathways between Ukraine and Hungary illustrates the importance of structural constraints, and the complex balance of power between regions and states in shaping both migration forms and an individual migrant's decisions regarding different forms of mobility (Glick Schiller and Faist 2010; de Haas 2010). It could also be read as a caution against celebrating a triple-win scheme of circular migration, and the migrants' capacities to overcome these constraints as development actors.

References

Baltes-Löhr, Christel et al. (2011). *Circular and Temporary Migration Empirical Evidence, Current Policy Practice and Future Options in Luxembourg*. Luxembourg: National Contact Point Luxembourg within the European Migration Network [online report], http://www.olai.public.lu/fr/publications/programmes-planactions-campagnes/programme_rem/etude_migration_circulaire_et_temporaire.pdf (accessed 28 July 2012).

Çağlar, Ayşe and Gereöffy, Andrea (2008). 'Ukrainian Migration to Hungary: A Fine Balance between Migration Policies and Diaspora Politics', *Journal of Immigrant & Refugee Studies*, 6(3): 326–43.

COM 390 final (2005a). *Migration and Development: Some Concrete Orientations*. Brussels: Communication from the Commission to the Council, the European Parliament, the European Social and Economic Committee and the Committee of Regions.

COM 669 final (2005b). *Policy Plan on Legal Migration*. Brussels: Communication from the Commission.

COM 248 final (2007). *Communication from the Commission of 16 May 2007 on Circular Migration and Mobility Partnerships between the European Union and Third Countries* [online]. http://eurlex.europa.eu/LexUriServ/LexUriServ.do?uri=COM:2007:0248: FIN:EN:PDF (accessed 28 July 2012).

Glick Schiller, Nina and Thomas F. (2010). *Migration, Development and Transnationalization: A Critical Stance (Critical Interventions)*. New York: Berghahn Books.

de Haas, Hein (2010). 'Migration and Development: A Theoretical Perspective', *International Migration Review*, 44(1), 227–64.

Hárs, Ágnes (1999). 'A munkaerőpiac védelme és a migráció', in Sik Endre és Tóth Judit (szerk.) *Átmenetek*. Budapest: MTA Politikai Tudományok Intézete, 67–74.

Hárs, Ágnes and Tóth, Judit (2010). *Változó Migráció Változó környezet* [Changing Migration—Changing Context]. Budapest: MTA Etnikai-nemzeti Kisebbsegkutato Intezet (Institute for Ethnic and National Minority Studies).

Juhász Judit, et al. (2011). New mobility trends in Europe (A preliminary analysis for further research), Eurofound. http://www.eurofound.europa.eu/areas/populationandsociety/mobility.htm

Kovács, M. and Tóth, J. (2007). 'Kin-State Responsibility and Ethnic Citizenship: The Hungarian Case', in R. Bauböck, B. Perchinig and W. Sievers (eds), *Citizenship Policies in the New Europe*, IMISCOE Research. Amsterdam: Amsterdam University Press, 135–59.

Kristóf, Tamás (1999). 'The Emergence of Migration Control Politics in Hungary', in G. Brochmann and T. Hammar (eds), *Mechanisms of Immigration Control. A Comparative Analysis of European Regulation Policies*. Oxford/New York: Berg, 261–96.

Kubatov, Márton (2011). *A mezőgazdasági foglalkoztatás sajátosságai, ágazati kollektív alku* [The characteristics of agricultural employment, sectorial collective bargaining]. Budapest: Corvinus University.

Malynovska, Olena (2006a). *Caught Between East and West, Ukraine Struggles with Its Migration Policy*. National Institute for International Security Problems, Kyiv [online report]. http://www.migrationinformation.org/USFocus/display.cfm?ID=365 (accessed 28 July 2012).

Malynovska, Olena (2006b). *Trans-border Migration of the Population of the Ukrainian Western Frontier Areas in the Context EU Enlargement*. Centre for International Relations Reports & Analyses, 6/06. Warsaw.

Osztapec, Yuri et al. (2010). *Transcarpathia 1919–2009: History, Politics and Culture*. Budapest: Argumentum, Institute of Ethnic and National Minority Research Institute.

State Statistics Committee of Ukraine (2009). ЗОВНІШНЯ ТРУДОВА МІГРАЦІЯ НАСЕЛЕННЯ УКРАЇНИ: ОСНОВНІ РЕЗУЛЬТАТИ ВИБІРКОВОГО ОБСТЕЖЕННЯ [External labour migration of the Ukrainian population].

Vertovec, Steven (2007). *Circular Migration: The Way Forward in Global Policy'*, Working Paper 4, University of Oxford: International Migration Institute [online report]. http://www.imi.ox.ac.uk/pdfs/imi-working-papers/wp4-circular-migration-policy.pdf (accessed 28 July 2012).

Wichramasekara, Piyasiri (2011). 'Circular Migration: A Triple Win or a Dead End?' *GURN Discussion Paper*, no.15, Geneva: International Labour Office [online report]. http://www.gurn.info/en/discussion-papers/no15-mar11-circular-migration-a-triple-win-or-a-dead-end (last accessed 5 September 2012).

World Bank, The (2006). *International Labor Migration: Eastern Europe and the Former Soviet Union*. Washington, DC: The World Bank, Europe and Central Asia Region.

Notes

1. This chapter is based on the research and fieldwork conducted by Tibor Sillo, Ignacy Jozwiak Kornélia Hires-László. For a more comprehensive report on the migration patterns between Ukraine and Hungary, see the report Caglar et al. 2011. I thank Tibor Silo, Ignacy Jozwiak, and Kornélia Hires-László for their research. I am also thankful to Alexandra Sindestrean for her careful reading of the chapter.
2. Majority of Ukanian migration is to Russia (48.5 per cent). This is followed by migration to Italy (13.4 per cent), to Czech Republic (12.8 per cent), to Poland (7.4 per cent), to Spain and Portugal (3.9 and 3 per cent respectively), and to other destinations (8.6 per cent) (Malynovska 2010, in Fedyuk 2011: 13).
3. For example, we know much less about Ukrainian women working in Hungary. Since irregular work such as care work rarely appears in statistics, it is difficult to get reliable data on irregular and undocumented migrants.
4. One of the researchers was a transnational migrant: while she was a student in Hungary, she was also based in Ukraine, and was going back and forth all the time
5. Source: www.mfa.gov.hu/kulkepviselet/Beregovo/hu/Konzuliinfo/altalanos_schengeni_taj.htm last accessed 2 September 2012.

6. This Amendment Act in 2010 and the following new Law on Citizenship in 2011 have to be considered within the context of a series of attempts to include Hungarians abroad (especially those living in neighbouring states) in the Hungarian citizenship regime, including the Status Law and the referendum on dual citizenship in 2004, which failed (see Kovacs and Toth 2007).
7. Interestingly, some of those interviewed went to some bigger cities in Ukraine, and they considered this mobility as part of their circular migration, without making much distinction between cross-border and internal circular migration.
8. This problem has been repeatedly flagged by transnational migration scholars (Vertovec 2007; Glick Schiller and Faist 2010; de Haas 2010).

8

Circular Migration Patterns between Ukraine and Poland

Krystyna Iglicka and Katarzyna Gmaj

8.1 Framing migration between Poland and Ukraine

Immigrants from Ukraine had often been perceived as those whose integration into Polish society might be achieved quite naturally owing to a long history of neighbourhood, kinship relations across the borders, as well as geographical, linguistic, and cultural proximity (Iglicka 2001; Koryś 2003; Iglicka 2010; Iglicka and Gmaj 2010). However, contrary to the expectations of experts and politicians at the turn of this century, Poland has not transformed from a country of emigration into a country of immigration. Instead, it has become an area of a vast shuttle and circular mobility, especially for those arriving from the former USSR.

As far as integration challenges are concerned, one should realize that opportunities for integration are quite limited owing to the circular character of the migration, and the main aim of the migrants involved in this type of mobility, which consists mainly of accumulating money and returning home. The irregular status of some migrants is another factor impeding their integration process. We are still unable to tell what the needs of both regular and irregular migrants are, and whether they would be interested in any integration programmes *per se*. Until the late 1990s, the main economic activity undertaken by Ukrainians was trade (Iglicka and Sword 1999). During their short stay in Poland (usually not longer than a week or two), Ukrainians tried to sell their goods directly at local markets or to middlemen. Gradually, thanks to informal contacts established during those short stays in Poland, and thanks to cheap transportation and accommodation, the time of their stays in Poland was extended. As a result, a kind of specialization was observed: some Ukrainians started reselling goods bought in warehouses in Poland in local market-places, while others were involved in trans-border transportation of goods. These activities were predominantly informal (Iglicka 1999). However, most probably as a result of the financial crisis in Russia (1998), the profitability of this form of economic activity decreased. Therefore, Ukrainian immigrants started to work in construction, renovation, or agriculture, and also got involved in the domestic services sector. That meant that the length of their stay in Poland had to become longer than the few weeks they would spend in the country previously (Konieczna 2000; Iglicka 2001a).

Since the beginning of the economic transformation in 1989, the foreign labour market in Poland was characterized by ethnic divisions. Only a small part of the Eastern flow could find employment in the primary labour market. The majority of Ukrainians who found legal jobs were hired in agriculture and forestry, industry, and construction. However, unskilled workers who found illegal employment in the secondary labour market constituted the predominant labour sector (Iglicka 2000).[1] It was observed that Ukrainian migrants evolved into a stable seasonal labour force arriving at the same farms every year (Antoniewski 1997, 2002). More recent research also confirmed that the strategy of short-term employment and shuttle migration is predominant among Ukrainian citizens working in Poland (Bieniecki and Pawlak 2009).

In the case of Central Eastern Europe, seasonality has become a way of life for a large proportion of migrants. This two-way mobility, also called circular migration, is undertaken by migrants who choose the strategy of minimizing their household risks. Since salaries in Ukraine are very low or paid with delay, circular migrants provide their families with predictable and stable money. As far as Ukraine is concerned, in the year 2006, migratory growth to cities and towns was equal to 0.3 people per 1,000 inhabitants, whereas the number of people living in the countryside decreased by 1.7 per 1,000 population owing to intensive external migration. Migrants from rural areas leave because of the lack of employment opportunities, unacceptably low wages, and poor working and living conditions. The labour supply in agriculture is twenty-five times higher than labour demand, in fact; there is no such disparity in any other branch of the economy (Kyzyma 2007).

Since Poland is not an economically attractive destination for immigrants, especially compared with other parts of the EU, it is not perceived as a place suitable for a longer-term stay or settlement. Although its economic success measured by GDP growth rates is indisputable, remuneration levels and living conditions are not encouraging enough to attract immigrants on a larger scale. For a majority of immigrants, it is much more reasonable to earn money in Poland and spend it in Ukraine than to undertake the effort of settling in Poland.[2]

According to a study published in 2008 by the Ukrainian Centre for Social Reform and the Derzhkomstat, the state statistics agency, a number of Ukrainian citizens who crossed the state border at least once in the previous thirty-nine months in search of work amounted to nearly 1,500,000 (in other words, 5.1 per cent of Ukraine's able-bodied adult population). Of these, 7.4 per cent went to Poland (Kaźmierkiewicz et al. 2009: 13). One third of the respondents reported that they crossed the border (with either Poland or Hungary) two to ten times per year, 14.8 per cent travelled monthly, 17.5 per cent two to three times per month, 17.7 per cent once per week, and 8.7 per cent several times per week. In 2003, before the introduction of visas, the purpose of a majority of the trips to Poland and Hungary was to buy or sell goods (57.9 per cent), and 8.7 per cent made trips for the purpose of foreign employment. Immigrants often find employment in the irregular economy, even though they cross the border legally with different types of visas.

A characteristic feature of Poland is 'suspended immigration'. The prognosis made at the very turn of the century—that Poland would smoothly become an immigration country—seems to have been precocious. At the end of the first decade of the twenty-first century, Poland is still 'caught in between sending, receiving and being a place of transit for migrants' (Triandafyllidou and Gropas 2007).

Focusing on western Ukraine, the region of origin for a majority of Ukrainian migrants to Poland, one can say that the border areas demarking Ukraine and Poland have traditionally been porous. The area of free travel established in the 1990s in Central Europe led not only to the development of friendly neighbour relations and cooperation between countries, but was also crucial for the survival of a certain category of Ukrainian citizens—especially the population of border areas, i.e. the regions that had experienced the strongest impact of the economic crisis that followed the transformation in the 1990s. According to a study conducted in three frontier regions (Volyn, Zakarpattya, and Lviv) in 2003, a large majority of Ukrainians (80 per cent) living in these areas had travelled to work either to Poland or Hungary (Malynovska 2006). While the introduction of visas did not significantly change the frequency of travelling to Poland, the population of Ukrainians living in the border areas was most strongly affected by this change.[3] The new visa regime, which brought about administrative and bureaucratic procedures, made mobility complicated from a logistical point of view.

Migrants often adapt to Polish realities, but, as we have mentioned before, a majority of them do not stay in Poland for a longer period or permanently. However, as has already been said, they belong to social networks consisting of both Ukrainians and Poles. A crucial role is played by a 'driver', who is a contact person, and a mediator between a potential employer and seasonal employees. Frequently, he offers complex migration services and transport to/from and within Poland. The other crucial element of the Polish labour market landscape is employment exchange, situated in the areas where there is stable demand for seasonal or occasional employment (Antoniewski 1997, 2002; Adamiec 2008; Bieniecki and Pawlak 2009). It leads to a self-sustaining process of chain migration. A gender division of available jobs is visible as well. Men are offered work in construction and renovation and clearing up gardens, sometimes loading/unloading. Women can take care of ill or elderly people or children, clean or pick fruit and vegetables, or work in the food processing industry. (Adamiec 2008). Remuneration is differentiated, and depends on the duration and kind of job.

Interestingly, there are also foreign domestic workers who, despite having a regular job, operate as work agents in the domestic services industry (Maroukis et al. 2011). Research relating to the demand for the domestic services sector (Golinowska 2004) revealed labour market segmentation by sex and ethnicity. Female immigrants originating mainly from Ukraine (but also from Belarus and the Russian Federation) usually find irregular employment in this sector. According to Golinowska's research (2004), approximately 925,000 of Polish households employed domestic service workers, and of those, 92,500 employed foreigners. The range of jobs undertaken by foreigners—cleaning, taking care of children and elderly or ill people—indicates that they are substitutes for Polish women in their traditional roles. Foreign females are also employed by rural households, where their duties usually include assisting in agricultural work undertaken by household members.

The predominance of Ukrainian females in the domestic services sector is so significant that the label 'Ukrainian woman' has almost become a synonym for a foreign housekeeper in Poland. They are hired not only because they are cheaper but also because they work hard and are ready to accept flexible hours. Women undertaking this kind of employment usually have secondary or vocational education. However, among these migrants one can also find women with a higher education degree. What is common among all these Ukrainian domestic workers is their motivation—to support their family, and especially their children. Thanks to circular mobility they are not separated from their families for a long period, but can spend a part of the year taking care of their household and family members in Ukraine (Slany and Małek 2006).

Ukrainians looking after children and elderly or ill people form a distinct category of female immigrants. Their contacts with employers are very intensive. In some cases they have twenty-four-hour shifts. It is estimated that approximately 15 per cent of Ukrainians working in the segment of domestic services are live-ins. It is observed that this type of work induces social isolation, and sometimes exposes migrants to abuse by their employers (Bojar et al. 2005; Kindler 2006).

8.2 Institutional and legal constraints which favour circular migration

Poland has no official policy on circular migration. In practice, however, owing to a set of actions (stemming from negotiations with the EU during the pre-accession period, and then those related to the Schengen Area), the regulations existing encourage this type of migrants' mobility.

It should be stressed here that EU requirements during the pre-accession period reduced Central and Eastern European countries to the status of EU immigration buffers. Further obligations related to admission into the Schengen Area have contributed to the restrictive character of immigration policies in these countries. Moreover, long-lasting political concerns about the maintenance of national and cultural identity in these countries prioritized the policies towards diasporas living in neighbouring countries and the return of co-ethnics over the economic migration of foreigners (Iglicka 1998; Hut 2002; Sik and Zakarias 2005; Futo 2010).

Only significant worker shortages in certain sectors after EU enlargement in 2004, when Poland started experiencing a huge outflow of its own citizens, forced the Polish government to open its labour market to seasonal workers from the eastern neighbouring countries. These regulations gave workers the right to work in Poland without work permits for three months during a six-month period, in the agricultural sector only. In 2006, the period of a single stay was extended to six months during a year, and the regulation has been expanded to all other sectors (and to citizens of Moldova and Georgia as well). It is this policy that has shaped the form of circularity.

8.3 Description of the types of circular migrants found

Referring to the above framework of migration, we have undertaken an effort to analyse more in depth the nature of circular migration between Poland and Ukraine. We focused on factors stimulating circular movements, and those deterring circularity as well. We believe that such an approach could help to broaden understanding of this phenomenon and its complex conditioning.

8.3.1 Methodology and research design

First interviews took place in Warsaw as early as April 2010. All in all, the fieldwork in Poland spanned a period from the beginning of April to the beginning of September 2010. Immigrants were interviewed in the Warsaw metropolitan area and in villages up to 60 kilometres from Warsaw. Most of the sixteen interviews were individual; however, in some cases respondents were accompanied by other migrants, who were more or less involved in the conversation. Potential interviewees were approached during meetings organized by various NGOs and after Ukrainian church services in Warsaw. It was an opportunity to arrange a proper appointment in a café, a park, an office, or an interviewee's place of residence. Informal contacts with people employing circular migrants were also used. In such situations, migrants were asked by their employer whether they agreed to have their telephone number passed on to the researcher. The same pattern was followed in the case of employment agencies. A snowball methodology was also used. Interviews were conducted mainly in Polish. Only in three cases did migrants just speak Ukrainian, and in one case a mixture of Ukrainian and Czech was used.

There were also eleven interviews conducted with experts working in the following institutions: Business Centre Club, Polish-Ukrainian Chamber of Commerce, Caritas Polska, Nasz Wybór Foundation (immigrants' NGO), Mazovian Province Office, Ministry of Labour and Social Policy, Ministry of the Economy, Ministry of the Interior and Administration, East West Link (employment agency), and FROG (Foundation for Development Beyond Borders—immigrants' NGO). About half of these interviews were individual, and for the rest more than one interviewee was involved.

The fieldwork in Ukraine took place in July 2010. Immigrants were reached in western and central Ukraine (Lviv, Zhitomir, Striy, Drohobych, Ivano-Frankivsk, Ternopil, Rivne, Vinnytsia, Lutsk—fifteen interviews), and experts in Kiev (five interviews). Potential migrant interviewees were approached at bus stations and in parks close to railway stations. When they agreed to talk, an interview was conducted directly afterwards or arranged for later in a public place, like a café or a park. Interviews were conducted in Ukrainian, Polish, or a mixture of both.

The experts interviewed worked for the following institutions: Ministry of Labour and Social Policy, Research Committee on Population Studies and Demographic Education of Sociology Association of Ukraine, International Organization for Migration Office, and the National Institute for International Security. Interviews with experts were arranged in advance, in Poland.

In our study, we considered three factors:

- the level of skills and education of the people involved (semi-/low-skilled versus high-skilled);
- the legal or irregular nature of the movement—and hence the regulated or unregulated character of the phenomenon;
- the time length of each stay and return (short-term, medium-term and long-term circularity).

8.3.2 *The level of skills and education of the people involved*

All migrants interviewed within the fieldwork, both in Ukraine and in Poland, had a secondary or tertiary level of education. The relatively high level of education represented by migrants moving between Poland and Ukraine is a characteristic that distinguishes Poland from Southern European countries dealing with circular migration that involves mainly uneducated or poorly educated people (*Ukrainian External Labour Migration* 2009: 29).

Unfortunately, migrants with secondary and even tertiary education are employed as unskilled manual workers (e.g., men and women employed as farm workers, cleaners, or men employed as unskilled builders) or semi-skilled workers (people working in construction or caring/cleaning jobs in specialised positions). In terms of using their education and skills, the few migrants (entrepreneurs, scientists, doctors, and managers) who have well-established sources of income in Ukraine (permanent employment or their own business) are in a much better situation. In their case, working in Poland is not purely economic, at least for the short term. Of course it brings income, but their real aim is to consolidate their position in Ukraine, and to facilitate access to certain goods and services.

8.4 The legal or irregular nature of the movement

Migrants moving between Poland and Ukraine are very aware of the necessity of having documents that confirm the legal purpose of their visit to Poland. Labour migrants use existing regulations that allow them to cross the Polish border and stay in Poland legally. In these terms, they can be described as circular migrants holding permits that allow them to engage in circular mobility between the two countries.

It is worth mentioning that in the Polish-Ukrainian reality, illegal stay deters circularity to some extent. An extreme situation is observed when, owiing to very different reasons, migrants prolong their stay in Poland without any legal basis. In such cases, falling into illegality stops circular migration, and turns them into illegal residents. It has been reported, though, that illegal migrants who are caught and deported to Ukraine are able to return to Poland quite quickly, with a new passport under a new name. The price for such corruptive procedure is approximately €500.

Although migrants are very careful about keeping their stay in Poland legal, they are not equally mindful of being employed on a regular basis. According to a survey report (*Ukrainian External Labour Migration* 2009: 33), Poland is characterized by the lowest percentage of migrants with duly formalized legal status of labour (around 22 per cent), and by the largest share of persons without any official status of employment (56 per cent of the total number of labour migrants from Ukraine to Poland do not have such a status).

During our research, we have learned that misemploying Polish regulations is a typical pattern. Therefore, migrants work in the shadow economy while staying legally in Poland. It should also be stressed that even those whose employment is registered will undertake unregistered supplementary jobs in order to accumulate more money during their stay in Poland.

8.5 The time length of each stay and return

Considering the length of each stay and return, one should notice that circularity is often a result of the passive attitude of human nature. Immigrants tend to follow well-established patterns created by their networks. The length of their stays depends on changing legal regulations that refer to short-term mobility. As has been mentioned before, Polish regulations encourage this circular migration, and lay the rules for the duration of stays in Poland.

Another factor influencing the duration of migrants' stays in Poland is economic in its nature. The recent economic crisis has forced migrants to economize, in the sense that they are limiting their trips home. They are afraid of losing their jobs, since it is more difficult to find employment than it used to be. Moreover, each trip means not only money spent on the journey but also losing an income.

Therefore, it seems that repeated short stays taking place within less than a year are being gradually replaced by short stays of six months in a year, which follow an annual cycle. This modification is influenced mainly by the change of Polish procedures.[4]

Long-term circular migration that involves stays of a couple of years in each country (origin and destination) is difficult, although not impossible in the Polish-Ukrainian case. It seems that in order to legalize their stay for more than a year, migrants have to invest so much in terms of both money and time spent overcoming bureaucratic procedures that they would rather prolong their stay in Poland instead of being involved in circulation.

8.6 Typology of Ukrainian economic circular migrants circulating between Ukraine and Poland

In relation to the above factors, such as levels of skills and education, legal or irregular nature of movement, and length of each stay, we have constructed a typology of circular migration between Ukraine and Poland (see Table 8.1).

Table 8.1 Types of Ukrainian economic circular migrants circulating between Ukraine and Poland

	Type 1 Females: Domestic Services, Nursing, Cleaning	Type 2 Males: Working in Construction	Type 3 'Individual' Agricultural Seasonal Workers	Type 4 Migrants employed by Agencies Offering Temporary Job	Type 5 Specialists
Legal status	Staying in Poland legally (since 2006, mainly on the basis of the simplified procedures for seasonal workers) but working in the shadow economy	Staying in Poland legally but working in the shadow economy (since 2006, mainly on the basis of the simplified procedures for seasonal workers) or staying legally and working on the basis of a work permit	Staying in Poland legally (since 2006) mainly on the basis of the simplified procedures for seasonal workers) but working in the shadow economy	Staying legally, officially employed on the basis of the simplified procedures for seasonal workers or on the basis of a work permit	Staying and working legally in Poland on the basis of a work permit
Family status, Nuclear family	Married or single (often divorced), most with children in Ukraine	Married or single, with or without children in Ukraine	Married or single, with or without children in Ukraine	Married or single, with or without children in Ukraine	Married or single, with or without children in Ukraine
Country of residence	Ukraine	Ukraine	Ukraine	Ukraine	Ukraine
Working status in Ukraine	Unemployed, pensioners, self-employed or employed on a short-term basis	Unemployed, pensioners	Unemployed, employed, students	Unemployed, students, employed	Permanently employed, business owners
Skill level in Poland	Low-skilled or semi-skilled	Low-skilled, semi-skilled, or highly skilled	Low-skilled	Low-skilled or semi-skilled, or highly skilled	Highly skilled

Source: Own research findings.

8.6.1 *Female circular migrants: domestic services, nursing, cleaning*

All migrants in the domestic care sector who were interviewed both in Ukraine and in Poland had secondary or even tertiary education. Their jobs and professions in Ukraine had nothing to do with household services. In fact, some women engaged in care for the elderly or ill had professional experience as nurses, but their certificates could not be recognized in Poland owing to huge differences and discrepancies in Polish and Ukrainian medical schools' curricula.

Some interviewees pointed out that in their case the flexibility of circular migration was the most optimal option:

> We receive 180-day visas. Sometimes I stay in Poland for a month, sometimes two months. I want to be at home and in Poland. I could not stay in Poland longer. I could not stand it. (Ukrainian female, 60)
>
> My kids need me. I cannot stay in Poland longer. Even when I am here, I make short trips to see them. (Ukrainian female, 31)

Some other interviewees said that they would be interested in prolonging their stays in Poland if they had secure employment with longer-term prospects, or if procedures did not require their return to Ukraine. It is worth noting that in our sample there were some migrants who were offered assistance in finding employment in Italy or Austria by relatives or friends, but they preferred Poland because of its geographical proximity and policies, which enabled them to visit their families more often.

On the basis of the interviews with female migrants, it might be said that a typical circular migrant is a married or divorced middle-aged woman with teenage or adult children. She comes from the underdeveloped regions of western Ukraine. It is important to note that younger women who are breadwinners in their families belong in this category as well. Although the reasons for their choice of circular migration are individual and depend on their life situation, it is possible to indicate certain commonalities. Most of these women are driven to migration by insufficient salaries, or more often by lack of employment possibilities at home. Ukrainian citizens experienced mass-scale redundancies twice in the past generation: firstly, owing to the economic, social and political upheaval that resulted from the break-up of the USSR, and secondly owing to the 2008 financial crisis.

During our interviews, we learnt that women with the longest migratory experience first visited Poland as tradespersons, and agriculture or industry workers, but they decided to move to domestic or caring services since it is much more financially advantageous. Circular migrants describe their career path in Poland:

> I started in an orchard. One man looked at me and noticed that the job was hard and I was small and that I would survive there no longer than a month. He was right. It was hard and I earned little. (Ukrainian female, 46

> I called the driver and I told him: find me another job since I cannot work here any longer. He responded: give me 50 zlotys and I will find you another place. He came. I gave him 50 zlotys and he took me to another place. I met another Ukrainian female there. She showed me everything. It was a lot to remember. There was an old woman without a leg. (Ukrainian female, 51)

As a result of the peculiarity of employment in household services, the relationship that develops between an employee and her employer is very close. In many cases it can lead to abuses on both sides. Maltreatment of female migrants is well described in the literature. In the Polish case it was analysed by Kindler (2006).

Domestic care services tend to be physically and mentally taxing, as caring for children and the elderly often requires that the worker be there 24/7, performing strenuous tasks. Many domestic workers suffer from social isolation, as they are tied to the ones whom they care for, Therefore, as soon as female migrants broaden their social network, some of them decide to move onto cleaning services, where they can earn more and are not exposed to such difficult psychological conditions.

None of the women interviewed in Ukraine were employed in their home country; rather, they described themselves as unemployed. Those interviewed in Poland, who were from a more diverse age group, described themselves as pensioners, unemployed, or even employed in Ukraine (usually meaning self-employed or employed for a short term, although it is extremely difficult and quite exceptional to find a Ukrainian employer who would accept an employee travelling between two countries). Several of these women describe their employment status here:

> There are no jobs for young people, especially for someone my age. (Ukrainian female, 53)

> I am a hairdresser. When I am in Ukraine, my clients come to my house. (Ukrainian female, 51)

> [regarding daughter who replaces her in Ukraine] In Ukraine she works in a grocery. She has a good, understanding employer. She understands that my daughter is in a difficult situation and that she needs money. (Ukrainian female woman, 60)

All of the interviewed women were staying in Poland legally. However, most of them abused Polish regulations owing to a well-developed social network of Ukrainians and Poles working in the shadow economy. Several migrants recount their employment experiences:

> My neighbour had worked here and she asked me whether I would like to work here. (Ukrainian female, 60)
>
> You know, officially I am supposed to work in agriculture. (Ukrainian female, 45)
>
> I was three months in Poland, three at home. And once again, here and there. Once two months. You know, they sent me an invitation and I received a guest visa. (Ukrainian female, 51)

It should also be stressed that even those with registered employment undertake supplementary jobs in order to accumulate more money during their stay in Poland.

During our field study, we came across one innovative method of earning extra money that was devised by migrants. Some Polish employers help their employees to bring other Ukrainians to Poland by signing a declaration that they need a worker, e.g. for seasonal work in the garden, although the demand does not really exist. Ukrainian women sell these declarations to their fellow-countrymen on average for a very steep price of between €200 and €450 for each document. The price depends on the geographical distance from Poland, and from the Polish consulates in Ukraine. Since it is highly profitable, some migrants involve all their Polish contacts in obtaining such declarations from employers, who do not realize that the documents are sold in Ukraine. A migrant tells about how the employer innocently complied to sign the document which would later be sold:

> Volodia took care of everything. He printed the declaration. My employer did not want to go to any office since she worked a lot. She only signed it. And then she told me that someone from the office had called her to find out whether she is still interested in it. And she forgot about that declaration and panicked. But I told her that she should not have. How can they check it? (Ukrainian female, 49)

Migrants taking advantage of this shady business rationalize their activities, as we are told by a Ukrainian who recently bought her declaration, 'It is cost-effective—they pay and they receive a legal working visa for six months and they can earn more than in Ukraine'. (Ukrainian female, 49)

8.6.2 *Male circular migrants: construction*

As construction requires at least a certain set of skills, migrants working in this sector tend to stay in this sector. In comparing migrants' activity abroad with their last place of employment in Ukraine, construction workers constitute the most numerous group of workers who do not change their occupation (Ukrainian External Labour Migration 2009).

Again, all of the interviewees assigned to this type of circular migration had secondary or tertiary education. As for their previous occupation in Ukraine, they worked in construction, military service, and industries related to military production.

Within the framework of our field study, we reached circular migrants with a longer migratory experience. They manage to prolong their stays in Poland by working with work permits. Normally when Ukrainian workers return home, they do not even search for a job, as they are usually occupied with work on their own houses. For the most part, they have wives and children in rural areas of western Ukraine. Their stays in Ukraine are short, except for when they are needed for hard seasonal work in agriculture. One labourer who is now in Poland explains:

> We live in a village. We have our own land, houses, and homesteads. We have to farm and then come back to Poland... Our family needs food, we need to collect it for winter time—potatoes, and vegetables, and cereal. (Ukrainian male, 38)

In Ukraine, we managed to reach men whose stays in Poland were legal, although they worked in the shadow economy. Some migrants talked about their experiences:

> It costs, but it is worth the money. It is safer. You have a working visa so when they check you at the border, you do not worry. You see how it is here. It is not wrong to work a bit in Poland. (Ukrainian male, 51)

> Formerly, you could stay in Poland for a long time. Even if they gave a stamp in our passports, we knew the way to overcome it. Now, it is different. It is better not to take risks. If they catch you on the border, the information spreads to Germany due to the Schengen System or whatever you call it. People do not take risks any longer. (Ukrainian male, 43)

Even though most of the construction workers interviewed are unemployed, there was one fifty-one-year-old man who described himself as a pensioner. In the past he used to work in the military. It seems that some migrants who benefit from an early retirement option (provided in Ukraine for particular occupational categories such as the military) use this early retirement as an opportunity to earn additional money abroad. The main motivating factors for the interviewees to migrate were insufficient earnings in Ukraine or unemployment. Most of the migrant construction workers, along with the domestic care migrants, originated from the underdeveloped western Ukraine region. Several recount their difficulties in managing to make ends meet in Ukraine:

> I am not saying that there is no job at all in Ukraine. However, when you convert it from our currency to zlotys, it is 300 zlotys per month. So please understand there is no use to go to that work. (Ukrainian male, 38)

> When I lost my job, I stayed at home for three weeks. I phoned different Polish companies. Eventually, one responded and I worked for a month. One of my acquaintances from Ukraine helped me at this time in Poland. Sometimes

> I dropped in and she fed me. She told me to visit market-places in order to find whether someone needed a worker. I can do everything. I can even build an entire house. And I found a job for a few weeks. And now I am staying in Ukraine but I have already an employer in Poland and after potato-harvesting I go to Poland. (Ukrainian male, 52)

8.6.3 'Individual' agricultural seasonal workers

Most of the migrant seasonal workers encountered are rather young, mainly in their twenties or early thirties, single or married. Generally speaking, one might find almost anyone among individual seasonal workers employed in the agriculture sector: students, graduates, people who lost their jobs during the recent economic crisis, Ukrainian peasants, or even teachers working during their summer holidays. However, working in agriculture may be just a starting point of a migrant's circular career, as women tend to move from it into domestic services, and some men move on to the construction sector.

For Ukrainian students, seasonal employment during summer holidays is also an occasion for becoming familiar with Poland. A student interviewee expressed her desire to continue circularity until the end of her studies in Ukraine. She was even considering settling in Poland because of her familiarity with the country through seasonal work. Another respondent (from Central Ukraine, secondary technical education) described his first visit as follows: 'In order to find a good job in Ukraine, you need to have "friends" or to pay for it. I was earning too little, just enough to survive, so I got a visa and "escaped" to Poland' (Ukrainian male, 29). This migrant was considering different options other than working in agriculture, and felt that construction would be the most profitable.

Seasonal workers employed in agriculture on an individual basis tend to stay in Poland legally, but they work in the irregular economy. It is worth mentioning at this point that in Poland, employment on farms is regulated mainly by informal mechanisms. in the case of Polish agricultural workers as well.

Migrants working in this sector originate from different parts of Ukraine, but those interviewed were from various towns in Central Ukraine. Most used the informal assistance of 'drivers', who are well known in Polish agricultural towns and Ukrainian villages. Migrants pay 'drivers', who for this fee sort out the work and accommodation arrangements. When one job is done, they take migrants to another destination, and finally, back to Ukraine. One seasonal worker talks about having taken advantage of such persons:

> My first and second job in Poland was arranged by a 'driver'. I gave him money and he took care of work and accommodation... When work is done in one place, he takes us to the next employer. Eventually, he takes us back to Ukraine. (Ukrainian female, 20)

8.6.4 *Migrants employed by agencies offering temporary jobs*

It seems that migrants ascribed to this category, like some migrants employed in the agricultural sector on an individual basis, are at the beginning of their migratory career. During interviews, some of them attempted to get more information about possible future employment outside the agency. 'I am already looking for other available options to stay in Poland for a longer time. Have you heard about any kind of vacancy?' (Ukrainian male, 27). Even though migrants try to build up their own social networks in Poland, their options are rather limited, owing to the character of their contract. They have to change places, or even regions, of employment and accommodation quite often. Accommodations are usually far away from social centres, and migrants are usually on a shift roster, with their free time at odd hours.

In order to fill this lack of networks, there are Polish agencies that collaborate with Ukrainian partners to offer official employment. The employment agency responds to its clients' (employers) needs for seasonal work, and migrants do not have to look for a job or housing. Once hired, their housing is provided for in their contract. This appears to be advantageous for circular migrants, as it is a good solution for residents from the far-eastern Ukrainian regions that are not covered by an informal Polish-Ukrainian network, such as the 'drivers' mentioned previously.

One of our respondents, who decided to turn to a formal job agency in order to be more secure, recalled an example of a more naïve female migrant 'who paid a huge equivalent of 2,500 PLN (about €600) in order to arrive to Poland and to have a job here—picking strawberries' (Ukrainian female, 25). Such a price was completely unreasonable; obviously, the woman was cheated by an informal mediator. In order to avoid such scams, an interviewee who had visited Poland several times before, but in a different context (training for teachers), decided to enlist an agency in western Ukraine first:

> Since the assistance of job agencies in central Ukraine is expensive...I turned to the one in Lviv (western Ukraine). Thanks to it, we spent only about PLN 100 per person. This agency found a place of employment. So arriving to Poland...everything was arranged, including a place of accommodation...I received a receipt 'for consultation'. (Ukrainian female, 25)

8.6.5 *Highly skilled circular migrants*

Even though highly skilled circular migrants are not significant in numbers, they do form an interesting part of circular migration between Poland and Ukraine. This form of migration is rather new, as it has developed over a dozen of years or so. For the context of this study, 'specialists' are people who have well-established sources of income in Ukraine, such as permanent employment or their own businesses. Therefore, they work in Poland not purely for money, at least in the short term, but for longer-term advancement of their enterprises. Their real aim is to consolidate their position in Ukraine, and to facilitate access to certain goods and services. Several highly skilled workers explain:

> A representative of a Polish company offered me a job in a research unit. Since then I have been working for them. They arranged all work permits... Yes, I am considering a long stay permit. Especially, since my daughter has settled in Greece. Being in Poland makes it easier for me to visit them [family]... I like Poland but it is difficult for me to give up my life in Ukraine. (Ukrainian female, 50)

> In Poland I see a different approach to the area of my academic interest. I learn new methods of teaching that are equally important. (Ukrainian academic, male 36)

We managed to reach two migrants who might be assigned to this type: a general practitioner working part time in Poland and running her private practice in Ukraine, she spends two weeks in Poland and two in Ukraine by turns; and an academic who has a permanent position at one of the Ukrainian state universities, and regularly travels to Poland to teach at a private university in the borderland region.

8.7 Is circularity good, and for whom?

One of the main challenges for both Poland and Ukraine is that of a declining population, mainly owing to natural causes and emigration. Circular migration may facilitate effective matching of supply and demand for migrant labour forces without a permanent loss of population through emigration. It seems that circular migration is beneficial for both countries. For Poland it responds to a demand for seasonal workers, and for Ukraine it does not result in a permanent loss of population, and provides remittances for the families left back home.

Attracting foreign seasonal workers from a country with a small cultural distance is a positive strategy adopted by the state, thus providing for an ever-expanding flow of seasonal circular migrants. On the other hand, however, most Ukrainian migrants do not treat Poland as a settlement country. Therefore, this strategy responds to short-term labour market demands, but not to the long-run demographic challenges of Poland.

The idea of circular migration seems ideal for labour markets experiencing shortages of workers in some sectors. However, migrants may be abused by individuals and cheated by the temporary agency work sector in terms of salaries, social insurance, and working hours. Therefore, it seems necessary to design policies preventing exploitation of seasonal migrant workers.

Poland and Ukraine still do not have a normative document that would establish the foundations of the countries' migration policies, recognizing their goals, objectives, mechanisms, and instruments. A Ministry of Labour representative from Poland and a Ukrainian migration expert explain:

> Any kind of integration should be preceded by a general decision: do we need immigrants who will work in Poland but who will not settle here, or do we need settlement immigration? In Poland, we still have not made this decision. (Ministry of Labour and Social Policy interview, 27 May 2010)

> The migration policy is completely unclear, the main instruments are unclear, and the central government and regional authorities are not determined. (Ukrainian migration expert interview, 16 August 2010)

As far as transnational Ukrainian families are concerned, migration leads to erosion of emotional ties and kinship. Since in the majority of cases migrants are trying to follow the lifestyle observed on emigration, it fosters consumerism. It also leads to alienation between family members. Migration may have positive effects on individual members of the family or on some aspects of family life, however, on the family as a whole it has a disintegrating impact. While labour migration may enhance the financial stability of the household, it also has a negative impact on the family economy, making the families who rely on remittances less prone to be active on their native labour market. Remittances are used primarily for family consumption, education of children, and housing. Around 60 to 80 per cent of remittances are invested into real estate. To a much lesser extent, they are invested in small family businesses, mainly because Ukraine has not created enough economic incentives for such endeavours (Tolstokorova 2009).

According to different estimates, about 1.3 to 3.25 million Ukrainian women work abroad (including Poland), almost 90 per cent of them illegally (Kyzyma 2007). Many of them come from mainly rural areas and are in the reproductive age. They have husbands and children left behind in Ukraine. Mass international migration of women leads to slow ageing of the rural population, fertility reduction, and losses in rural labour potential; and it prevents further agricultural and rural development (Kyzyma 2007).

The great involvement of Ukrainian women in the care industry in Western European countries affects the redistribution of traditional gender roles. It is particularly visible among rural families in western Ukraine. The definition of masculinity has changed, and furthermore it has been observed that males from these regions refuse to accept available local jobs even when the remuneration offered exceeds average income rates for the capital of Ukraine, where the salaries are the highest. Since remittances received from migrant wives exceed by far the wages offered by local employers, men are reluctant to work even for high salaries. Instead, some of them find the roles of childminders and home-makers acceptable for themselves, although in most cases only for the period when their wives are absent through migration (Tolstokorova 2009).

8.8 Conclusion

Many statements associated with migration have been rooted in the perception of population outflows and influxes as settlement migrations. When analysing migration, people use such words as 'exodus' (in the case of sending countries) or 'flooding' (in the case of receiving countries). However, as Hugo (2003) noticed, in the current situation, a question arises whether temporary migration is really a prelude to permanent settlement. Returning to Ukraine, in the case of Polish-Ukrainian circularity, it is not often a spontaneous or a desired activity, but it is forced by procedures operating within the scheme of the short-term visa systems. Migrants moving between Poland and Ukraine know that they need documents to cross the border and stay legally, even if it means additional money paid to informal mediators. In the Polish-Ukrainian reality, illegal stay makes it to a great extent impossible to be involved in circular migration.

There are two basic types of circular migrants in Poland: firstly, there are labour migrants who spontaneously choose circularity as an option for modernizing their households in Ukraine, to collect money for their own business, or provide money for their households without leaving their families for too long. Secondly, there are Ukrainian migrants who are engaged in circularity owing to the lack of entrepreneurial spirit and policy constraints. In this context, Skeldon (2011) elaborates on the nuances of circular migration:

> Nevertheless, a large number of different systems of more regulated temporary migration do exist and the fact that migrants must go back to their areas of origin gives the impression that these systems are essentially circulatory in nature. However, these temporary migrations are different from circulation in terms of spontaneity, frequency and distance. (Skeldon 2011: 58)

In the Polish-Ukrainian case, circularity seems to be the female domain. Among other economic reasons, women who are engaged in circular mobility do not want to break family ties for good. Their activities are shaped by the need to stay close to their family—children, elderly parents, or a husband—and by the working roles in a transnational dimension. Interestingly, traditional division of gender roles leads to a situation where men can prolong their stays abroad without strong social labelling as being bad parents or spouses. Men are more often driven by their traditional role of breadwinners. The above-mentioned observation is a part of the 'new economics of migration' approach, which points out that migrants act as family or household members rather than as individuals. Therefore, migration is a family's or a household's strategy of minimizing risks as well as of increasing the income of the family unit (Massey et al. 1998).

However, one should realize that over time, circulation may be gradually transformed into a more permanent migration. Migrants may stay longer in destination countries, for example when they have secure employment with longer-term prospects, or they get married, or decide to have a child (Skeldon 2011). In Poland, the latter options are more probable in the case of women. It is confirmed by statistics on mixed (international) marriages of Poles, which show that Ukrainian women are the predominant nationality married to Polish males. It is important to mention here, however, that experiences of circular migration in the Central Eastern European region indicate that one does not have to settle down in order to protect oneself from exploitation; keeping in touch with fellow-nationals and locals who work in a labour niche is a much more important condition (Maroukis et al. 2011).

References

Adamiec, W. (2008). 'Nieformalna giełda pracy—przypadek instytucji ekonomicznej skupiającej Ukraińców', in A. Grzymała-Kazłowska (ed), *Między jednością a wielością. Integracja odmiennych grup i kategorii imigrantów w Polsce*. Warszawa: Ośrodek Badań nad Migracjami, 141–62.

Antoniewski, R. (1997). 'Przyczynek do badań nad nieformalnym rynkiem pracy cudzoziemców', *ISS Working Paper, Seria Prace Migracyjne (3)*, Warszawa: UW.

Antoniewski, R. (2002). 'Cudzoziemcy o nieuregulowanym statusie w Polsce. Pracownicy ukraińscy w jednym z "zagłębi" owocowo-warzywnych na Mazowszu', CMR Working Papers, (47). Warszawa: UW, 33–66.

Bieniecki, M. and Pawlak, M. (2009). *Strategie przetrwania. Adaptacja ukraińskich migrantów zarobkowych do polskiej rzeczywistości instytucjonalnej*. Warszawa: ISP.

Bojar, H. et al. (2005). *Migranci na rynku pracy w Polsce*, Warszawa: Instytut Spraw Publicznych.

Futo, P. (2010). 'Hungary: A Quantitative Overview of Irregular Migration', in A. Triandafyllidou (ed), *Irregular Migration in Europe: Myths and Realities*. Ashgate: Farnham, 167–86.

Golinowska, S. (2004). *Popyt na pracę cudzoziemców. Polska i sąsiedzi*. Warszawa: IPiSS.

Hugo, G. (2003). 'Circular Migration: Keeping Development Rolling?' *Migration Information Source*, June 2003. Washington: Migration Policy Institute [online]. http://www.migrationinformation.org/Feature/display.cfm?ID=129 (accessed 29 July 2012).

Hut, P. (2002). *Warunki życia i proces adaptacji repatriantów w Polsce w latach 1992–2000*. Warszawa: Institute of Social Policy, Warsaw University (IPS UW).

Iglicka, K. (1998). 'The Migration of Ethnic Poles from Kazakhstan to Poland', *International Migration Review*, 32 (Winter), 995–1015.

Iglicka, K. (1999). 'The Economics of Petty Trade on the Eastern Polish Border', in K. Iglicka and K. Sword (eds), *The Challenge of East-West Migration for Poland*. London: Macmillan Press Ltd, 120–45.

Iglicka, K. (2000). 'Ethnic Division on Emerging Foreign Labour Markets in Poland During the Transition Period', *Europe-Asia Studies*, (7), 1237–55.

Iglicka, K. (2001). 'Shuttling from the Former Soviet Union to Poland: From "Primitive Mobility" to Migration', *Journal of Ethnic and Migration Studies*, 27 (3), 505–18.

Iglicka, K. (2001a). *Poland's Post-War Dynamic of Migration*. Aldershot: Ashgate.

Iglicka, K. (2010). 'Migration Research in a Transformation Country: The Polish Case', in D. Thranhardt and M. Bommes (eds), *National Paradigms of Migration Research*. Osnabruck: V&R Unipress Universitatsverlag, 259–66.

Iglicka, K. and Gmaj K. (2010). 'Poland', in A. Triandafyllidou (ed), *Irregular Migration in Europe. Myths and Realities*. Aldershot: Ashgate.

Iglicka, K. and Sword, K. (1999). *The Challenge of East-West Migration for Poland*. London: Macmillan Press Ltd.

Kaźmierkiewicz, P., Lvolva, O. and Chumak, V (2009). *Coordinating Migration Policy in Ukraine. Lessons from Poland*. Kyiv: IPA [online]. www.icps.com.ua/files/articles/55/1/Migration_UP_ENG_Last.pdf (accessed 28 July 2012).

Kindler, M. (2006). 'Migrant Domestic Workers in Poland—Balancing the Risk', in H. Lutz (ed.), *Migration and Domestic Work: A European Perspective on a Global Theme*. Aldershot: Ashgate.

Konieczna, J. (2000). *Polska–Ukraina. Wzajemny wizerunek*. Warszawa: Instytut Spraw Publicznych.

Koryś, I. (2003). Migration Trends in Selected EU Applicant Countries: Poland, *CEFMR Working Paper 5/2003, Warsaw: Central European Forum For Migration Research [online]*. http://www.cefmr.pan.pl/docs/cefmr_wp_2003-05.pdf

Kyzyma, I. (2007). *Determinants and Consequences of Female Labor Migration from Rural Areas: The Case of Ukraine* [online]. www.mace-events.org/greenweek2009/5808-MACE.html (18 March 2010).

Malynovska, O. (2006). 'Trans-Border Migration of the Population of the Ukrainian Western Frontier Areas in the Context of EU Enlargement', in K. Iglicka (ed.), *Transnational Migration Dilemmas*. Warsaw: Centre for International Migrations, 81–9.

Maroukis, T., Iglicka, K. and Gmaj, K. (2011). 'Irregular Migration and Informal Economy in Southern and Central-Eastern Europe: Breaking the Vicious Cycle?' *International Migration*, 49 (5), 129–56.

Massey, D. et al. (1998). *Worlds in Motion: Understanding International Migration at the End of the Millennium*. Oxford: Clarendon Press.

Piore, M. J. (1979). *Birds of Passage: Migrant Labour and Industrial Societies, Cambridge*: Cambridge University Press.

Sik, E., Zakarias, I. (2005). *Active Civic Participation of Immigrants in Hungary*. Country report prepared for the European Research Project POLITIS, Oldenburg: University of Olenburg [online]. http://www.politis-europe.uni-oldenburg.de/download/Hungary.pdf (accessed 29 July 2012).

Skeldon, R. (2011). 'The Impact of Temporary and Circular Migration on Families and Areas of Origin', in S. McLoughlin et al. (eds), *Temporary and Circular Migration: Opportunities and Challenges. Working Paper No. 35*. Brussels: European Policy Centre.

Slany, K. and Małek, A. (2006). 'Integration of New Female Migrants in Polish Labor Market and Society and Policies Affecting Integration: State of the Art', *Working Paper No. 9—WP4*, Kraków: Jagiellonian University [online]. www.femipol.uni-frankfurt.de (accessed 29 July 2012).

Tolstokorova, A. (2009). 'Costs and Benefits of Labour Migration for Ukrainian Transnational Families: Connection or Consumption?', *Cahier de l'URMIS (Unité de recherche migrations et société)*, 12/2009[online]. urmis.revues.org/index868.html (accessed 29 July 2012).

Triandafyllidou, A. and Gropas, R. (2007). *European Immigration: A Sourcebook*. Aldershot: Ashgate.

Ukrainian External Labour Migration. Survey report. (2009). Kyiv: Ukrainian Centre for Social Reforms (UCSR), State Statistics Committee of Ukraine (SSCU).

Notes

1. According to Piore's theory (1979) in modern market economies one can distinguish primary and secondary sectors of the labour market. In a contrary to the primary one the secondary contains jobs that offer unfavourable and unstable conditions. Immigrants, in an opposite to native population, accept low wages and uncertain conditions. Therefore, they respond to labour market shortages.
2. It is worth mentioning at this point that a number of Ukrainian citizens staying in Poland on the basis of a settlement and stay permit has been increasing steadily; however, it is still not very high. At the end of 2008, it was at the level of 22,801. At the end of 2009, 13,787 Ukrainians held permanent residency cards, while 11,074 held temporary residency permits (Office for Foreigners data).
3. The total number of visits to Poland in 2004 remained at the previous year's level of 3.8 million.
4. Ordinance of the Minister of Labour and Social Policy on foreigners' employment without work permit from 30 August 2006; Ordinance of the Minister Labour and Social Policy from 27 June 2007; Ordinance of the Minister Labour and Social Policy of signed 29 January 2008. The regulations stemming from the last ordinance are still in force.

9

A Transnational Double Presence: Circular Migration between Ukraine and Italy

Francesca Alice Vianello

9.1 Introduction

Abdelmalek Sayad (1999), in his illuminating analysis of the migration of male Algerians, introduces the concept of 'double absence'. He writes that in order for emigration to be considered not as a 'pure absence', an impossible ubiquity is required: the migrant must be present in spite of absence, and at the same time must continue to be completely present in the place where he is actually present. Besides being doubly absent, Ukrainian migrant women are also doubly present both in Italian and Ukrainian societies. In Italy, their work provides a necessary support to an inadequate and insufficient welfare state, while in Ukraine they are constantly developing new strategies to be present in spite of distance. Circular migration is one of these strategies.

This study explores the phenomenon of circular migration between Ukraine and Italy. In particular, it investigates the circular migration of Ukrainian women, as they represent the majority of Ukrainians who reside in Italy. Interviews given by women who have moved to Italy since the second half of the 1990s are analysed, in order to identify their migratory trajectories and circular practices. Specifically, the analysis examines the social, emotional, and economic reasons that are behind the migrants' choice of circular migratory patterns, as well as the legal and employment related obstacles encountered by migrants.

This study is organized as follows: the second part of this section describes the research and the methodology adopted; the second section illustrates the history of migration between the Ukraine and Italy; the third section presents the main features of Ukrainian immigration to Italy; and the fourth section provides examples of migrant women's experiences of circular migration.

9.1.1 Methodological introduction

This chapter is mainly based both on a secondary analysis of forty-five in-depth interviews with migrant women (see Table 9.1 and 9.2)—thirty-three of which were conducted in Italy, in particular in the region of Veneto[1] (Figure 9.1), and twelve in Ukraine (Figure 9.2), in the regions of L'viv[2] and Ivano Frankivsk[3]—and on the information gathered through thirty-two interviews with key informants such as diplomats, civil servants, members of NGOs and intergovernmental organizations, journalists, church ministers, researchers, and cultural mediators (See Table 9.3).

The interviews were collected by the author mainly between 2005 and 2008 as part of a wider doctoral research project which focused on migratory practices among Ukrainian women and was published in Italy with the title *Migrando sole. Legami transnazionali tra Ucraina e Italia* (Migrating alone. Transnational bonds between the Ukraine and Italy) (Vianello 2009).[4] Another section of the interviews was conducted between 2009 and 2010

Table 9.1 Socio-demographic characteristics of the migrant women interviewed I

	Total	Married	Divorced	Widows	Unmarried	With Children	Age 20–29	Age 30–39	Age 40–49	Age 50<
Migrant women	33	10	16	3	4	30	1	12	11	9
Returned migrant women	12	8	3	1		12	1	1	5	5
Total	45	18	19	4	4	42	2	13	16	

Source: Vianello 2009; Sacchetto 2011.

Table 9.2 Socio-demographic characteristics of the migrant women interviewed II

	Total	High school diploma	University degree	Care workers	Domestic workers (paid by the hour)	Other occupations
Migrant women	33	20	13	12	9	12
Returned migrant women	12	7	5	8	2	2
Total	45	27	18	20	11	14

Source: Vianello 2009; Sacchetto 2011.

A Transnational Double Presence: Circular Migration between Ukraine and Italy

Figure 9.1 Map of Ukraine, highlighting the regions of L'viv (Львівська область) and Ivano Frankivsk (Івано-Франківська область) where in-depth interviews were conducted
© OpenStreetMap contributors, CC BY-SA
Source: www.openstreetmap.org

for a study funded by Veneto Lavoro, which investigated economic change and the social repercussions of migration and delocalization in some Central Eastern European countries (Ukraine, Moldova, and Romania) (Sacchetto 2011).[5]

Both studies were characterized by a multi-sited approach (Marcus 1995), prompted by the awareness that, in order to achieve a full understanding of the different aspects and dynamics of migration, it is necessary to analyse the two social contexts of departure and destination (Sayad 1999). Following this approach, interviews were collected both in Italy and in Ukraine. Moreover, the women interviewed in Ukraine had returned only for a short period, or were return migrants who had stated that they had finished their experience of international mobility.

The majority of the women interviewed were between thirty and fifty-nine years old, single mothers—divorcees or widows—and had a high school diploma or a university degree. In their country of origin they had been factory workers, teachers, nurses, factory technicians, shop assistants, office clerks, and journalists, while in Italy they had found employment

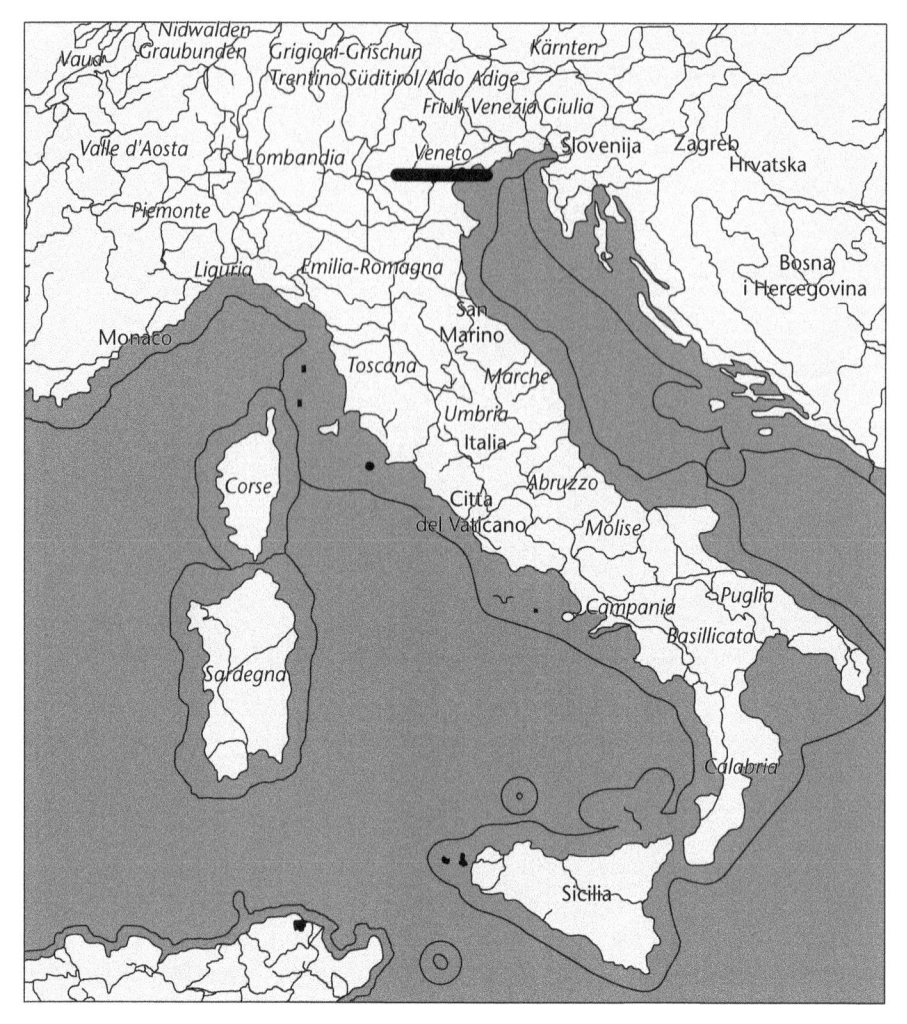

Figure 9.2 Map of Italy, highlighting the region of Veneto where in-depth interviews were conducted

© OpenStreetMap contributors, CC BY-SA

Source: www.openstreetmap.org

Table 9.3 Interviews with key informants

Civil servants	2
Journalists	3
Cultural mediators	3
Members of NGOs and intergovernmental organizations	8
Recruitment agency representatives	1
Diplomats	3
Researchers	4
Church ministers	8
Total	32

Source: Vianello 2009; Sacchetto 2011.

mainly as care or domestic workers. The migrants interviewed had left their affective bonds and their social identities back in Ukraine. Their stories recount how they left home in order to guarantee their children an opportunity to study. The migrants' age, the presence of a family left behind, and their 'Italian job' are some of the features of this type of female migration, which significantly distinguishes itself from migrations of young, unmarried women who are probably looking to achieve self-realization abroad, far from the social control wielded by their community of origin (Pedraza 1991; Decimo 2005).

9.2. Moving around Europe: from cross-border traders to care workers

9.2.1 A historical perspective

Ukrainian emigration towards countries outside the former Soviet area has historically been directed toward Israel, Germany, and the United States; these flows, at least initially, were composed of Ukrainians of Jewish, Greek, German, and Polish origins (Fassmann and Munz 1994; Codagnone 1998). In 1990, 93 per cent of Ukrainian migrants migrated to Israel, 3 per cent went to Greece, and 1.5 per cent migrated to Germany and Hungary (Shamshur 1992). Alongside these long-distance migrations, the early 1990s saw the emergence of a particular form of transborder migration, commonly known as petty trade or suitcase trade. Since the end of the 1980s, because of the progressive liberalization and streamlining of Soviet citizens' mobility—both inside and outside the Soviet Union—a large number of Ukrainians, especially women, reinvented themselves as small-time traders specialized in making profits across national borders. According to some opinion surveys conducted in the early 1990s, commercial trips abroad had become a key activity for 5 per cent of Ukraine's working population and an occasional activity for another 20 per cent (Frejka et al. 1999: 6).[6] Since the early 2000s, the suitcase trade phenomenon has been reducing in size, but is still present: those who travel for commercial reasons are directed towards Russia, Poland, and Turkey. In Russia they usually buy housewares, domestic appliances, detergents, and cosmetics; craftwork, clothes, shoes, and leather products in Poland; hides, carpets, and knitwear in Turkey (Homra et al. 2003). As an example of this phenomenon, here is how Myroslava, an Ukrainian migrant describes her experience:

> I used to have a job that I really liked, I used to be an engraver. I had a small store of just about two square metres in the town centre and I wrote things, a lot of people stopped by and I liked it. People used to come from Moldova, from Ivano Frankivsk

and L'viv to have engravings done by me. I engraved with sterling and gold. I loved it and it also gave me a lot, I used to work all day long. Then I met some people and I started going to Turkey to do business. I didn't resign, I gave my job to a friend, who was twenty and already had two kids. I went to Turkey for the first time in 1994, but before that I went to Romania, then Poland, Czech Republic. I kept my old job for my retirement pension. I started making good money there, and this guy who was making money with me used to have a big apartment that we shared, then he accumulated a lot of debts and we lost all the money. Yes, my associate had his own things going on and that's why we lost everything. We exported ridiculous things to Poland, underwear, bras, things for the house that they didn't have over there. We lived better here than in Poland and Hungary. We imported sweets from Turkey to Ukraine, then when we started earning some more money we bought another van and we brought hides, trousers, shoes and sold them in markets. We took this van, bought things, brought them here and then we went to the big market where we had another van where we unloaded the products which were sold by our employees. I could go there and be back in three days. I'm also that kind of person who smiles at customs, I used to bring gifts, and Turkish men liked blonde women like me so they asked me how I was, how my family was, a smile was enough and they relaxed. If they decided to search the truck they had to take all the stuff out and then it was just impossible to put everything back in its place. (Myroslava, Chernivtsi, 9 August 2006)

Transnational trade was particularly profitable in the years of great unrest and transformation, when public stores were suddenly empty, and access to consumables was a thrilling discovery for a large part of the ex-Soviet population. The early 1990s consequently witnessed the appearance of a vast number of markets. However, small-scale cross-border trade soon became an insufficient source of income owing to the regulation of customs and of import-export activities: small traders have been slowly crushed by larger and more structured companies. The case of Poland is particularly symbolic. Many Ukrainians usually work for short periods in Poland, where one of the most frequent activities is the sale of cigarettes, alcohol, or petrol, which are cheaper in Ukraine.[7] Over time, this form of trade has become more and more structured, with the opening of agencies that assist the small traders in the organization of their journeys, and transporting them by bus to the main Polish markets (Okolski 2001).

Destinations for international worker migrations have also changed over the years. Israel was an important destination between 1990 and 1991, attracting more than 100,000 people, but at the end of the decade, this flow had already reduced to 20,000 people. New receiving areas, such as Southern and Central Europe, are emerging. In 2004, the data provided by Ukrainian embassies abroad—whose figures are usually underestimated, but nonetheless useful to understand the main trends—registered the following distribution: about 300,000 workers living in Poland, 200,000 in Italy and Czech Republic,

100,000 in Spain, 35,000 in Turkey, 20,000 in the USA, and 15,000 in Portugal, while they calculated that approximately 1 million people were working in the Russian Federation (Malynovska 2004).

Migratory flows are influenced by two factors: gender and the area of origin. Ukraine is a divided country on linguistic, political, religious, and economic levels: on the right side of the river Dnepr lies the Russophone, Orthodox, industrial area. On its left side is western Ukraine, whose centre is Galicia, with the city of L'viv, where Ukrainian independent and nationalist movements have grown, Ukrainian is the main language, the Greek-Catholic Church is predominant, and there are deep historical ties with Poland.

From southern and eastern Ukraine, migration is mainly directed towards the Russian Federation, but there is also a large number of workers from western Ukraine that chooses the same destination. Russia is traditionally the most important destination for Ukrainian men, and has continued to be so even after Ukraine's declaration of independence. These migratory habits can be traced back to the Soviet era: in the beginning there were forced migrations towards Siberia, the extreme north, and the far east, which later became voluntary (Korobkov and Zaionchkovskaia 2004; Malynovska 2004).

Migrants from the western regions, instead, are mainly directed towards Southern and Central Europe. Obtaining a visa in Portugal is a relatively easy procedure, therefore in recent years this country has been attracting an increasing number of Ukrainian migrants, both men and women. Moreover, in March 2005, Ukraine and Portugal signed an agreement that opened the frontiers to Ukrainian seasonal workers (Fonseca et al. 2004; Gois and Marques 2007). In Spain, Ukrainian citizens are employed in different sectors: agriculture, construction, assistance and care for children, care for the elderly and people with medical conditions, hotels, catering, and entertainment (Cipko 2006; Tymczuk 2012). Italy particularly attracts women who find employment as care or domestic workers (Mazzacurati 2005; Näre 2007; Vianello 2009, 2011; Solari 2010; Fedyuk 2012). Lastly, even former socialist countries that are now EU members, like Poland and the Czech Republic, have become the destination for large migratory flows from Ukraine (see Iglicka and Gmaj in this volume, but also Wallace et al. 1997; Wallace et al. 1998; Iglicka 2003; Kindler 2008; Iglicka et al. 2011; Volodko 2011).

9.2.2 The birth of a female migratory flow

We have seen how, during the 1990s, new migratory practices were introduced into the pre-existing migratory tradition, directing the migrant population towards new receiving countries. For many of the women interviewed, Italy was not the first choice of destination, but merely a stage in a more complex migratory experience. In the initial years after the declaration of independence, migrant women moved to the countries closest to the border, to enable cross-border trading or subordinate labour. Several interviewees, for example, recounted how they travelled and worked in the Czech Republic and Poland. For example, Alla stated that she worked in Poland for three months but then went back to Ukraine because her salary was too low.[8] Sofia, instead, was employed for a year in a Czech poultry farm before returning to Ukraine and ending up in Venice:

> I worked in Czechoslovakia for one year, I was a shop assistant in a factory... where they raised these hens for thirty-six days...3 kilos...they're not hens... chickens, 3 kilos in a month.
>
> *And what did you do there?*
>
> First I was...I took the eggs and close to the factory there was a shop where they sold them, I worked there as a shop assistant... but something bad happened... In the meantime, I heard from Italy...I wanted to come to Italy, but I didn't have money, because you needed a lot of money to cross the border. That year the owner didn't give us money because the factory failed.
>
> *Failed?*
>
> Failed... because there was an epidemic and half the chickens died... He didn't pay me and I decided to go home also to work, I don't know how you say, the land. (Sofia, Venice, 27 June 2006)

Oksana, who, immediately after 1991, was on maternity leave, decided to supplement her allowance with cross-border trading: she started buying clothes in Poland and selling them at the market in her hometown.[9] Then, between 1995 and 1996, her husband started receiving his salary with substantial delays, and her family's financial condition rapidly worsened: cross-border trading was no longer a sufficient supplement to their income. Oksana then decided to migrate abroad. Her first work experience was in an Italian textile factory located in the Czech Republic, where she worked for a few months with Ukrainian and Polish colleagues. However, because of low wages and long working days, she decided to move back to the Ukraine after six months, before leaving again for Italy.

In other cases, husbands also migrated to neighbouring countries, but in many instances they soon returned home owing to harsh working conditions and the salaries, which were deemed too low to justify the human cost of emigration.

> First my husband left for Poland and Czech Republic for three months; in Poland he worked as a gardener and in the Czech Republic as a construction worker. Two, three months later he came back home and then left again. The money was very little. In the Czech Republic he earned 300–400 dollars, half of that in Poland. So

> he left that job and came back home and I left. We talked about it, with my husband, with our children, do I go or do you go? And I said, I'll go, because he had already left. (Svetlana, Drohobich, 26 August 2006)

Female migration towards Italy started in the second half of the 1990s. The first pioneers left almost blindly, basing their knowledge of the country only on fragmented, word-of-mouth information from friends and acquaintances, who told them of good work opportunities for women in Italy. Often this information would come from Poland, a country which had been an important source of female migration to Italy for several years. Migration from Ukraine, on the other hand, was yet to be organized by agencies based in Poland and specialized in the planning of trips to Italy: thus, these pioneers generally travelled via Poland.

> We went by train to Poland, and there we took the tourist bus and left directly for Rome, but we stopped in Austria first and saw many beautiful things. We stopped for one night close to the sea, but I can't remember the name of the town.
> *What did you do once you got there?*
> There were thirty of us, we stopped next to Porta Portese, we got out and many people met with friends and we were left alone, we didn't have anybody. Many of us left for Naples. (Liuba, Sambir, 17 August 2006)

The network of Polish women and, more generally, of women from Eastern European, also represented an important reference point for these pioneers, who arrived in Italy without a permit of stay or contacts to help them look for accommodation and employment. This is how Liuba recalls her arrival:

> While we were in this square a woman walks up to us and says: 'I heard you speaking Russian, I am Polish, are you looking for a job?' We answer we are and she says: 'I work with an old person and I want to leave this job because I'm going back to Poland.' My friend says: 'I'll go!' Because she didn't speak Italian, the lady was a little angry and our friend said she felt bad, she didn't understand anything. We told her: 'No, Oksana, don't leave it, don't talk, I don't know, but don't go, if you work you can help us with the money, if you don't work we die too.' Then this Italian, a Jehovah's Witness, tells us there is a job with three kids, my friends say: 'Liuba, since you have no husband and you left your kids, you go.' Ah, I forgot one thing, when we got to the hotel there was a young girl who spoke Russian, we were so happy, she was a cleaning lady. She was from Estonia. She helped us so much, she brought us food, a piece of bread. When the Italian man said to my friend that there was a job with kids, this Estonian girl, because she already spoke some Italian, she called this lady and the lady said she wanted to see me so we made an appointment. We talked to this lady and she said: 'Yes, Liuba, come with us.' After one week I moved to their house and I stayed with this family for twenty months. I worked twenty-four hours a day and I didn't have the usual day off on Thursday. (Liuba, Sambir, 17 August 2006)

The narratives and experiences offered by the pioneers built the foundation for the growth of a migratory culture, which has since gradually normalized and legitimized the women's departure, although a heated debate regarding this matter is still continuing. Through these pioneers, more and more detailed information about Italy reached Ukraine, and when these women managed to return for short holidays to their country of origin, they told their sisters, cousins, friends, and colleagues about their work experience abroad, showing the results of their migration through the purchase of apartments and luxury items. The pioneers' stories and their visibly increasing wealth excited the desires and ambitions of other women, who eventually made the decision to leave themselves. Therefore, once the pioneers explored a new pattern of geographical mobility, the migratory flow took shape accordingly, by waves of attraction.

Nowadays, an increasing number of women of different origins and social classes have access to the basic resources that are necessary for geographical mobility. This is made possible by the existence of a complex migratory system, which conveys information regarding the most desirable destinations, the wage differentials, the documents that are necessary, as well as helpful information regarding job applications, and formal and informal services for migrants, such as loans, tourist visas, and transportation. Ana, a cultural mediator, explains:

> With the first wave of migration came women with higher education, with degrees and PhDs. With the second wave, instead, there were also all the people from the countryside. The ones from western Ukraine were the ones who had more money and the right mentality to leave. They knew the language. Only a few knew English, German, French, and that's not bad, but they didn't know who Dante was, or Umberto Eco. Then the second wave happened when the news started to get around. For example, now there are a lot of them in Portugal, both men and women, but especially men because there are more manual jobs. Greece, Spain, France, more women, or Germany... but especially Italy. Almost every family in western Ukraine has someone that now works abroad. (cultural mediator, Padua, 18 February 2006)

The differentiation of migration patterns partially depends on a diversification of the labour demand, but it is also generated by the ethnic specialization phenomenon, which develops in receiving countries and consists in the association of a particular nationality with an occupation, which in turn can be gender-specific (Scrinzi 2004). As Oleksandra explains, 'One of the reasons why women leave is because in Italy you can find jobs for women but not for men. So it's the women who leave.'[10] Thus, a central aspect of Ukrainian migration is the ethnicization of the labour market, which in this case is favourable for female emigration. In Italy, there are in fact many sectors where a foreign male labour force is employed, but access to these workplaces is blocked by the predominant presence of other national groups.[11]

To arrange their trips, migrants rely on tourist agencies that specialize in organizing tours of Europe with Italy as a final destination. Aside from planning their journey, these agencies also deal with the bureaucratic procedures for obtaining the tourist visa, and provide contacts with informal employment agencies. These contacts are usually Polish or Ukrainian women who have been in Italy for some time—in certain cases can be Italian—and offer reception and employment services. The price of the employment service is half of the first salary, while the visa and trip package used to be sold at $300–400 during the 1990s, and had reached the price of €3,000 by 2006.

Once they have arrived in Naples, Rome, or other Italian cities, migrants find illegal employment as domestic or care workers, and overstay their tourist visa. This sector is particularly suitable for the employment of a low-cost, migrant labour force, usually without a permit of stay, because inspections from the law enforcement bodies are extremely rare, if not completely absent. As a consequence, Ukrainian migrants can work for several years for Italian families, while waiting to obtain a permanent visa through one of the cyclical mass regularizations of irregular immigrants (Ambrosini 2011; Ambrosini and Triandafyllidou 2011).

9.3 Ukrainian migration towards Italy, and its circularity in figures and numbers

Although Ukrainian immigration started in the 1990s, the migrants' presence has only been registered by Italian statistics after the general immigration amnesty of 2002. In 2001 the Istat (Italian National Institute of Statistics) estimated a mere 6,567 Ukrainian citizens with a permit of stay; in 2004, the permits issued to Ukrainian citizens had rapidly increased to 117,161 (Istat 2001, 2004).

As of 2009, 170,440 Ukrainian citizens had a permit of stay. They now represent the fifth largest national group among foreign citizens in Italy, after Romanians, Albanians, Moroccans, and Chinese (Istat 2009). The majority of regular migrants are women (80.8 per cent), and minors only amount to 8 per cent. The purpose of their presence is mainly work (73.7 per cent) (see Table 9.4), which is also the most important purpose of the legal entries that have been registered during 2008 (82.2 per cent of a total 22,000 entries).

Among the people who have legally entered the country in 2008 (Tables 9.5 and 9.6), a trend reversal can be observed from the immigration figures of the previous years, which were characterized by a prevalence of adult women—in their forties and fifties—who were married, divorced, or widowed (Chumalo

Table 9.4 Ukrainian citizens with a permit of stay by purpose of presence, and sex as of 1 January 2009—male and female: absolute numbers

	Work	Family[12]	Religion	Residence	Study	Asylum request	Asylum	Humanitarian	Health	Other[13]	Total
M + F	123,634	42,459	244	336	903	27	7	98	421	2,311	170,440
M	19,580	11,998	182	18	367	19	2	27	65	550	32,808
F	104,054	30,461	62	318	536	8	5	71	356	1,761	137,632

Source: Istat www.demo.istat.it

2005; Conti et al. 2010). Instead, the current majority consists of unmarried adults (54.2 per cent, 11,937) and a more equal distribution among the different age groups. Although the largest number of entries is still represented by people between forty and forty-nine years of age (27.1 per cent), there is a significant number of young people between eighteen and twenty-nine years old (19.6 per cent). This new trend can probably be seen as the result of the process of reunification between mothers and children, who have come of age and left for Italy for work or study purposes.

Most Ukrainian migrant women are employed in the domestic work sector, where undeclared labour is particularly common.[14] According to the most recent INPS/Caritas report, in 2007 these women represented 16.4 per cent (78,000) of those insured (618,032) (INPS/Caritas 2011). However, this data does not account for the immigration amnesty of 2009, which regularized about 26,000 Ukrainian women who worked for Italian families as housemaids, or caregivers for non-self-sufficient people.[15]

The majority of Ukrainian workers are employed as live-in domestic workers, or caregivers for the elderly who are not self-sufficient. The national collective labour agreement that regulates domestic work has currently expired, and a renewal is being discussed. Working conditions, therefore, are still regulated by the old collective labour agreement of 2007, which established some distinctions between different professional roles and different duties. One of the most important distinctions is between live-in and non-live-in workers: the number of working hours for live-in housemaids is set at a maximum of fifty-four per week, while for non-live-in ones it is forty per week (Ioli 2010). Another distinction concerns the health conditions of the person who requires assistance. If it is a live-in post with a non-self-sufficient person, the minimum monthly wage for the caregiver is set at €897, while if the client is self-sufficient it drops to €791.[16]

The 2007 labour agreement also introduced the possibility of job sharing, an important new opportunity that has significantly encouraged circular migratory practices. Workers are allowed to share their job with another person, and to manage independently the organization of the work schedule. Both the

Table 9.5 Ukrainian citizens who entered in 2008 and were legally resident as of 1 January 2009, by sex and marital status: absolute numbers and percentages

	MALE AND FEMALE				MALE				FEMALE			
	Unmarried	Married	Other	Total	Unmarried	Married	Other	Total	Unmarried	Married	Other	Total
Absolute numbers	11,937	9,294	809	22,040	2,727	1,980	19	4,726	9,210	7,314	790	17,314
Percentages	54.2	42.2	3.7	100.0	57.7	4.9	0.4	100.0	53.2	42.2	4.6	100.0

Source: Istat www.demo.istat.it

Table 9.6 Ukrainian citizens entered in 2008 and legally present as of 1 January 2009, by sex and age group: absolute numbers and percentages

MALE AND FEMALE								MALE								FEMALE							
>17	18–29	30–39	40–49	50–59	60<	TOT	>17	18–29	30–39	40–49	50–59	60<	TOT	>17	18–29	30–39	40–49	50–59	60<	TOT
1,502	4,329	4,523	5,982	4,848	856	22,040	765	1,641	1,104	771	358	87	4,726	737	2,688	3,419	5,211	4,490	769	17,314
6.8	19.6	20.5	27.1	22.0	3.9	100.0	16.2	34.7	23.4	16.3	7.6	1.8	100.0	4.3	15.5	19.7	30.1	25.9	4.4	100.0

Source: Istat www.demo.istat.it

women involved are directly and personally responsible for the entire duty to work. Turns can be arranged vertically (usually, migrants work for three or six months each), or horizontally (during the same working day).

The habit of sharing jobs between friends and sisters was already customary among migrants from Eastern European—especially among Romanian and Croatian women, who were allowed to cross Italian borders with a tourist visa and stay for a maximum of three months—although it was still an informal, unregulated practice. Today, the legal recognition of this working arrangement—which is particularly advantageous for employers—makes it relatively easy even for workers with a limited freedom of movement, like Ukrainians and Moldavians, to adopt circular migratory practices while maintaining their contract, and consequently their permit of stay.[17] Nevertheless, a key informant of Acli-Colf claims that such labour contracts are often used by employers to exploit domestic workers, in particular when working shifts are arranged horizontally: they have two workers available for the price of one, who are mutually responsible.[18] Moreover, Acli-Colf suggests that vertical shifts should be managed according to a different system that would protect workers better, such as the part-time system. In their opinion it would be better to operate two independent working relationships, and to suspend the worker's salary during her absence period.

If INPS (National Institute of Social Security) disclosed the data regarding the number of contracts that allow job sharing, it would be possible to quantify the circular migration of Ukrainian citizens employed in the domestic and care work sector, who, as we have seen, represent an increasing share of the Ukrainian women who reside in Italy. However, since such data is still unavailable, it is almost impossible to estimate the real dimensions of this migratory practice, since there are no other sources of information regarding this phenomenon.[19]

Data regarding expired permits of stay can, however, provide some insight into return migrations. As of 2009, 8,423 Ukrainian citizens who had been registered as legal sojourners at the end of 2008 did not have a permit of stay. Presumably, only a small percentage of this group have lost their job and their permit owing to the recent economic crisis, since the demand for domestic workers has not decreased significantly. These departures can probably be better defined as voluntary and permanent return migrations, since those workers who are planning on moving back to Italy are usually very careful about renewing their documents.

Finally, data regarding seasonal labour, which represents an important source of information regarding circular migrations of other nationalities, is almost irrelevant for the study of Ukrainian workers: in 2009, the Ukrainian citizens hired as seasonal workers were less than a thousand (753 in the agricultural sector and 306 in the tourism industry) (Attanasio et al. 2010).

A Transnational Double Presence: Circular Migration between Ukraine and Italy

Table 9.7 Types of Ukrainian migration

	Adult women	Adult men	Girls and boys
Family in Ukraine	Intermittent circular migrants: main residence in Italy; married, divorced or widowed; manual workers.	Seasonal workers: main residence in Ukraine; both married and unmarried; manual workers.	Ideal circular migrants: main residence in Ukraine; students, high-skilled workers and entrepreneurs.
Family in Italy	Stationary migrants: main residence in Italy; married, divorced or widowed; reunited with some of their relatives; manual workers.	Stationary migrants: main residence in Italy; married; reached their wives in Italy; manual workers.	Cosmopolitans: members of migrant families; live both in Italy and in Ukraine; students, high-skilled workers and entrepreneurs.

We see this low number probably because there is not any agreement for international cooperation in migratory matters between Italy and the Ukraine.

To sum up, it is possible to schematize Ukrainian migration through the ideal types laid out in Table 9.7.

The biggest group is composed of intermittent circular migrants, and for this reason the next section focuses on this category. As already described, the majority of migrants are adult women, who keep their main residence in Italy. They are usually employed in the care and domestic sector, and they have left their families behind (children and husbands). Even if the majority plan to return to Ukraine soon, some women are trying to reunite their families by bringing their children and husbands to Italy. This process of family reunification is producing three new types of migrants: stationary migrant women; stationary migrant men; and cosmopolitan girls and boys (the migrants' children). In addition, there are two other types of Ukrainian migrants. The first one is the seasonal worker: an adult man employed mainly in agriculture. The second one is the group of ideal circular migrants: an elite group of people performing the ideal forms of circular migrations promoted by the EU Commission (COM 2007 248 final).[20] They are the new guest workers, and they are functional to the paradigm of flexibility (Gallino 2007).

9.4 Intermittent circular migrants

The majority of the interviewed migrants—both in Italy and in Ukraine—think of migration as a short-term or circular experience. Many of them recall having left their country with the intention of working in Italy only for a brief period: the time necessary to improve their family's financial situation, pay debts, and provide for their children's studies, as well as for their elderly parents and their husbands. However, a large number of these migrants have been trapped in Italy for a much longer time.

The reasons for the extension of the migratory experience are many. First of all, being irregular workers prevents the migrants from returning to Ukraine even for short periods, because they would be allowed back in Italy only with a tourist visa. Many migrants have stated how they had been forced to stay as irregular immigrants, waiting for years for a general amnesty. For instance, Oleksandra arrived in 1998 and obtained a permit of stay only in 2002, after working for three years for many Italian families:

> I arrived in Naples in 1998. I found a job in the countryside close to Naples and I worked there for one year and seven months. Then the lady died and I left for Mestre. I found another job in Vicenza, I worked for a short period with a ninety-four-year-old man. He fell and hurt himself so I was again without a job. Found another job in Verona thanks to a lady from the Red Cross. The job was very hard because this man was paralysed and so you had to do everything: change diapers, cook food, clean. Then the lady decided to give me the papers so I had to go back to Kiev to get my papers. So I lived in Italy without documents for three years and ten days. (Oleksandra, Venice, 2 June 2006)

When migrants manage to regularize their legal status, they generally decide to profit from their permit of stay—also considering the consistent human and economic investment that was necessary to obtain it—and therefore extend their stay abroad for some years, as they are now free to travel back and forth between Italy and Ukraine.

Upon returning home for the first time, they realize that work opportunities are few, and that, because of high inflation, the small capital that they accumulated is still insufficient to fulfil some of the goals they had set for themselves, such as the purchase of a house, or the creation of a 'pension fund' for their retirement. Moreover, remittances have become an essential source of income for their children who remained at home, and it is difficult to force them to live without that money.

Therefore, many migrants continue to work in Italy, often as caregivers or domestic workers, and return to Ukraine once or twice a year, for periods that range from two weeks in the summer to two or three months. These movements can be defined as spontaneous and intermittent circular labour migration of adult women (mothers or grandmothers) with high skills but low-wage jobs, who are temporary (short-term) migrants and desire to maintain strong ties with the country of origin. Generally, these women are between forty and sixty years old, and have adult children who are independent from their mothers but still need financial support. The migrants' advanced age reduces their

A Transnational Double Presence: Circular Migration between Ukraine and Italy

opportunities to find employment in Ukraine. They prefer to conclude their productive life in Italy, and to accumulate enough money to grant themselves a dignified retirement, considering the low retirement pensions that they will receive in their home country.

One of the reasons why they cannot stay for long in Ukraine is the risk of losing their jobs in Italy, something that has happened to Liuba:

> After three years I went back home because they had my papers done and I went home. I stayed home for three months and they told me that it was too long for them so I lost my job. It was difficult to go back because in the beginning you can't come back because you don't have the documents, so if you go out then you never go back. With the permit it's easier. (Liuba, Sambir, 17 August 2006)

Employers are rarely inclined to let their employees take long vacations, because this would mean not only finding a substitute who is willing to work only for a few months, but also establishing a new relationship of trust and intimacy. Care workers are not as easily replaceable as other types of workers. This job is characterized by a strong relational and emotional dimension, which often makes the relationship between the caregiver and the care receiver a unique one, especially when receivers are elderly people or people with medical conditions. Often, the relationship between the worker and the family becomes one of interdependence, since, on the one hand, the migrants need a contract, and, on the other, families are unable to deal on their own with the needs of the dependent person. Moreover, caregivers develop feelings of gratitude for the families that regularize their legal status, as well as of loyalty toward the care receivers, and often decide to stay with them until their death.

The returns that last two or three months generally coincide with the death of the care receiver and the search for a new job. They almost become sabbatical leaves, which the workers take to mourn (Fedyuk 2009) and rest before beginning a new job. Therefore, although it does not have an immediate financial purpose, this period of suspension of working activity is functional in improving the worker's well-being and, consequently, the quality of the care service. During these months, migrants stay with their families, re-establish social ties which have been weakened by distance, and monitor the investment of their remittances—usually the renovation of their house, or the purchase/construction of a new one.

Others, instead, manage to find a less demanding occupation, and arrange a more flexible working schedule with their employers in order to be able to return often to their country of origin. When asked how often a female Ukrainian migrant is able to come home, she responded:

> Often. Last year my daughter was pregnant and I had my bags ready to leave. My daughter delivered on 4 February and I was home on the 6th. My grandson is

> beautiful, his name is Oreste and now he's one year old. We have some pictures. I stayed home to help my daughter for almost two months. I didn't lose my job, because to every family I asked: 'Do you need someone permanent or are you able to be on your own when I am away?' For some families I have friends who replaced me, in others they don't always need me and then when I go back I work some extra hours. Then Oxana got married and I went back one more time. (Tatiana, L'viv, 24 August 2006)

The interview with Tatiana gives us some insight into an important dimension of Ukrainian female migration, that is how these women have managed to re-elaborate their 'double presence' (Balbo 1978) on a transnational level (Vianello 2012). We can see how Tatiana is able to reconcile the paid labour she does in Italy, which is care work, with the unpaid reproductive labour for her family, which she continues to attend to in her country of origin. In this case, the model of choice within the family/work system falls into an action space which has transnational extension (Balsamo 2006).

Thus, Ukrainian migrants become used to mediating between reproductive labour and market labour. In their case, the female identity based on the experience of the 'double presence' (Bimbi 1985) has to face the challenge represented by the integration of extremely different spheres of living, and consequently acquires new dimensions. Their experience goes beyond the simple identity contradiction between the public and the private dimensions: they have to conciliate different cultural, spatial, and temporal spheres, through a commuting that is both mental and physical.

Although physically distant from their children, migrants keep them spiritually close with letters, messages, telephone calls, gifts, remittances. They can also actually visit them because of the short geographical distances, which allow fast and low-cost travelling. Transnational double presence, therefore, refuses to coincide with a totalizing, exclusive experience. Rather, it represents the foundation for the multiple identity with which the women migrants identify themselves: beside being workers, they want to be mothers, grandmothers, and, in a few cases, even wives.[21]

Finally, the habit of sharing jobs (formally and informally) is becoming a common practice among Ukrainian migrants. Those who choose to share their job accept to receive only half of their annual salary (around €6,000), in exchange for the possibility of returning to Ukraine for six months a year. This choice significantly affects the household income, and it is acceptable only when the migrant is not the sole breadwinner. In fact, among the women I interviewed, the ones who had chosen this working arrangement had husbands who worked in Ukraine and received a medium-high wage.

> Our engine drivers retire at fifty-five, five years earlier than usual, because it's a hard job. He's fifty-seven years old, is already retired but he kept on working

A Transnational Double Presence: Circular Migration between Ukraine and Italy

because in the last years he was responsible for the movements: there are four of them, they are responsible for the departures of trains, there is also the depot where trains stop and he's responsible if the trains need fixing. The pension is high compared to the others: €200. The salary is also high, €300. After all he has €500 a month. He's independent. He spent all his money on the house. Now he wants to build a fireplace... What can I do with this money? Buy a few shoes. I worked in the spring and all of the money went to my daughter... My husband always says that he thinks I can go back home, because he's got some money. He doesn't want me to help my daughter, because he thinks she's old enough to provide for herself, we paid for her studies and now it's enough. (Alexandra, Venice, 11 September 2009)

Migrants who share jobs have adopted high-intensity circular migratory practices. They perceive this working arrangement as a positive opportunity, because it allows them to conciliate their desire for financial independence with their private lives, and to live a transnational life where they are able to keep their identities as migrant workers. The women interviewed often think of the possibility of going home as one of the most positive aspects of the shift-system: it helps them maintain ties with their society of origin, relieve the emotional stress typical of care work (Hochschild 1983; Macdonald and Sirianni 1996; Hunter 2001), and thereby reduce the risk of burnout (Maslach 2003).

Cyclical and regular returns also allow the migrants to participate actively in the informal domestic economy of their extended family. Although they do not do paid work during the months they spend in Ukraine, they work in the family's vegetable gardens and participate in care activities.

9.5 Conclusion

The aim of this chapter has been to investigate Ukrainian women's circular migration between their country of origin and Italy. First, we could observe how the professional and migratory patterns of Ukrainian women who work in Italy are extremely articulated, and that Italy only represents a stage in their experience. These women—who are generally in their forties and fifties, with an education and a long working experience—have undertaken international migration to survive the economic crisis of the 1990s. In the earlier years they were engaged in a circular trans-border mobility, but later shifted to longer-distance circular migrations.

Italian restrictive migration policies represent an obstacle to Ukrainian women's migratory plans, since, once they have crossed the country's borders, they become trapped for many years without being able to return to Ukraine even for short visits. They wait for several years to obtain a permit of stay, and find irregular employment in the domestic work sector. Moreover, the poor employment opportunities in Ukraine, owing to the migrants' advanced age and the low wages, make their return even more problematic. Ukraine, on the other hand, has not implemented any policy for the social and economic reintegration of circular migrants.

According to some key informants, the experience of returning is deeply traumatic, and many women suffer from psychological distress caused by the migratory experience.[22] Besides, only a few women manage to make their return coincide with the beginning of a new entrepreneurial project. However, such difficulties are not only made worse by the absence of a support programme to help them cope with their return, but also by the fact that they are middle-aged women with specific skills that are rarely recognized within the Ukrainian care service sector.

The long absence from their country of origin also contributes to the transformation of the role and the social identity with which the migrants identify. Therefore, when they eventually obtain a permit of stay, many of these women have already abandoned their initial project of a short-term migration and prefer to adopt a circular migratory pattern.[23] They do not have a permanent residence in Italy or in Ukraine, but they have interests to protect in both countries. With circular migration, they manage to maintain their financial independence, and the freedom and social life that they have come to know in Italy, as well as their affective bonds left behind.

The action space of migrant women has become wider. National borders and restrictive immigration laws represent an obstacle for the circular migratory practices employed by the women interviewed. They wish to be able to cross borders without restrictions, and to spend their lives in a transnational space between the sending and the receiving countries.

According to the women interviewed, the experience of circular migration has generated positive results. However, we cannot forget that they are part of a very specific group in a particular moment of their life, whose life has been deeply upset by the dissolution of the Soviet Union. This revolutionary event has turned them into a low-cost labour force, which is perfectly functional to the needs of the Italian labour market.

In conclusion, I define the circular migratory practices of Ukrainian women as a transnational double presence. This is a specific way of reinterpreting the 'double presence' model (Balbo 1978; Bimbi and Pristinger 1985)—which usually identifies women's simultaneous presence in two different realities, like the public and the private spheres, paid labour and the family—in the transnational social space, defined as that multiplicity of circular flows that connects the societies of emigration and immigration (Basch, Glick Schiller, and Szanton Blanc 1994).

References

Ambrosini, M. (2011). 'Undocumented Migrants and Invisible Welfare: Survival Practices in the Domestic Environment', *Migration Letters*, 8(1), 34–42.

Ambrosini, M. and Triandafyllidou, A. (2011). 'Irregular Immigration Control in Italy and Greece: Strong Fencing and Weak Gate-keeping serving the Labour Market', *European Journal of Migration and Law*, 13(3), 251–73.

Attanasio, P., Pittau, F. and Ricci, A. (2010). *Migrazione temporanea e circolare in italia: evidenze empiriche, prassi politiche attuali e opzioni per il futuro*. Roma: European Migration Network e Centro Studi e Ricerche IDOS.

Balbo, L. (1978), 'La doppia presenza', *Inchiesta*, VIII (32), 3–6.

Balsamo, F. (2006). 'Madri migranti, diversamente sole', in F. Bimbi and R. Trifiletti (eds), *Madri sole e nuove famiglie*. Roma: Edizioni Lavoro, 195–234.

Basch, L., Glick Schiller, N. and Szanton Blanc, C. (1994). *Nations Unbound: Transnational Projects, Postcolonial Predicaments, and Deterritorialized Nation-states*. OPA Amsterdam: Gordon and Breach Publishers.

Bimbi, F. (1985). 'La doppia presenza: diffusione di un modello e trasformazione dell'identità', in F. Bimbi and F. Pristinger (eds), *Profili sovrapposti: la doppia presenza delle donne in un'area ad economia diffusa*. Milano: Franco Angeli, 11–92.

Bimbi, F. and Pristinger, F. (eds) (1985), *Profili sovrapposti: la doppia presenza delle donne in un'area ad economia diffusa*. Milano: Franco Angeli.

Censis (2010). *VI Rapporto Censis sulla situazione sociale del Paese*, Roma.

Chumalo, M. (2005). 'Ukrains'ki schinki na zarobitkach v Italii', in I. Markov (ed.), *Ukrajins'ka trudova migracija u contesti zmin suchasnogo svitu*. L'viv: Kompanija Manuskript, 78–89.

Cipko, S. (2006). 'Contemporary Migration from Ukraine', in R. Rodriguez Rios (ed.), *Migration Perspectives: Eastern Europe and Central Asia*. Vienna: IOM, 117–32 [online]. http://publications.iom.int/bookstore/free/MigrationPerspectives.pdf

Codagnone, C. (1998). 'The New Migration in Russia in the 1990s', in K. Koser and H. Lutz (eds), *The New Migration in Europe*. London: Macmillan Press Ltd, 39–59.

Conti, C. et al. (2010). *From East to West: the Former USSR Citizens in Italy*, paper presented at European Population Conference (EPC 2010), Vienna, Austria, 1–4 September 2010.

Decimo, F. (2005). *Quando emigrano le donne*, Bologna: Il Mulino.

Fassmann, H. and Munz, R. (1994). 'European East-West Migration, 1945–1992', *International Migration Review*, 28(3), 520–38.

Fedyuk, O. (2009). 'Death in the life of Ukrainian labor migrants in Italy', *Migration Online*, 20, [online]. www.migrationonline.cz/e-library/?x=2162690

Fedyuk, O. (2012). 'Images of Transnational Motherhood: The Role of Photographs in Measuring Time and Maintaining Connections between Ukraine and Italy', *Journal of Ethnic and Migration Studies*, 38(2), 279–300.

Fonseca, M., João, A. and Nunes, A. (2004). 'Immigration to medium sized cities and rural areas: the case of Eastern Europeans in the Évora Region (Southern Portugal)', in M. Ioannis Baganha and M. L. Fonseca (eds), *New waves: migration from eastern to Southern Europe*, Luso-American Foundation, Lisbon.

Frejka, T., Okolski, M. and Sword, K. (1999). *In-depth Studies on Migration in Central and Eastern Europe: The Case of Ukraine*. New York-Geneva: United Nations Press.

Gallino, L. (2007). *Il lavoro non è una merce. Contro la flessibilità*, Roma-Bari: Laterza.

Gois, P. and Marques, J. C. (2007). 'Ukrainian Migration to Portugal. From Non-Existence to One of the Top Three Immigrant Groups', *Migration Online*. http://aa.ecn.cz/img_upload/3bfc4ddc48d13ae0415c78ceae108bf5/JCMarquesPGois_Ukraniansin Portugal.pdf.

Hochschild, A. R. (1983). *The Managed Heart*. Berkeley-Los Angeles-London: University of California Press.

Homra, A., Malynovska, O. and Pirozhkov, S. (2003). *Foreign Labour Migration in Ukraine: Socio-Economic Aspect*. Kyiv: IOM.

Huner, B. (2001). 'Emotion work in midwifery: a review of current knowledge', *Journal of Advanced Nursing*, 34 (4), 436–44.

Iglicka, K. (2003). *Migration and Labour Markets in Poland and Ukraine*. Warsaw: Institute of Public Affairs.

Iglicka, K., Gmaj, K. and Borodzicz-Smoliński, W. (2011). *Circular migration patterns. Migration between Ukraine and Poland*. San Domenico di Fiesole: Metoikos Project.

INPS/Caritas, *IV Rapporto sui lavoratori di origine immigrata negli archivi INPS. La regolarità del lavoro come fattore di integrazione*, Roma: Edizioni Idos.

Ioli, A. (2010). 'Dal primo contratto collettivo sul lavoro domestico ai giorni nostri', in R. Sarti (ed.), *Lavoro domestico e di cura:quali diritti?* Roma: Ediesse.

Istat (2001). *Permessi di soggiorno per sesso, area geografica e singolo paese di cittadinanza al 1° gennaio 2001*. Roma: Istat.

Istat (2004). *Permessi di soggiorno per sesso e paese di cittadinanza al 1° gennaio 2004. Primi cinquanta paesi*. Roma: Istat.

Istat (2009). *Cittadini non comunitari entrati nel 2008 regolarmente presenti al 1/1/2009, per sesso e stato civile, per area geografica e principali paesi di cittadinanza*. Roma: Istat.

Istat (2009). *Cittadini non comunitari regolarmente presenti per motivo di lavoro, area geografica e principali paesi di cittadinanza, per sesso, al 1° gennaio 2009—Maschi e femmine*. Roma: Istat.

Ivano Frankivsk Region (2005). *Statistical Reference Book*, Ivano Frankivsk: Statistical Rregional Committee.

Kindler, M. (2006). *Irregular Migration in Central and Eastern Europe: The Case of Ukrainian Workers in Poland*, Paper for the conference 'Irregular Migration: Research, Policy and Practice', University of Oxford, 8–9 July, Oxford.

Kindler, M. (2008). 'Risk and Risk Strategies in Migration: Ukrainian Domestic Workers in Poland, Migration and Domestic Work: A European Perspective on a Global Theme', in H. Lutz (ed.), *Migration and Domestic Work: A European Perspective on a Global Theme*. London: Ashgate, 154–60.

Korobkov, A. V., Zaionchkovskaia, Z. A. (2004). 'The Changes in the Migration Patterns in the Post-Soviet States: the First Decade', *Communist and Post-Communist Studies*, 37, 481–508.

Macdonald, L. C. and Sirianni, C. (1996). *Working in the Service Society*. Philadelphia: Temple University Press.

Malynovska, O. (2004). 'International Migration in Contemporary Ukraine: Trends and Policy', *Global Migration Perspectives*, (14), Geneva: Global Commission on International Migration.

Maslach, C. (2003). *Burnout: The Cost of Caring*. Los Altos: ISHK.

Mazzacurati, C. (2005). 'Dal blat alla vendita del lavoro. Come sono cambiate colf e badanti ucraine e moldave a Padova', in T. Caponio and A. Colombo (eds), *Migrazioni globali e integrazioni locali*. Bologna: Il Mulino, 145–74.

Ministero dell'Interno (2010). *Colf e badanti, i dati riepilogativi al 5 luglio* [online]. www.interno.it (accessed 29 July 2012).

Näre, L. (2007). 'Ukrainian and Polish Domestic Workers in Naples—A Case of East-South Migration', *Migration Online*, http://aa.ecn.cz/img_upload/3bfc4ddc48d13ae0415c78ceae108bf5/LNare_UkrainianandPolishDomesticWorkersinNaplesACaseofEast_1.pdf

Okolski, M. (2001). 'Incomplete Migration: A New Form of Mobility in Central and Eastern Europe. The Case of Polish and Ukrainian Migrants', in C. Wallace and D. Stola (eds), *Patterns of Migration in Central Europe*. Houndmills: Palgrave Macmillan, 105–29.

Pasquinelli, S. and Rusmini, G. (2010). 'La sanatoria delle assistenti familiari: un bilancio'. http://www.qualificare.info/upload/Pasquinelli-Rusmini_NNA-2010.pdf

Pedraza, S. (1991). 'Women and Migration: The Social Consequences of Gender', *Annual Review of Sociology*, 17, 203–325.

Sacchetto, D. (ed.) (2011). *Ai margini dell'Unione Europea*. Roma: Carocci.

Sayad, A. (1999). *La double absence. Des illusions de l'émigré aux souffrances de l'immigré*. Paris: Seuil.

Scrinzi, F. (2004). 'Donne migranti e mercato del lavoro domestico', *Polis*, vol. XVIII(1), 107–36.

Shamshur, O. (1992). 'Ukraine in the Context of New European Migrations', *International Migration Review*, vol. XXVI(2), 258–68.

Solari, C. (2010). 'Resource drain vs. constitutive circularity: comparing the gendered effects of Post-Soviet migration patterns in Ukraine', *The Anthropology of East Europe Review*, 28(1), 215–38.

Tymczuk, A. and Leifsen, E. (2012). 'Care at a distance: Ukrainian and Ecuadorian transnational parenthood from Spain', *Journal of Ethnic and Migration Studies*, 38(2), 219–36.

Vianello, F. A. (2009). *Migrando sole. Legami transnazionali tra Ucraina e Italia*. Milano: Franco Angeli.

Vianello, F. A. (2011). 'Suspended migrants. Return migration to Ukraine', in M. Nowak and M. Nowosielski M. (eds), *(Post)trans-formational Migration*. Berlin: Peter Lang, 251–74.

Vianello, F. A. (2012), 'Continuità e confini tra vita pubblica e vita privata. La doppia presenza delle assistenti familiari', *AG About Gender*, 1(2), 175–203.

Volodko, V. (2011). 'Transnational Family Practices of Ukrainian Female Labour Migrants in Poland', in J. Luczys (ed.), *Selling One's Favourite Piano to Emigrate Mobility Patterns in Central Europe at the Beginning of the 21st Century*. Newcastle: Cambridge Scholars Publishing, 105–18.

Wallace, C., Bedezir, V. and Chmoulir, O. (1997). *Spending, saving or investing social capital: the case of shuttle traders in post-communist Central Europe.* Vienna: Institute for Advanced Studies.

Wallace, C. et al. (1998). *Some Characteristics of Labour Migration and the Central European Buffer Zone.* Vienna: Institute for Advanced Studies.

Notes

1. Ukrainians living in Veneto mainly come from western Ukraine, but there are also people from the south and the centre of the country.
2. L'viv is the regional capital of Galicia, as well as the main political and cultural centre of western Ukraine. Its economy is based on the service sector (commerce, finance and tourism), while the surrounding region is characterized by a predominantly agricultural economy.
3. Ivano Frankivsk has a population of about 220,000 people and is located in eastern Galicia. Ivano Frankivsk, with the smaller towns of Kalush, Kolomyia, Nadvirna, is an important centre for mechanical engineering, wood processing, and chemical and light industry.
4. PhD programme in Sociology of Intercultural and Communication Processes in the Public Sphere, Department of Sociology, University of Padua.
5. Veneto Lavoro is a local public agency on labour policies.
6. Ukraine's working population at the time reached 20 million people.
7. The sale of a carton of cigarettes, two litres of alcohol or a tank of gasoline in Poland or Hungary is worth around $20 a day (Malynovska 2006).
8. Venice, 12 February 2006.
9. Sambir, 18 August 2006.
10. L'viv, 11 September 2006.
11. This may still be true in the near future; however, there is a strong possibility that, in the long term, Ukrainian men will be able to be employed in the Italian labour market. For example, a few Ukrainians are already present in the construction sector in Bologna.
12. These figures include individual permits of stay issued for family reasons as well as minors accompanied by an adult, even if entered for other purposes.
13. These figures include permanent visas that do not indicate a purpose of presence (about 15,000 cases).
14. In Italy, the incidence of the underground economy on GNP amounts to 17.6 per cent, of which 37.2 per cent is related to the irregular work phenomenon (Censis 2010). The number of domestic workers is estimated to be 840,000, of which 90 per cent are foreigners. Migrant women workers without a permit amount to 40 per cent of this figure, that is 300,000 people (Pasquinelli and Rusmini 2010).
15. Law no. 102/2009 allowed families that employed domestic workers and caregivers who were illegally living in Italy to apply for regularization. When the law was passed, 295,000 applications were submitted (Ministero dell'Interno 2010), although the public authorities had anticipated to receive at least twice as many.

16. Agreement signed on 21 January 2011 at the Ministry of Labour and Social Policies, regarding the new minimum wage adjusted according to the variations in the cost of living.
17. The fundamental principle of Italian migration policies is represented by the contract of residence for subordinate labour, which is necessary to obtain a permit of stay. This contract regulates the relationship between an employer and an employee from a non-EU country, and guarantees the migrant's legal residence in Italy (law no. 189, 30 July 2002).
18. Acli-Colf is an association dedicated to the defence, protection and social and professional promotion of caregivers and domestic workers, both Italian and immigrant.
19. For technical reasons.
20. 'The Commission indicates that the two main forms of circular migration which could be most relevant in the EU context are: that of third-country nationals residing in the EU, such as business people from third countries working in the EU and wishing to start an activity in their country of origin or in another third country; that of third-country nationals established outside the EU, such as nationals wishing to engage in seasonal or temporary work within the EU or to study there before returning to their country' [online]. http://europa.eu (accessed: 29 July 2012).
21. Many migrant women are divorced.
22. Commonly known as 'Italian syndrome'.
23. Others, instead, prefer to settle in Italy, where they have built a new life (Vianello 2009). Such a decision is connected with the life cycle of both women and their relatives.

10

Circular Migration at the Periphery of Europe: Choice, Opportunity, or Necessity?

Anna Triandafyllidou

10.1 Introduction

The aim of this chapter is to compare the three sets of case studies presented in this book with a view to identifying circular migration types that are valid across cases, and eventually propose a refined set of circular migration types. In addition here we pay attention to identify through comparative analysis the common factors that foster or indeed impede the development of circular migration. We also focus on issues of migrant integration and reintegration, as these are crucial for the understanding of who benefits from circular migration, and what the challenges are for sending countries, receiving states, and indeed the migrants themselves. The chapter concludes with a critical appraisal of how circular migration fits the post-fordist paradigm of production (Venturini 2004) and the securitized temporariness approach that seems to dominate policymaking both at EU and at member state level (see Cassarino in this volume).

10.2 Circular migration in the south-western and central Mediterranean: Spain, Italy, and Morocco

Moroccan immigration in Spain and Italy is largely sedentary. People migrate with the view of finding employment and staying at the destination country for a number of years. The fact that most Moroccan immigrants arrived in Spain or Italy without documents (even if later they regularized) is an important factor that has from the beginning limited any consideration of circularity and of economic activity that would engage travelling between the two countries. In addition, the necessity to prove that one is employed so as to periodically renew one's stay permit makes Moroccan immigrants in both Italy and Spain cling onto their jobs in the destination country, and not risk losing them by lengthy trips back to Morocco. Indeed, both Spanish and Italian employers want reliable, stable, year-round migrant workers, and do not appreciate people who need to be absent from work for long periods. Circularity or seasonality is actually a by-product of the Italian and Spanish labour markets, and of the migration opportunities and restrictions that the Spanish and Italian migration policy offers, as we shall explain below.

As the Italy-Morocco case study proposes, we need to distinguish between circular migrants who have the destination country (Italy) as their base, and circular migrants who have the origin country (Morocco) as their main place of residence. In the case of Spain, the circular migrants identified indeed had their lives mostly in Morocco, spending on average two months a year working in Spanish agriculture.

On the basis of the findings from the Italian and Spanish case studies we have identified two types of circular migrants who engage in economic activity in either country but have their basis in the country of origin, namely Morocco.

The type 'seasonal agricultural work at the destination country' involves Moroccan women in Spain, who come from rural regions of Morocco (and are employed in agriculture at home too), who travel to Spain each year to work in the harvesting of strawberries (in the region of Huelva) or in other cultivations, at greenhouses mostly in the region of Almeria (both regions in southern Spain). In the case of Italy, this category mainly involves Moroccan men, who are either self-employed in semi-low-skilled work or unemployed in Morocco, who come to Italy on a legal basis in order to work in agriculture for six months a year. These individuals were resident in Italy for more than ten years before embarking on circulation. There is only a limited number of Moroccans working in Italian agriculture on a seasonal basis today in Italy.

The type 'seasonal street-selling at the destination country' is not present in Spain, as street peddling is an activity mostly undertaken by Sub-Saharan Africans. In Italy it involves mainly Moroccan men, who are farmers at home in Morocco for most of the year, and travel to Italy for two to three months a year to work as street-sellers. While Moroccan street hawkers are numerous and often undocumented, those engaged upon this activity on a circular basis hold Italian stay permits, which allow them to work in Italy as self-employed. They are usually first-generation Moroccan immigrants in Italy who came early on, and hence had acquired their long-term stay permits.

They decided to return to Morocco, but still engage into this circular economic activity to supplement their income in Morocco.

This is a type of circular migration that is found mostly in southern Italy, and these Moroccan circular migrants spend the summer holiday months selling Chinese goods (bought in Italy) in Italy by the seaside. These migrants spend about three months a year in the country, and are engaged in street selling. They have mostly been coming to Italy for more than ten years.

Both these types of circular migration are small in size and somewhat declining in Italy. They have their roots in the times of free circularity before the introduction of the visa regimes between Morocco and Italy, and respond to the particularities of southern Italian regions where street hawking, selling, and buying in open air markets is not only an economic activity but also perhaps a cultural trait.

Circular migration to work on a seasonal basis in agriculture is by contrast an increasing trend in Spain. Rather than being a legacy that comes from the period of free circulation in the case of Spain, this pattern has been designed by Spanish authorities to respond to the needs for a seasonal labour force in agriculture in specific Spanish regions, where the agricultural sector has developed and intensified during the last decade with important positive developments for the entire regions concerned (Almeria, Huelva, Lleida).

This type of circularity has been fostered by EU-funded programmes, initially through the AENEAS programme and later through other lines of the EU and the Spanish national budget. Hence these programmes are managed at a bilateral level between Spain and Morocco, with the involvement of trade unions and authorities in the selection (of migrant workers) process, and in monitoring the living and working conditions of the circular migrants. Such a programme may be cited as a good practice example, to the extent that it provides for the possibility for Moroccan women to earn a much higher salary from agricultural work than they would have done in their own country; have decent working and living conditions at the destination country; be escorted and helped with translation for all their paperwork by Moroccan and Spanish authorities or civil society actors; not being separated from their families and children for too long a period.

It is worth noting that ANAPEC (*Agence Nationale de Promotion de l'Emploi et des Compétences*), the Moroccan Employment Service, has tried to establish such a bilateral scheme with Italy too, but to no avail. Apparently the demand for seasonal workers in agriculture in Italy is much more fragmented among many small employers, and very few immigrants and employers take advantage of the precedence clause available in the law (inviting again the worker who was employed the previous year).

With regard to circular migrants who have their base in the destination country and periodically return to the country of origin, it is important to note that we found no such occurrences in the case of Moroccan immigration to Spain. Moroccan immigrants who are settled in Spain generally do not engage in circular migration between the two countries. By contrast, in Italy, especially in the northern regions, there are several types of Moroccan economic circular migration between the two countries. Two of these types are similar to those outlined above, with the main difference being that they are principally based in Italy rather than in Morocco. Thus, the 'seasonal agricultural work at the country of origin' type involves low-skill or semi-skilled Moroccans employed in northern or southern Italy in unstable jobs (e.g., in the construction sector), who return to Morocco to work on the family farm (between three and six months annually). The type 'economizing in Morocco' encapsulates Moroccans based in the south of Italy who spend a couple of months a year in Morocco in order to save money, because they do not have stable employment in Italy. People belonging to either category have generally been legally resident in Italy for more or less than ten years, and are in and out of employment.

There are, however, two additional types of circular migration between Italy and Morocco, where the migrant is based in Italy, which are more related to business and trade. The first type entitled 'circular trade and transport' involves semi-skilled Moroccans who do not hold regular employment in Italy but are legally resident in Italy or in possession of dual citizenship. They buy goods[1] from Italy which they sell in Morocco—usually secondhand goods, or for instance electronic appliances—and also transport the goods of co-nationals to Morocco. The transportation of merchandise to sell or other people's belongings is usually done with vans which are overloaded with all sorts of goods. There are several problems with this kind of activity, as the Italian authorities are unable to register and categorize it (but generally tend to be permissive and allow this kind of trade to take place), while Moroccan customs officers generally ask for bribes to let the merchandise pass the border. The second type we may call brain circulation, as it involves people who are self-employed and engage in circular migration with a view to doing business and development cooperation in Morocco. These Moroccan circular migrants are relatively few, and live in northern Italy. Generally they have been residing legally in Italy for more than ten years.

10.2.1 *Factors and policies affecting circularity*

The analysis of the Italy-Morocco and Spain-Morocco cases shows that there are several factors that affect the possibility and profitability of circular migration between each pair of countries.

The first factor is the existence of a specific policy programme that organizes circular migration. In the case of Spain and Morocco, the development of a special bilateral programme that organizes and promotes repeated seasonal stays of Moroccan women in Spain to work in agriculture has greatly affected the size of these flows as well as their character. It is the programme itself that sets the conditions (working hours, salary, accommodation, insurance, but also lack of possibility to stay longer or to engage in different labour market sectors) and organizes the recruitment in Morocco. The programme promotes the return of the same workers every year, provided that they have complied with the conditions and that, of course, they wish to return (our study shows that they generally do). Such programmes do not exist between Italy and Morocco.

In the case of Italy, the possibility of having a self-employment permit fosters circularity. This facilitates the kind of spontaneous circular migration that we have identified in Italy, of Moroccan people working (a) in agriculture, (b) in street selling, (c) doing trade and offering transport services, (d) developing some kind of business between Italy and Morocco. In addition, Moroccans also circulate between Italy and Morocco with permits for employment, long-term residency status, and dual citizenship. In Spain, since would-be migrants cannot enter the country legally, claiming their will to work as self-employed, this kind of circularity is constricted. Migrants can become self-employed (and hence possibly engage in this type of circularity) after five years of legal stay, when they become permanent residents.

In addition to the specific policies that on purpose (as in the case of the seasonal agriculture programme between Morocco and Spain) or by accident (the self-employment permit) promote circular migration, a third factor is the level of skills. Clearly migrants with a medium level of skills and with a long residency at the country of destination are better placed to develop a cooperation and development business or a small trade between Italy and Morocco. Here, perhaps, as part of the human capital that circular migrants have, we should add the importance of speaking the language and being familiar with the country of destination. We assume that this is an important precondition, as all spontaneous circular migrants between Italy and Morocco (regardless of whether they are based now in Italy or Morocco) are people who have lived at the destination country for more than five years, and usually around ten years.

Last but not least, we note an important gender bias in the circularity patterns identified: women are only found in Spain in the organized bilateral circular migration programme between Morocco and Spain. All spontaneous circular migration emerging between Italy and Morocco involves only men. This probably derives from the gender roles assigned to women and men in the country of origin. Women would probably not engage in circular migration at all if ANAPEC did not actively recruit them for the seasonal migration scheme.

10.2.2 Benefits and challenges of circularity

Moroccan circular migrants in Spain and Italy are largely low- or semi-skilled people, mostly coming from rural areas, earning relatively low incomes, and not likely to make business investments in Morocco. At the most they will buy property with the money saved or develop their own family farm. There are no special provisions for their reintegration in Morocco, even though, with the onset of the global financial crisis during the last couple of years, the Moroccan government has introduced medical coverage for Moroccans residing abroad (*Mutuelle des Maroccains a l'Etranger*) who return to Morocco temporarily or permanently from a country with which there is no bilateral agreement. Other than this, reintegration in Morocco takes place through family ties at the village or town of origin.

Informal trade and transport, as practised by an increasing number of Moroccans who are based in Italy, is mainly a strategy of coping with temporary unemployment or underemployment during the crisis rather than a strategy for economic advancement. These circular migrants are usually resident in Italy for at least five years, and are well acquainted with the Italian socio-economic and political context. Despite the longevity of their presence in Italy, many of them do not feel accepted or understood by Italians. This inadequate social integration provides an indirect incentive for pursuing economic projects in the country of origin. Their integration in the destination country (Italy), for example by means of inter-marriage, facilitates economic circularity by providing migrants with access to social networks and social and cultural capital. However, the circular migrants and the families that stay behind (in Italy) cope with the challenges of circularity (absence of one parent for longer periods, economic instability) as best they can through extended family ties and co-ethnic network support.

Attention to circular migrants' specific necessities in the immigration country would facilitate circulation, for example the possibility for them to avail themselves of special services, including the provision of extra lessons for children who have missed school owing to absences abroad, and the organization of subletting among circular migrants, in order to cover the cost of paying rent while abroad. These migrants generally do not have to reintegrate in Morocco during circulation, as they often spend very short periods there and make use of their existing family and social networks. Nevertheless, instruction in Arabic is crucial to maintaining ties with Morocco and circularity among the second generation, and should continue to be supported by Moroccan institutions.

Circularity between Spain and Morocco is framed within the seasonal agricultural employment programme, and is thus more controlled but also more 'protected' for the people involved. The programme provides support for the paperwork and oversees the living and working conditions of the women involved. However, this also means that their contacts with the local population are scarce, as hostels are usually outside villages. Interaction with local people is hampered by the migrant women's lack of fluency in (or complete ignorance of) Spanish, the short period of stay, and residence in hostels scattered in the countryside. Workers visit the villages from time to time, but they limit their visits to buying or solving personal affairs.

> I do not see coexistence among locals and Moroccan women. The main reason is the language, a barrier that separates people and the second reason is that they come here to work. Their habit/life style is working, going to the village to buy and returning. So, there is not much coexistence and "interculturality" does not exist. (Huelva, NGO devoted to immigrants)

Half of the interviewed women have registered in Spanish courses offered by the organization of the programme. Some others could not partake in the language lessons because of the lack of places. Reintegration in normal life after returning to Morocco seems not to be problematic. All interviewed workers state that they have not faced any integration difficulty once back in their family and village. The average stay of two months allows them to keep communication and links with relatives alive. However, several Moroccan stakeholders interviewed pointed out a problem: many husbands reject their wives' participation in seasonal work in Spain for cultural reasons. As a matter of fact, the unease of husbands seems to pose a greater challenge to the circular experience than the care of children. Moroccan villages are still traditional and patriarchal, and the departure of a married woman to work in a foreign country can be seen as a sign of the husband's incompetence, or even of the woman's supposed indecent behaviour. Sources also relate cases of husbands who marry other women while their first wives are in Spain.

Circularity between Italy and Morocco on one hand and Spain and Morocco on the other is quite different in nature. In the former case, and in its different types identified earlier (see Devitt in this volume), circularity is a spontaneous response of the worker to the difficulties that she or he faces at the home or destination country. Circularity is an entrepreneurial type of reaction to poverty, unemployment, or underemployment, taking advantage of a long-term permit acquired previously through 'normal' long-term migration, and of familiarity and networks in either country. In other words, circularity is here a new form of migrant entrepreneurship. In the case of Spain and Morocco, such entrepreneurship has not yet arisen, and circularity takes rather a more classical form of repeated seasonal migration of people based in the home country and periodically staying in the destination country. In both sets of cases, circularity responds to the needs of the migrants to increase their income and/or find (better) employment. In the case of Spain-Morocco, circularity clearly fills a labour market niche without raising the challenges of long-term migrant integration. In the case of Italy, circularity rather creates a new employment niche (petty trade and street peddling in the summer) that responds to a need in the Italian labour market. In either case, the home country may be said to benefit, from the extent that circularity increases the populations' income and economic activity in the country, while at the same time not involving so-called brain drain.

10.3 Circular migration in South-eastern Europe: Greece, Italy, and Albania

Albanian migration to Greece and Italy has been strongly motivated by economic necessity. It started as an irregular movement, and hence circularity was not possible because of the difficulty and risk involved in crossing borders regularly. However, there were and still are important differences between Greece and Italy as destination countries. While Italy was seen as a more desired destination (Mai 2010), Greece was a more affordable one, as crossing the mountainous borders could be done on foot, on one's own, in small groups, or with the assistance of a local smuggler. By contrast, crossing the Otranto Straits from Albania to the Italian region of Apulia was more expensive and more dangerous.

Hence, while irregular Albanian immigrants to Italy stayed put, Albanian immigrants to Greece were more prone to circulate back and forth. Part of this circulation was also a forced one, as in the mid-1990s Greece systematically raided public places where migrants used to gather, rounded up thousands of Albanians without documents, and expelled them overnight to Albania. These operations cost the Greek state several billion drachmas without having any long-term effect, as the repatriated Albanians would cross the Greek border again after a few weeks or months.

The two case studies on circular migration between Italy and Greece have investigated both legal and irregular patterns of circular migration between each pair of countries. We have identified four main types of circular migration which are present in both pairs of countries. These four patterns are distinguished by the legal or irregular nature of the movement (legal seasonal migration for work purposes versus irregular seasonal or other types of circular migration also for employment), and by the level of skills (low or medium skills versus high-skill circular migration, or else termed brain circulation, between Italy or Greece and Albania).

The four types of circular migration between Greece or Italy and Albania identified are the following: legal seasonal migration in agriculture or other seasonal employment, such as herding or tourism; irregular seasonal migration for employment in agriculture, construction, or tourism; legal circular migration of low-skill or semi-skilled workers for employment in construction (this form is mainly present in Greece, less so in Italy); legal circular migration of semi-skilled and highly skilled people with a secure stay status in Greece (long-term stay permit or ethnic Greek Albanians) or Italy (long-term stay permit), who travel between Greece and Albania for high-skilled work or for their own small business development.

The first two types of circular migration may have an equal share of time spent in both countries. However, the 'home', the place where the family and the social cycle of the migrant is situated, is in Albania. The third and fourth types involve the destination country as the circular migrant's main country of residence; with the propensity to return to Albania becoming even more pertinent in the current economic climate.

Vullnetari (2009) notes that being a male, having a lower education level, originating from a rural area, and having positive short-term migration experiences are all factors that indicated a propensity to be involved in temporary or circular migration. Indeed, the first two types of our typology here confirm her findings. The 'legal seasonal migration' type involves young and middle-aged men who live in rural areas in Albania, and go to Italy and Greece every year for a few months per year (up to six months, as the respective laws and bilateral agreements specify) to work in agriculture in northern Greece, and also in Italian regions with intensive agricultural production.

In the case of Greece, this type of Albanian circular migrant consists predominantly of men aged thirty-five to fifty-eight, who first came to Greece in the early 1990s as irregular migrants. Throughout the 1990s, the time Albanians spent in Greece was dependent on police controls and on the work opportunities available. If there was work, the return to Albania was delayed, unless they were apprehended and deported by the police.

The introduction of a seasonal work scheme in agriculture in 2001 gave a strong incentive to formerly irregular circular migrants to make their movement seasonal and stick to their seasonal stay permit requirements. Even if they had an opportunity for a longer period of work, many of these migrants would not risk it. The possibility of finally attaining legal entry and stay is too strong to ignore for people who have experienced illegality for many years. At the same time, the fact that they have to leave after six months and cannot stay in the host country works as an incentive to invest towards some activity or property back home.

In the case of Greece, this system of legal seasonal migration has given rise to informal networks between employers and seasonal workers, which lead to a number of informal arrangements that actually violate the seasonal migration law. First, a common informal arrangement is that employers invite more workers than they need. Invited workers pay the employer who formally invites them a fee (which can range from €200 to €250), so they have the chance to engage in legal circular migration towards Greece. They may stay in the same geographical region where their employer is, but work in other sectors (e.g., construction), or they may move to another region to work there in agriculture, construction, or other manual jobs. Second, Albanian middle-men who facilitate the initial contact between the prospective migrant and the fake formal employer also obtain a fee for their mediation. Third, the migrant labourers may work for multiple employers: they may start working for a month with the employer who formally invited them but then change to a different employer. Fourth, employers sometimes retain a small part of the worker's daily wage (about 5 per cent) if they promise to invite him again the following year.

The second type of circularity that we have found between Italy or Greece and Albania is that of irregular seasonal migration for work in agriculture and other areas of temporary employment, such as construction or tourism. Such irregular seasonal migration is facilitated by the geographical proximity between the destination and origin countries. In both Greece and Italy, the socio-economic features of the people involved in this kind of circular migration patterns is very similar to that of those employed as legal seasonal workers in agriculture. There is one main difference between the two: that for some reason they cannot be invited by a Greek employer, or they cannot take part in the Italian quota system for seasonal migration. The reason may be in either case that in the past they were irregular migrants who were caught, and expelled to Albania with a no-entry ban for five years. Thus, during these five years they cannot enter Greece or Italy legally, and hence resort to irregular circularity. In Greece, these irregular seasonal migration patterns sometimes involve young men between fifteen and twenty-one years of age, who come with their fathers (who are part of the legal seasonal migration schemes) for work in agriculture in northern Greece, violating the minimum age requirement (of twenty-one years of age) that the invitation system requires.

The third type of circular migration between Greece or Italy and Albania may be called 'legal circular low-skilled or semi-skilled migration', and involves different types of economic activity and employment. This migration concerns not only low-skilled but also semi-skilled Albanian citizens, who in Albania have a farm or a small shop and engage in temporary legal circular migration to Greece or Italy to work temporarily in agriculture, construction, tourism, or other services, to supplement their income in Albania.

In the case of Greece, these are previously sedentary migrants who hold the usual two-year or in some cases the ten-year long permit, and who have been pushed to circularity because of unstable employment or underemployment in Greece owing to the current economic crisis.[2] They thus spend several months a year in Albania, with a view to either save money or to take advantage of employment opportunities there. If the economic crisis deepens in Greece, these migrants are more likely to spend more time in Albania. These circular migrants usually make some form of investment or savings in Albania, which may have to do with the development of their own farm there, or opening up a small shop or other business (such as a restaurant or café).

The fieldwork research has shown that there are increasing numbers of Albanians who divide their time between Greece and Albania depending on the employment opportunities in either country. Their families in some cases have migrated back to Albania because it was too expensive to continue living in Greece. In some other cases, when the family can afford it, the mother and the children are based in Greece, and it is only the father who circulates.

Unlike the interviewees working in the service sector (waiters and cooks in restaurants and cafeterias, cleaners in businesses and private homes), almost all of the construction sector workers interviewed had their families settled in Albania from the onset of their emigration experience, and have been going back and forth ever since. They circulate between Greece and Albania in order to see their families back home, and build a viable way of earning a living that their family can rely on and cushions against their return/retirement. Their investments range from technical equipment, such as tractors and water pumps for their fields, to the purchase of various crops and livestock.

The circular migrants working in the service sector in Greece take different entrepreneurial paths in Albania from the construction sector workers. They draw support from family networks, and invest more in new businesses than existing ones. Apart from the different ways their families experience migration (family reunification and family established in Greece as opposed to single male migration and family remaining in Albania), they invest in tourism or other work that follows a seasonal pattern. This is because the tourism and catering employment that they have in Greece is also seasonal, and hence they can organize their circularity accordingly. By contrast, people working in the construction sector and circulating between Greece and Albania cannot adopt a seasonal pattern, since this type of work requires continued presence on-site, and regular trips to Albania are often out of the question. Indeed, all the construction sector workers interviewed came from towns and rural areas in southern Albania, and when back in Albania they were also involved in work at their own farms or houses.

The fourth and last category of circular migration between Italy or Greece and Albania is that which may be called brain circulation. This involves semi-skilled or highly skilled people in Italy or Greece who engage in business development or trade in Albania, and for reasons related to their work or business have to travel between and spend time in both countries.

This category of circular migrant between Italy or Greece and Albania is probably the smallest one in terms of the number of people involved, but at the same time probably the most interesting and internally diverse one. It involves people who graduated from university in Albania, or even had professional experience in highly skilled jobs there. When they came to Greece or Italy they managed to climb up the socio-economic ladder and find semi-skilled or highly skilled employment. It also involves young people who came to Greece or Italy with their parents (or without them, when they finished high school), and graduated from a Greek or Italian university. Last but not least, in the case of Greece, it involves in particular ethnic Greek Albanians, who since 1998 have had secure stay-status and equal socio-economic rights with Greek citizens, in Greece. In fact, some of them are now Greek citizens. In the case of Italy, this category also involves naturalized Italian citizens. As regards non-citizens, this category of brain circularity generally involves people with a five-year plus stay permit in the case of Italy, and a two-year or ten-year permit in the case of Greece.

In other words, the brain circulation category involves people with a stable legal stay status at the destination country, with medium or high skills, and in particular people with a strong motivation to work in their sector of expertise in the destination country, and to develop their career through taking advantage of their social capital (knowledge of both countries, networks in both countries).

These people may exercise very different professions. They may be Albanian graduates from Italy who are recruited by Albanian higher education colleges or in public administration, and whose tasks require the maintenance of an active relationship with Italy. They may be entrepreneurs or artists in either Italy or Greece, whose art or business profits from circulating (for instance because it involves import and export, because the business in Albania is a branch of a Greek or Italian business, because they bring together theatres or art exhibitions and activities in Greece or Italy and Albania).

It is worth noting that this type of circular migration and business development is qualitatively different from that of the former category of semi-skilled or low-skilled migrants. These migrants circulate between Italy or Greece and Albania with a view to making ends meet and developing their farm or small shop in rural Albania. The capital required for someone to invest in the Albanian services industry in Tirana, or in a desirable tourist destination, is of a different scale compared with the capital required for farm expansion in rural parts of Albania.

10.3.1 *Challenges and opportunities of circular migration between Greece or Italy and Albania*

The four circular migration types identified in the Greece-Albania and in the Italy-Albania case studies share similarities, and are clearly affected by Greek and Italian migration policies as well as by the Greek and Italian labour markets. Legal seasonal migration with repeated stays is a type of circularity actively promoted by the Greek and Italian states to cater for the need of a seasonal workforce in agriculture. Informally, these workers may also cover the needs for temporary workers in other low-skill sectors, such as construction, tourism, or generic manual jobs.

Irregular seasonal migration with repeated stays is a by-product of the restrictive Greek and Italian immigration policies, which have led many Albanians, especially in earlier periods, to migrate illegally to Greece and Italy. After having been expelled from Greece, they could not regularize their situation for a number of years, and hence could not take advantage of the legal seasonal migration programmes enacted. Interestingly, the legal seasonal migration programmes for employment in agriculture promote the invitation of the same worker for several years, but employers make the migrant worker pay for this advantage. People involved in these two categories have usually spent a number of years as sedentary migrants in Greece or Italy, mostly as irregular ones initially who are later regularized through one of the amnesty programmes that the two countries have implemented during the past two decades. However, because of unstable employment or because of nostalgia, they have later returned to Albania, and have adopted this seasonal migration pattern.

Thus, similarly to the case of Moroccans in Italy, we witness here the emergence of certain circular migration movements that we may qualify as an entrepreneurial response to unstable employment or lack of better prospects at the country of destination, which make migrants develop their own business plans. Our informants noted that while rural development plans may receive some subsidies from the Albanian state, people aspiring to open a shop or business face important hurdles such as corruption, red tape, and lack of infrastructure (e.g., transport network), as well as high taxation, which some complain makes the business non-profitable. At the same time, the Italian case study also points to the non-viability of some of the business plans developed by circulating Albanian immigrants, who have opened up too many leisure facilities, such as restaurants or cafés, which cannot realistically survive in Albania, a country where consumption standards are still relatively low.

Overall, circularity from Albania to Greece caters for specific labour market niches in Greece, and offers a viable strategy of survival for Albanian workers and their families who live in Albania or, more often, have been long-term migrants in Greece before but were unable or unwilling to settle there permanently. Like circular migration from Morocco to Spain, this kind of movement caters for a specific labour market niche. It does not, however, contribute towards the migrant's building a better future, as the income gained is rather low and there is a continuous need to circulate in order to secure employment.

In the long run, people involved are likely to face important alienation problems, as they live neither here nor there.

In the case of circulating migrants who seek to open up a business in the home country, this is potentially a dynamic aspect of circular migration that could indeed lead to a triple-win situation. However, more often than not, this is not the case, as many of these new businesses are not viable; they develop in specific sectors such as catering and leisure, rather than in a more innovative or productive type of industry. While such movements allow for medium-skilled and highly skilled circulation, their positive impact is yet to be proven. The triple-win potential is often blocked when faced with the reality on the ground, which is economically harsher than it may seem.

10.4 Circular migration in Central Eastern Europe: Poland, Hungary, and Ukraine

For Poland, emigration towards other EU countries rather than immigration has been the main migration policy concern in the last decade. Nonetheless, the continuous inflows of third country nationals even if at still low levels, have gained some attention by policymakers with a view to managing and controlling the phenomenon. The case of Hungary is different, as Hungarians have not emigrated in any significant numbers, while they have admitted a limited level of immigrants, predominantly of Hungarian ethnicity, from Romania (even before Romania's accession to the EU) and Ukraine. Contrary to the previous two sets of cases, where migration was in its bulk sedentary and circular migration was the exception to the rule, in the case of Poland and Hungary, circularity plays an important part in overall Ukrainian migration to these two countries.

In the case of Poland, this circularity was originally encouraged by the lack of visa requirements (until October 2003), and later via their liberal visa policy (between October 2003 and December 2007 when Poland joined the Schengen Area) towards Ukrainians. Until October 2003, Ukrainians benefited from non-visa entrance; once visas were instated, they then had easy access to free of charge tourist visas. As a result, until December 2007 and the enlargement of the Schengen Area, the most characteristic feature of the Ukrainian immigrant group was irregular work on the basis of legal residence visas and documents. It was easily possible, since Ukrainians who are engaged in circular migration in and out of Poland do not differ in terms of appearance from Poles (Iglicka and Gmaj 2010). Significant worker shortages in certain sectors, caused by the Polish outflow to the UK and Ireland after 1 May 2004, forced the Polish government to open its labour market to seasonal workers from the eastern neighbouring countries. These regulations, introduced in 2006 in spite of strong opposition from the trade unions, were even liberalized, extending the period of a single stay to six months within a year, and to all economic sectors.

Poland has no official policy that has circularity in its name, or that consciously promotes the circular mobility of immigrants. However, in practice there are regulations in Poland that encourage this type of migrant mobility. Such regulations are driven by several factors, including regional labour market needs and EU migration control policies. Migrants moving between Poland and Ukraine are very careful to have their documents in order as regards their stay, even if it means additional money paid to informal mediators. In the Polish-Ukrainian reality, illegal stay stops circularity.

Similarly to Poland, after 21 December 2007, with the entry of Hungary to the Schengen Area, the number of visas issued to Ukrainian citizens decreased, and became much more difficult to obtain. Different types of visas were also introduced, such as the local border traffic permit (*kishatárforgalmi engedély*). Up to April 2010, 40,000 Ukrainians had obtained this type of visa, which is valid in the seventy kilometre border zone. One needs no supporting document from Hungary, and health insurance and the visa cost only €20.

It is worth noting that neither the national visas nor the national residence permits authorize their holders to work or engage in any paid activity in Hungary;[3] both limit their holder to enter and stay only in Hungary, and no other member state in the Schengen Area. The holders may enter Hungary to pursue objectives of a cultural or educational nature, either (a) to preserve and further the Hungarian language; (b) to preserve their cultural and national identity; (c) to enroll in education activities outside the statutory secondary and higher education system; and (d) to strengthen family ties other than family (re)unification. In conclusion, while the Schengen visa has greatly reduced the regional cross-border and circular migration patterns, both Poland and Hungary have issued entry visas that are valid for their territory only, and which directly or indirectly cater to the needs for economic circularity.

In the case of Italy, circularity has been facilitated in particular by the introduction of a provision in the 2007 labour agreement which allows for job sharing when one is a domestic worker or care giver (see Vianello in this volume). This encourages circularity while maintaining legal status, and seems to respond well to the needs of Ukrainian women who wish to visit family back home at regular intervals, and to the needs of Italian families who require continuous care for elderly people or children.

Four main types of circular migration have been identified in the cases of Ukraine and Poland or Hungary or Italy. In all four types, the circular migrants have their main residence in Ukraine. The first type is that of low-skilled semi-legal circular migration. This involves both men and women, but they have different backgrounds and they work in different sectors. In the Poland-Ukraine and in the Italy-Ukraine cases, circularity is predominantly a female domain. Women who are engaged in circular mobility seek to make a living while also maintaining their family role, i.e. looking after children, elderly parents, or husband. The women concerned are usually middle-aged with teenage or adult children, and they are married, divorced, or widowed. However, this type of circular migration also embraces younger women who are the main breadwinners in their families.

This type of circularity concerns also Ukrainian men from rural areas, who go to Poland periodically to work in construction. They come and go as long as there is employment. They go back home to Ukraine when they need to work in agriculture there. For the most part, they have no stable employment in Ukraine, but just like the women, their families are based there, and this is home for them.

Although the reasons for Ukrainian citizens' engaging into circular migration are individual and can vary, there is a single common trait: insufficient income and unemployment in Ukraine. For middle-aged women in particular, it is hardly possible to find a job in Ukraine if they have been made redundant in their fifties. The Ukrainian economy has been hit hard both during the early period of economic transformation (early 1990s) and during this last economic crisis (from 2008 onwards).

In the case of Hungary, our fieldwork shows a decrease in this form of low-skilled circular migration, because the crisis has hit Hungary very hard, and because Ukrainian citizens have been oriented to other EU countries further west or south. In Poland, women with the longest migrant experience started their visits in Poland, from trade, agriculture, or industry. They moved to domestic services or caring, since they are paid better in these jobs. In Hungary, the women who engage in repeated temporary stays generally engage in farm work and some cleaning. Ukrainian men in both Poland and Hungary are mainly employed in construction, whereas in Hungary they are also employed in agriculture. We call this type of circular migration semi-legal, because both in Hungary and Poland the migrants involved have a legal stay, but abuse their terms of stay by engaging in employment.

This type of semi-legal low-skilled circular migration is classified as such with regards to the job, but the people involved are generally semi- or highly skilled—with secondary or even higher education. Women's professions in Ukraine had nothing to do with cleaning or caring, while men were previously employed in industry, but also in agriculture and construction. This kind of circularity is spontaneous, and primarily depends on Polish-Ukrainian and Hungarian-Ukrainian networks. This is a circular migration of a regional character: the migrants concerned originate from the less developed areas of Western Ukraine. Circular mobility is a strategy for survival, or for improving their future and that of their children (providing for education, supporting a youth who is entering adulthood or grandchildren, building or renovating a house, etc.).

There is a variant of this type of low-skilled semi-legal circular migration, in which jobs and accommodation are not arranged through informal ethnic networks at the two sides of the borders but rather through employment or travel agencies. While these agencies bring together offer and demand for people who have no good regional ethnic networks, they can be less trustworthy than informal contacts through friends and relatives. Fieldwork has shown that these travel and employment agencies sometimes charge too high a fee for the job opportunity that they arrange.

A second type of low-skilled irregular circular migration is that of individual agriculture seasonal workers in Poland and Hungary, but not Italy. These are usually young men or women who may have recently finished university, or lost their job, or have a long summer holiday (teachers), and seek to make some extra money through temporary employment in Hungary or Poland. Since they work in agriculture, they are typically seasonal workers. Their movement, like that of the previous category, is spontaneous, and they usually repeat their 'working holidays' for more than one year. For some, this is the beginning of a circular career, which brings us back to the first type of circular migration discussed above. For others, this seasonal circular mobility ends after a few years. The cultural proximity between Ukraine and Poland or Hungary in the regions close to the borders, and the feeling that people are still close to home, the existence of the informal networks of 'drivers' who bring people back and forth, are very important pieces of the puzzle that form this type of circularity.

The third type of circular migration identified is that of cross-border movement. Again, this is a type of circularity that concerns Ukrainian men and women who continue to engage in shuttle cross-border trade in Transcarpathia between Ukraine and Hungary. Malynovska's calculations in 2006 showed that by crossing the border to Hungary or Poland with a block of cigarettes and two litres of alcohol allowed by the customs rules, or with a full tank of petrol, one could have earned up to $20 per day. Being employed at the other side of the border, one could earn about $200 per month, which was a much higher income than working in Ukraine would provide. Today, the rules allow for only two packs of cigarettes and one litre of alcohol, but the fuel cost is still 60 per cent lower in Ukraine. Shuttle trade in the borderlands, earlier practised by Ukrainians, has to a large extent been taken over by Hungarians, who can enter the Ukrainian territory without visas.

A fourth type of circular migration between Ukraine and Hungary or Poland is that of legal highly skilled circular migrants. Such a type of migration of Ukrainian women in Italy has not been identified in our case study. Even in Poland or Hungary this type of circularity only concerns a small number of people (compared with the previous categories), and concerns people who have well-established sources of income in Ukraine (permanent employment or their own business). For them, this type of circularity simply adds some income, and also adds prestige to their own work. An example of the profile of this type of migrant could be a GP doctor who works part-time in Poland and has his own private practice in Ukraine, or an academic with a permanent post at one of the Ukrainian state universities, who regularly travels to Poland to teach at a private university in the borderland region.

10.4.1 *Challenges and opportunities of circular migration between Ukraine and Hungary or Poland or Italy*

All circular mobility between Ukraine and Hungary or Poland is spontaneous and regional in character. The case of Ukraine-Italy, by contrast, corresponds rather to the general post-Communist gendered migration to old EU member states (see also Gockel et al. 2009). Within the Central Eastern European region, such circular mobility presents the natural continuation of several decades of porous borders and of intensive cross-border movement and repeated temporary stays for trade or employment. The stiffening of this movement because of the entry of Poland and Hungary to the Schengen Area has led to their reduction, but has also channelled migrants into semi-formal ways of moving back and forth. Thus, the Ukrainian circular migrant workers in Poland and Hungary are legal as regards their stay, through cross border or national visas in Hungary or short-term visas in Poland. However, many migrants abuse the terms of their stay by engaging into employment. They work in sectors where informal work is the norm for Polish workers too (e.g., agriculture and construction), and take up jobs (especially women in the cleaning and caring sector) that Polish women do not wish to take. The difference in the incomes between Poland or Hungary and Ukraine is such that circular mobility is worth the effort. In the case of Italy, it was mainly the previous migration experience in the neighbouring countries, and the proliferation and expansion of ethnic networks, that opened up Italy (and other countries) as a new destination for Ukrainian migrants.

There are two main factors that shape circular mobility between Ukraine and the three countries studied: insufficient income and unemployment in Ukraine, and the need to reconcile reproductive work with work outside the home. These are common in all the cases, and as our case studies show, they shape the migration plans of circular migrants. Interestingly, most migrants interviewed initially thought they would only do it once, or they would spend a short time and then return; but eventually this circular mobility becomes a way of life for several years. This is particularly true for female circular migrants. We may actually talk about intermittent circularity (see Vianello in this volume), as the same migrant may alternate periods of circular mobility with longer periods when she or he stays at the country of destination. This is often linked to the initial irregular status of the migrants concerned, and the difficulty then in circulating.

In the case of circularity between Poland or Hungary and Ukraine, there are additional factors that facilitate circular migration, notably the existence of special stay visas that allow for a legal circulation even if employment is in the shadow economy, and the pre-existing ethnic networks between the two sides of the border. In the case of Italy, these visas do not exist and initially circularity is completely illegal, but with time the migrants concerned eventually manage to arrange their papers and then circulate legally. The legal system in Italy now allows for the possibility of job sharing by formally recognizing this condition of circularity, in private care jobs in particular.

Circularity within Italy and Ukraine is different from the other two countries studied to the extent that while it starts as a sort of entrepreneurial reaction of the migrants to hardship at home (poverty, unemployment, underemployment), it takes advantage of concrete policies which facilitate this type of movement, builds on pre-existing ethnic and cultural ties, and at the same time caters for specific labour market niches in domestic work and agriculture. This circular movement may be seen to satisfy the triple-win situation, to the extent that it covers labour market needs at destination, releases some unemployment pressure at the home country, and also provides for a flexible employment pattern, which allows for interested migrants to gain additional income while not being completely cut off from their families.

10.5 A new typology for circular migration

Having compared our findings in the three sets of case studies, and having identified the different forms and types of circular migration and employment involved within each pair of countries, we shall here attempt the construction of a general typology of circular migration.

We have identified three main types of legal circular migration. The first and perhaps most common type is that of repeated seasonal labour migration in which migrants are based in the country of origin, which may take both a regulated form (within a programme) or take place spontaneously (outside such programmes). This happens mainly in agriculture, regulated by bilateral agreements between specific member states and specific countries of origin and/or by special types of permits. They may take the form of organized programmes (as between Morocco and Spain) or of general provisions for seasonal migration (as between Albania and Greece). Seasonal stays are not longer than six months, and normally employment permits are for one sector and one employer. It may also take place on the basis of special short-term visas. This kind of legal seasonal migration may also give the possibility for people to be informally employed in other sectors, such as tourism or catering, which are also seasonal in nature.

A second type is that of circular legal labour migration in which migrants are based in the country of origin and circularity arises spontaneously. It concerns mainly highly skilled people or businesspersons. People may circulate between two countries holding a stay permit (of indefinite stay) or indeed a passport or ID card (e.g., co-ethnic migrants, such as ethnic Greek Albanians in Greece) that allows them to do so. They tend to spend a few weeks or months in each country (origin and destination), either because of the nature of their employment (e.g., IT experts, economists), or because they are businesspersons doing trade or developing a business in between the two countries, or because they hold two part-time jobs, one in each country (e.g., the Ukrainian doctor and the Ukrainian academic, employed both in Ukraine and in Poland). This is probably the category of repeated temporary movement that is closest to what has been described as circular migration in the European Commission's Communication of May 2007.

A third type of legal circular migration is also spontaneous: migrants are based in the destination country, travelling back and forth to the country of origin. These are usually people with low or medium skills, who are long-term migrants at the destination country but are having difficulties finding a job in this period (e.g., because of the current economic crisis), or are underemployed (have temporary or unstable jobs). These people engage into circular migration with the country of origin to do repair work in the household or, for instance, farm work in the fields.

We also found two types of semi-legal circular migration. In the first type migrants are based in the country of origin, it may or may not follow a seasonal pattern, the stay is legal, and work is informal. This type of migration involves a number of employment sectors, such as construction, domestic work, tourism, and catering. This type of seasonal migration is technically legal as regards the stay of the migrant: the migrant enters with a tourist visa for the Schengen Area, or a special short-term visa valid in the specific member state (e.g., for Ukrainians in Poland), or a special status 'Magyar Igazolvany' (e.g., for ethnic Hungarians who are Ukrainian citizens in Hungary), or some other cross border document (e.g., for Ukrainians in Hungary). But her/his employment is irregular, as her/his visa does not provide for the right to work.

The people involved are semi-skilled or highly skilled people who are unemployed and/or cannot make ends meet in the country of origin and for various reasons (family reasons or simply the impossibility to migrate legally) do not wish to migrate for longer periods. They take advantage of established ethnic networks (e.g., Poland-Ukraine, or Hungary-Ukraine) and engage in circular migration. They work in the caring and cleaning sector (women) or in construction and farm work (men).

The second type of semi-legal circular labour migration concerns migrants based in the country of destination; it is also spontaneous (outside regulated programmes). It concerns people with low or medium skills who are long-term migrants in the destination country but are having difficulties finding a job (e.g., because of the current economic crisis) or are under-employed (have temporary or unstable jobs). These people engage into circular migration with the country of origin to conduct small-scale trade between the two countries, buying goods usually from the destination country and selling them in the country of origin. This is an informal trade without licence. They may also offer transport services to fellow nationals (transporting house belongings or large items from the destination country to the country of origin). This is also a service offered without the appropriate licence.

Both in this and the case above, custom officers in the countries involved (in Italy and Morocco for instance, or in Albania and Greece), may ask the people involved to pay fines or may ask for bribes to let them through. The business is still profitable. The main difference with the category referred to above as circular legal labour migration with migrants based in the destination country, is that while the travelling is legal here, the economic activity undertaken is informal and not properly registered. It takes place because it is tolerated by the authorities.

Last but not least, we have also identified irregular circular migration. In this case, the migrant enters without the necessary documents, and finds employment in the informal labour market in seasonal or other temporary jobs in agriculture, catering, tourism, cleaning, and private care. These are sectors where native workers also often work without registration in the informal economy.

Of the above six types identified, all are spontaneous, emanating from economic necessity, made possible by the social capital of migrants (i.e., their involvement in informal networks and their knowledge of both countries at destination and origin). They are legal to the extent that migrants hold long-term permits of various kinds, or they are semi-legal if migrants can take advantage of specific national policies that provide for special visas which make the stay legal, but their employment or other economic activity is usually irregular. Migrants consciously engage in informal economic activities out of economic necessity. The possibility to travel back and forth legally is of course crucial. We may largely distinguish between circularity that arises as an entrepreneurial response of the migrant to hardship at home or at destination, and as a dynamic solution to her/his problems. Another type of circularity emerges as a form of managed repeated seasonal migration (mostly in the case of agriculture schemes involving Moroccans in Spain, or Albanians in Greece, and Ukrainian men in Poland and Hungary). Rare is the case that circularity is fostered by the wish to advance one's career or improve one's professional position at the country of origin or destination. These are the highly skilled circular migrants, a small even if very interesting minority.

The concept of circularity is useful in describing the patterns of repeated temporary migration of various lengths, and indeed our case studies have shown that there are interesting patterns of economic activity that emerge out of the migrants' initiative. The role of policies is important in shaping the type and conditions of circularity. But one may argue, on the basis of our findings, that circularity is mainly agent-driven. Naturally, when migrants hold identity or residence documents that allow both circulation and employment in either country, circularity is favoured, but the mere existence of the possibility is not enough to trigger a circular movement.

10.6 Conclusion: is circular migration a triple-win situation?

Overall, circular migration is not a preferred option for migrants and their families. Migrants would rather stay put in one of the two countries, but they cannot stay in their country of origin because they do not have the means of subsistence and/or the possibility of creating a better life for themselves and their children. They do not migrate on a long-term basis either, because this is not an available option (no channels for legal economic immigration that involve longer stays), or because they (especially women) have family obligations at home (young or adolescent children, elderly parents), and are not able to be away for long periods. They engage into circularity also when based in the country of destination (but more rarely) when they are underemployed or unemployed. Thus circular migration involves moderate economic gains for the circular migrant and her/his family. It is mainly a means of survival—a dynamic response aimed at surviving, and improving their living conditions and the future of their children to the extent possible.

Our case studies and the comparative analysis show that there are no other social capital gains for circular migrants, except for the category of highly skilled circular migrants (brain circulation) which, however, involves a very small number of people engaging into business, trade, or development projects between the two countries. Most circular migrants engage into low-skill, low-pay jobs (farm work, construction work, cleaning or private care, street peddling, or other petty trade). They do not build any skills at the destination country. They do not receive any training, and they are not even taught the language of the destination country (with the exception of the Spanish-Moroccan programme for seasonal migration). By contrast, some (e.g., Ukrainian women in Poland) face important de-skilling, as they may have university diplomas, and end up working in the fields or in the private care sector.

Circular migration involves important personal hardship, when the migrant is separated from their young children. The frequent and repeated absence of the parent can affect the child's emotional well-being, even if children are usually left with close family members (grandparents, aunt/uncle). In addition, the migrant feels alienated from either country, standing somewhere in between the two.

Circular migration involves moderate gains for the country of origin, though. The country of origin has fewer people unemployed, and benefits from modest remittances from the circular migrants. These remittances are not high enough to shape the socio-economic development of the origin country, because the circular migrant only spends a few months a year in the destination country, hence their income is barely enough for subsistence at home. None of the countries of origin studied here (Albania, Morocco, Ukraine) have implemented any policies for reintegrating circular migrants. Thus, even when there is a potential that the circular migrant develops a business, a small trade, brings back some expertise or know how, or even just her/his contacts from abroad (her/his social capital), this cannot be put to fruition because basic conditions are lacking: red tape is high, corruption is high, infrastructure is poor, the national economy may be unstable, and therefore any investment is highly risky. Of course one might consider that countries of origin find it hard to reintegrate returning migrants who are going back to stay for good. It would probably be a touch too optimistic to expect these countries to provide for circular migrants too. In any case, any hardship and difficulties that circular migrants face when returning to the country of origin are dealt with by family and friends, not by state policies.

The country of destination benefits from legal circular migration in two specific ways: it satisfies specific labour market needs in sectors where natives do not want to work because employment is temporary/seasonal, work is hard, and jobs offer low pay and low prestige. It generally needs not worry about special integration issues of circular migrants and their families, because either circular migrants and their families are long-term settled at the destination country and well integrated, or the family is at the country of origin. However, countries of destination also face two important drawbacks of circular migration. They often cannot check whether circular migrants violate the terms of their stay, i.e. work in different sectors or regions from those initially agreed, and they cannot deal with their demographic problem if migrants are circular and eventually go back to their country of origin.

Overall, our study shows that circular migration on the ground is quite different from what has been promoted in recent years by EU initiatives to foster circular migration and mobility partnership schemes. Circular migration is shaped by labour market dynamics, and driven by the agency of the migrants who seek innovative solutions to pressing economic problems. In this process, policies can facilitate or shape the forms of circular migration, but they do not appear to be the main drivers behind it. Of course, the importance of legal possibilities for circulating is paramount for the migrants. We have seen clearly that this is the case for settled Moroccans or Albanians, who circulate back to the country of origin as a means for improving their income and/or dealing with periods of unemployment. The same is true for Ukrainians who benefit from special visa schemes in Hungary, Poland, or Italy.

This finding runs counter to the main rationale behind circular migration programmes proposed as part of the EU's global approach to migration, which linked the possibility of legal circular migration opportunities for non EU citizens to their country's willingness and ability to ensure better migration controls. Circular migration on the ground seems to defy the logic of securitized temporariness that the EU indirectly promotes (see Cassarino in this volume).

What is, however, clearly lacking in the case of circular migration is the perspective that this migration will change the life of the migrant for the better. For the most part, circular migration addresses pressing economic needs and provides a provisional solution to unemployment or insufficient income, but generally does not allow for a more long-term perspective either in the country of destination or in the country of origin. Remittances are too low to make a difference at the place of origin, while labour market insertion and social integration at the destination country are only partial and generally not secure. Even in the case of migrants with long-term permits, as happens with Moroccans who circulate between Italy and Morocco, or Albanians who circulate between Albania and Greece, circularity testifies to an incomplete or only partly successful integration at destination. In very few cases, circularity is aimed to improve the migrant's livelihood and job prospects. In fact, this is the case only for a handful of circular migrants in the countries studied, with high skills, for whom circularity is an opportunity to develop further a career or to engage into development projects and community service.

Circular migration realities actually fit very well the post-fordist system of production. They are a perfect match to flexicurity approaches to the labour market. Circular migrants become entrepreneurs of their own selves. Facing difficult conditions at home or at destination, they use their human capital (their skills) and their social capital (their networks at the country of origin and destination) to create employment for themselves. What remains to be seen, however, is what kind of challenges such lives-in-circulation pose to democracy both at home and in the destination countries, as circular migrants are likely to belong to and participate in neither. The impact of circularity on welfare states is also an open and very important research question. Circular migrants who provide for care in EU countries leave a welfare gap back home, where children and elderly parents are left to look after each other. In addition, circular migrants are likely to reach old age without having a pension anywhere. EU policies encouraging circularity need to address these inherent gaps in circular migration, in order to allow for an actual triple-win situation.

Notes

1. This kind of trade activity is also found between Morocco and the cities of Ceuta and Melilla, which are Spanish territories but located in Morocco. However, there it takes the form of daily commuting and trade.
2. In Greece, stay permits for dependent employment are routinely issued for two years, and must be renewed every two years until one completes a ten-year period of legal stay in Greece; after which one can apply and obtain the ten-year stay permit. At the end of 2010, there were 62,000 Albanians holding a ten-year stay permit in Greece, from a total of approximately 400,000 stay permit holders.
3. *Magyar igazolvány* Hungarian pass valid only with a visa.

Index

absence 17, 29, 58, 64, 66, 91, 95–6, 111, 134, 145, 187, 200, 206, 209, 217, 234
agriculture 52–3, 60, 69–70, 84–5, 89–93, 99, 104–10, 118–19, 125–6, 133, 137, 145, 147, 152, 155, 160, 167, 175, 177–9, 193, 201, 213, 216–24, 227, 229–33
   agricultural seasonal workers 179
   agricultural work 17, 73, 78, 98, 108, 122–3, 125, 139, 169, 213–15
   Greek agriculture 70, 84
Albanian migrants 16, 42, 47, 49, 53, 61–4, 68, 70, 72, 79–84, 88
   Albanian circular migration 68, 76, 78
   Albanian diaspora 53, 81
   Albanian reintegration policies 81
   irregular Albanian migrants 69
annual quotas (system of) 70, 91

bilateralism 30, 38
Blue Card Directive 31
Brain Gain Programme 81, 88

care work 153, 162, 164, 188, 191, 197, 200, 204
   caregiver 198, 202–3, 201, 211
   care receiver 203
   care workers 188, 191, 197, 203
circular migrants 1, 5, 12–13, 15, 19, 23–5, 35, 48, 70–4, 78, 80–4, 90, 95–100, 107–9, 117, 120–6, 136, 144, 147, 154, 159–60, 162, 167, 170–3, 175–83, 201, 206, 213–18, 220, 226, 228, 233–6
   back and forth irregular movements 70
   highly skilled circular migrants 76, 180, 228, 233
   legal circular migration
      of low-semi skilled worker 74, 220
      of semi- and high-skilled worker 73, 76
   patterns of circular migrants 71
   spontaneous circular migration 74, 121–2, 136, 151, 216
   types of circular migration 5, 72, 96, 151, 161, 214–15, 219–20, 226, 230

circular mobility 3–5, 12–14, 26, 52, 97, 122, 138, 166, 169, 172, 183, 226–30
circular practices 187
circularity 197, 213–35
   embedded 25
   hindered 24, 26
   regulated 137
citizenship 29, 49, 52–3, 60, 78, 97, 98–9, 101, 111, 115, 121, 123–4, 136, 139, 150–3, 162–5, 215–16
construction sector 73–5, 78–9, 89, 118, 124, 126, 160, 179, 210, 215, 222
country of origin 3–4, 6–7, 9, 12–13, 15, 17, 21, 23, 25, 41, 60, 66, 71–2, 76, 83–5, 87, 89–90, 97, 105, 108–9, 114, 125, 152–4, 189, 196, 202–6, 211, 213–17, 230–5
cross-border migration 71

domestic workers 169, 176, 185, 188, 191, 193, 198, 200, 202, 208, 210–11
double presence 187, 189, 204, 206

economic depression 78
elderly people 60, 169, 203, 226
employability 28, 63
employer 4, 10, 17, 26–7, 35–7, 57, 59, 70–2, 76–8, 84, 91, 96, 101–9, 111, 117, 127–31, 134, 168–71, 176–7, 179–80, 183, 200, 203, 211, 213–14, 220–4, 231

family 4, 6, 13, 17–18, 27–28, 36, 49, 53–4, 57–64, 70, 72, 75, 77, 79, 90, 95, 97, 99, 103–4, 107, 110, 125, 128, 131–5, 149, 154, 169, 178, 181–2, 191–2, 194–6, 201, 203–5
   Family Reunion Directive 30
foreign worker invitation 72, 77–8

G5 (today's G6) 30
Gastarbeiter programme 26
gender roles 182–3
Global Approach to Migration 31, 37, 39–41, 235

Index

Global Commission on International Migration 22
Greek Labour Force Survey 68, 89
Greek state authorities 89

high unemployment 78, 86
host country 17, 19, 36, 38, 71–2, 74–6, 80–5, 220
human resources 28, 62, 65, 115
human rights 8, 28, 128

in-depth interviews 145, 189–90
International Labour Organization 39
investment 12, 27, 58, 71, 75–6, 82, 98, 105–6, 109–13, 131, 135, 137, 142, 160, 202–3, 217, 222, 234
irregular movements 10–11, 70, 74
Ivano Frankivsk 171, 188–9, 191, 208, 210

job flexibility 28, 34
 job sharing 198, 200, 226, 230

L'viv 188–9, 192–3, 204, 207, 210
labour migration 5, 11, 20, 26, 36, 111, 113, 115, 127, 152–5, 164, 172, 177, 182, 186, 202, 208, 210, 230–2
legalization procedures 70
local labour markets 77, 82, 84–5

mass deportations 69
mass emigration flows 68
migrant women 79, 137, 187–8, 194, 198, 201, 206, 211, 218
 female migrants 175–6, 186
migration patterns 5, 14–15, 18, 22, 69, 72, 83, 85, 111, 144, 161–2, 164, 166, 196, 208–9, 221, 226
 migratory trajectories 187
mobility partnership 1, 7–11, 31–2, 37, 39, 41, 111, 142, 163, 235
Morocco 2, 15, 17–18, 38, 40, 64, 86, 90–1, 95–113, 114–38, 212–18, 224, 230, 232, 234–6

new economics of migration (or new economics of labour migration) 36, 184

Poland 2, 11, 15, 18, 30, 41, 125, 128–9, 148, 164, 166–86, 192–5
presence 27, 29, 54, 79, 84, 96, 110, 115, 120–3, 143, 187, 191, 193, 195, 197, 204, 206, 210, 217, 222

Quadro Group 30

readmission 8, 30–2, 35, 37–8
reintegration 9, 17, 35, 61, 64, 80–1, 135, 142, 206, 212, 217–18
 reintegration policies 17, 80–1
remittances 4, 46, 51, 53, 65, 68, 86–7, 101, 106, 123, 142, 181–2, 202–4, 234–5
restrictive immigration policies 4, 9, 24, 26, 70
return migration 18, 21, 38–9, 61, 65, 79–80, 87, 152, 161–2, 200, 209
 return programmes 28

seasonal migration 3–4, 10, 14, 69, 72, 111, 124, 126, 130, 133, 161, 216, 218–21, 224, 230–1, 233
 seasonal worker invitation visas 77
 seasonal invitation (system of) 70, 72, 76–7, 85–6
security paradigm 33
self-employed 30, 58, 93–4, 97, 102, 106, 121, 155, 213, 215–16
shadow economy 173, 176, 178, 230
shuttle mobility 166
social insurance contribution 70, 75, 89
social integration 29, 80, 87, 119, 131, 217, 235
stay permit 17, 70, 74–5, 78, 83–4, 89, 118, 181, 186, 213, 220, 223, 231, 236
strategies 20, 47, 59, 79, 187, 208
street-selling 90, 99, 107, 213

temporariness 22–5, 29, 31, 33–41, 151, 212, 235
 temporary jobs 131, 155, 180, 232
 temporary migrants 75, 126
tourism industry 71
trade unions 27, 34, 37, 116, 127, 129, 131, 138, 214, 226
transnationalism 3–4, 19–20
transport 17, 58–9, 93, 96, 98, 100, 102–3, 145, 166, 169, 192, 196, 215–17, 232
Treaty of Lisbon 30
 Treaty on European Union 29
 Treaty on the Functioning of the European Union (TFEU) 30

Ukraine 15, 17–18, 125, 140, 142–96, 201–10, 225–30

Veneto 92–3, 188–9, 210
visa facilitation 31–2
 visa-free regime 75

worker shortages 170, 225

238